MURDER ON THE MARCO POLO

Well, n

A CRUISE UP THE AMAZ

Well, nc

C000302736

ISBN 978-1-905328-61-1

ISBN 978-1-905328-78-9

'Perhaps it's the friction between his sense of where he is and where he would rather be that makes *The Virgin Whore and Other Chinese Characters* so good. He is best at trying to get along with people, and his attempt to unpick the Chinese character manages to be comic without being condescending.'
The Independent on Sunday

'Alert and observant of the dying social mores and customs of a changing Korea ... Several episodes with the opposite sex are described with breathtaking details and skill ... This book is not only delightful reading but also a valuable and original literary feat.'
The Journal of Asian Studies

OTHER BOOKS BY CLIVE LEATHERDALE INCLUDE:

INTERNATIONAL RELATIONS:
  Britain and Saudi Arabia 1925-1939: The Imperial Oasis
LITERARY CRITICISM:
  Dracula: The Novel & the Legend: A Study of Bram Stoker's Gothic Masterpiece
  The Origins of Dracula: The Background to Bram Stoker's Gothic Masterpiece
  Dracula Unearthed (annotated)
  The Jewel of Seven Stars (annotated)
EDUCATION:
  So You Want to Teach English to Foreigners
SPORT:
  England's Quest for the World Cup: A Complete Record
  Scotland's Quest for the World Cup; Ireland's Quest for the World Cup;
  Aberdeen: European Era; Wimbledon: from Southern League; West Ham (various)

Murder on the Marco Polo

WELL, NOT QUITE
A Cruise up the Amazon and the Orinoco
WELL, NOT QUITE

EDITED BY

Clive Leatherdale

DESERT ISLAND BOOKS

First published in 2011
by
DESERT ISLAND BOOKS LIMITED
16 Imperial Park, Rawreth lane, Rayleigh, Essex SS6 9RS
www.desertislandbooks.com

© 2011 all named contributors and photographers

British Library Cataloguing-in-Publication Data
A catalogue record for this book is available from the British Library

ISBN 978-1-905328-90-1

All rights reserved. No part of this book may be reproduced or utilised in any form or by any means, electronic or mechanical, including photocopying, recording or by any information storage and retrieval system, without prior permission in writing from the Publisher

Printed in Great Britain
by
4edge Ltd, Hockley.

Desert Island Books gratefully acknowledges Malcolm Whatcott for the
photographs used for the book cover and all those appearing on pages 129-160.
Front cover: Amazon, 3rd February 2011. The *Marco Polo* moored at Fazendinha,
in the noon-day equatorial sun, with tenders taking people ashore to Macapá.
Back cover: Amazon sunset, 2nd February. At the end of a day's cruising downstream,
the sun dipped below the horizon giving this incredible sky for just a few minutes

'With apologies to all those youthful, sprightly contributors whom I
disparaged as "geriatric scribblers" on the back cover of this book'
CLIVE LEATHERDALE (editor)

Editor's Note by Clive Leatherdale

She creaks, she groans; she squeaks, she moans. The *Marco Polo* does all this and more. As cruise ships go, she is more than merely old; the words stately and venerable come to mind. Yes, she is old. In fact she is very old.

So are her passengers. The *Marco Polo* has no facilities for children, so it markets itself as an adults-only cruise ship. Those able to sail on her for six weeks to South America are likely to be retired, which pushes the age up still further. The average vintage aboard the 2011 'Amazon & Orinoco Discovery' cruise was 65.

Even before I embarked, I knew a book would emerge from my scribblings. To my knowledge, no diary of a cruise had ever been published before. A book on a cruise? How trite! Clearly this had to be a cruise with a difference. In fact, it needed to be different in three respects.

First, the cruise had to be long. Long enough for the ship to act as a home rather than a hotel. Most cruises last one or two weeks; insufficient time for human interaction to really take a grip, for friendships to form and to fracture, love to blossom, hatreds to fester. We would be aboard the *Marco Polo* for six weeks, 42 nights, long enough for life-changing thrills for some, tantrums or tedium for others. Hardly any cruises last longer than six weeks, so that ticked the first box.

Second, the destination needed to be exotic. Pottering around the Med for a few days was hardly likely to provoke anything steamy except in the climatic sense. The chilly North Sea would see most passengers wrapped up or indoors. But the Amazon and Orinoco? They don't come much more exotic than that. Box number two, happily ticked.

Third, the ship had to be small, small enough to function as a village rather than as a town. Modern tower-block cruise ships with 3,000 or 4,000 passengers, where almost everyone else starts and stays a stranger, can't hope to foster the human joys and tensions possible on a smaller ship. And with just 800 passengers, the *Marco Polo* is comparatively snug. Of course, you can't hope to enjoy first-name terms with 800 over the course of six weeks, but a warm smile can chalk up a fair few. Box number three, signed and delivered.

No sooner was I on board than I transformed my cabin into a floating office – computers, guidebooks and maps at the ready. I was all set. But where to start? What had initially seemed so straightforward now appeared so daunting. What chance had I, working alone, of probing anywhere beneath the surface? My fellow passengers could offer so much more. In ways soon to be explained, I swooped them up and set them loose. *Murder on the Marco Polo* is the fruit of their enterprise.

Alphabetical list of contributors, and the days for which they contributed:

	NAME	DAY
1	J Armitage	16
2	Norma Pascua Artajos	36
3	Margaret Atkinson	1, 2, 23, 28, 42
4	Sarah Broadbent	23
5	Judith Buckley	18
6	Daphne Carden	23
7	Judy Chapman	4, 5, 6, 7, 24, 39
8	Caroline Clifford	major contributor throughout
9	James Coleman	13, 16, 36
10	Marion Cox	2, 5, 7, 14, 16, 17, 21, 27
11	Jill Crocker	major contributor throughout
12	Mave Eaton	major contributor throughout
13	Mark Edwards	major contributor throughout
14	Sue Edwards	major contributor throughout
15	Catharine Fox	20, 25
16	Jan and Poppy Greefkes	29
17	Dianne Hall	26
18	Margit Latter	11, 12, 23, 30, 32, 33
19	Clive Leatherdale (editor)	major contributor throughout
20	Jenny Liddell	16
21	Sue MacPherson	8, 14, 33
22	David Mackenzie-Crooks	9, 36
23	Jean McGinley	5, 22, 35, 36, 41
24	Tim Major	15, 17, 18, 23, 25, 27
25	Marie Martyn	40
26	Dick Mayes	3, 23
27	Lizzie Mayes	major contributor throughout
28	Pat Pickering	25, 28
29	Piet Pieterse	2, 16, 24
30	Kay Rainsley	major contributor throughout
31	Dinah Read	major contributor throughout
32	Steve Ragnall (ship lecturer)	6
33	Bernadine Ryan	23
34	Aileen Singh	23
35	Neville Singh	23, 31
36	Alan Smith	18
37	Richard Sykes (cruise director)	11, 20, 33
38	Jeremy Tait	20, 21, 23, 31, 36, 41
39	Alan Waite	24
40	Valerie Waite	42
41	Vivian Walsh	7, 23
42	Malcolm Whatcott	photos for book cover and pages 129-160
43	Jack White	23
44	Steve and Marion Wright	35

Day 1. Welcome Aboard

'On behalf of Captain Zhukov, his officers, staff and crew, welcome aboard the MS Marco Polo.
We hope you have a pleasant and enjoyable stay with us and that you enjoy the majestic splendour of your Amazon & Orinoco Discovery.'

by Clive Leatherdale (Cabin 725)

Even though Gerry Rafferty died almost a week ago, I still can't stop singing *Baker Street*. I remember the room in which I first heard it in the summer of 1978 and the Trotskyist girlfriend with whom I shared one set of headphones. That saxophone still has the capacity to 'wow'.

The pretty, sharp-nosed lady taxi driver who drove me to the train station asked if I was going far. 'Tilbury,' I said. 'And after that,' I teased, 'six weeks up the Amazon.'

'Wow,' she gasped. When I told her I would be writing a book, she asked if she could be in it, as the woman who said 'wow'. The Amazon has the capacity to 'wow'.

On board, no sooner were my bags unpacked and computer plugged in than Richard Sykes, cruise director, announced the Passenger Lifeboat Drill, which he assured us was 'compulsory' (heavy emphasis on 'pul'), a lovely word which carries more oomph than 'mandatory' or 'essential', leaving no excuse for absentees or slackers.

We traipsed after everyone else in a solemn conga to assemble by our lovely lifeboat – No 5 – alongside which a young, pert, east European crew member screeched instructions. These were completely inaudible except to those at the front because of the hubbub from those to our right, who were craning their necks to hear what was required of lifeboat 6. Oh well, they'll never be needed!

We didn't depart until 5.40pm, over an hour late. I asked the woman who came to sort out my malfunctioning cabin safe-box why the delay. 'Provisions arrived late,' she said.

At the dinner table I made my first *faux pas*. 'Why are we reversing towards Hammersmith?' I asked Carmen, my frustrated wine waitress – frustrated, though she hid it well, because I declined to order wine or anything else. Only then did I sort out my port from my starboard and realise we were in fact going forward in the direction of 'Sarfend-on-Sea'. I think she took pity on me from then on, though she hid it well.

I had been allocated to table 14 in the Waldorf restaurant. A helpful layout card should have guided me there, except that table numbers printed on it were so tiny as to be unreadable. This corner of the restaurant is surrounded by floor-to-ceiling mirrors, so it was difficult to choose a seat that would not allow my reflection to bounce back into my eyes. I was there on time, 5.45, on a table for eight, but the next person did not show until 6.25, Grace, on her own, Welsh, clad in peacock blue, and undertaking her first cruise. She ran a caravan business and had recently broken her ankle. Grace never graced our table again. Perhaps it was something I said.

Not long afterwards, Jack (85) and Dinah (80) joined us, Dinah to my immediate right, though as she was deaf in her left ear it was not a wise location, for our conversation floundered for her constant need to keep twisting her neck through 180 degrees. Jack – with his magnificent eyebrows like giant toothbrushes, each a different colour – asked me to settle an argument. Were Gravesend and Sheerness on our port side? No, I replied, now pretty cocky about my navigational skills; they are starboard. He gave a little victorious grin of contentment. Dinah just smiled. Or was it a wince?

A warning sign has been stuck on Reception. *The ship is sailing at full capacity. No cabin transfers are available. We apologise for the inconvenience.* This is obviously twaddle. The ship can't be full, otherwise what would happen to passengers whose cabin was accidentally flooded, or whose ceiling panels came crashing down, or ponged because of a blocked toilet? You can't ask them to sleep on the piano or in the jacuzzi. But at least the reception girls wear smiles. Perhaps they, too, are excited about heading up the Amazon. 'Wow.'

by Dinah Read (Cabin 422)

This cruise was a present to me from my sweetheart Jack [aged 85] on the occasion of my 80th birthday. I had no expectation of such a gift, generous and unprecedented. Travel I have always loved, and by sea above all. This was a dream that I had had since childhood.

We went with the blessing of his children and mine, although Jack had been tense and anxious for several weeks. We were looking forward to some 'quality time' with no distractions from our delight in each other's company. We are both happy at sea, both born for it.

We were bound for Jack's brother Gordon's house near Ongar, where we would stay overnight with him and his wife, Pat, and leave my car,

Gordon driving us to Tilbury in the morning. I had not met either of them before and was looking forward to it. The house, an old rectory, was beautifully furnished with antique pieces and well presented. Pat was obviously proud of it, and one might say that it was her life's work. Her 80th birthday was on the Tuesday, and I took her a picture or two as a present. Jack helped me pick out four from which she could choose and he proved to be a fair judge of her taste. Gordon I liked very much, and he was just as I thought he would be. He and Jack obviously wanted each other's company, and Pat and I talked for hours, covering a lot of ground. She was curious of course about my relationship with Jack. I do not think that anyone *quite* understands that. We had a fine Sunday lunch and a good night's sleep. This morning we transferred our luggage to Gordon's car and he drove us to the cruise terminal.

Our ship is the *Marco Polo*. She is a handsome vessel – originally built in East Germany in the 1960s as an ice-breaker but sailing under the Russian flag as the *Alexandr Pushkin*. She has been converted for the passenger business and totally refurbished. She is now Greek-owned and her crew are decidedly multi-racial.

Embarkation was a rather wearying process, and unpacking in our cabin (422 Pacific Deck) hard work, too, but at last it was finished and we were able to relax. We were due to sail at 4.30pm but were an hour late. During the afternoon we had a lifeboat drill as a matter of course and then looked around the ship a little.

We had our dinner in the Waldorf restaurant, after some difficulty in finding our rightful places, and then went to the show lounge where we watched an introductory show, sampling what entertainment and facilities are on offer. After that we retired to our cabin very happy with each other (although we have twin beds that cannot be pushed together and are too narrow for us to lie beside each other in comfort). We would ask for an upgrade but the ship is full to capacity.

by Lizzie Mayes (Cabin 494)
Arrived at Tilbury at noon for the Great Adventure – 'The Amazon & Orinoco Discovery'. Our first cruise. Oh my God, what a sight – rows of grey-haired, grey-skinned, grey-clad old people – walking sticks, wheelchairs. I felt really young and sprightly [aged 65]! A very camp man who was in a sort of 'meet and greet' role started to eulogise about our cruise director [Richard Sykes] and informed us that many people only cruised on the *Marco Polo* because of him. Anyway we embarked very quickly so didn't have long to dwell on the fact that the only people able to indulge a six-week holiday would be retired.

We were shocked to see how small our upgraded inside cabin actually was – it seemed about 9ft x 9ft with 2ft 6in beds. How am I going to survive in this box – no windows, no light, no air? Can't help thinking of home, scruffy but spacious and light, surrounded by some of the most beautiful countryside in the world – yes, in the world. I have to remind myself – but you are going to see the Amazon and the sun will shine and it will be raining in Somerset.

We had compulsory lifeboat drill – which instils great confidence as one's first activity. Went into dinner in the Waldorf restaurant (shock horror, first sitting at 5.45 – who eats dinner at 5.45?) after unpacking and taking a quick walk round the ship. Dinner was delicious – five courses and lots of choice.

We were on a huge table [for eight] with one other couple – John and Sue, brother and sister. Intrepid travellers both – had been on countless holidays and cruises together after they had been widowed. Seemed really nice and interesting – Sue from Jersey, a nurse, and John from Abingdon, a retired business travel advisor.

From there we went to our first cruise entertainment in the Marco Polo Lounge – the culture shock was complete. A tall, blond, curly headed man ran down the side of the theatre singing *Fly me to the Moon* and Mr Hi de Hi introduced himself as our cruise director. My nightmare that we had made a terrible mistake was complete. He went on with great enthusiasm to introduce the show team and left us in no doubt that we *would* enjoy our six weeks on board the *Marco Polo* – like it or not. I managed to escape the rest of the entertainment on the pretext I felt a bit queasy. I didn't say anything of my misgivings to Dick, who had on his fixed cheerful face.

The bed was surprisingly comfortable and the throbbing of the engines and some other noises, together with the gentle rocking from side to side, sent me off to sleep very quickly. My two seasickness wristbands in place made it look as if I was in double mourning. It felt a bit like that. Anyway, I slept for twelve hours.

by Margaret Atkinson (Cabin 504)

At Tilbury an orderly queue formed, a format the British do so well. It was a little tiresome, but expected. The immediate impression of the cabin was favourable. Pleasant decor – a hint of Art Deco. But perhaps rather small for a 43-day cruise. The hangers in the wardrobe were the usual irritating [non-removable] type, but appropriate for ships. We noticed a window was short of a rivet and had had some 'patching up' done at some time. Will it be secure to take us across the Atlantic?

'Diary of a Supernumerary' (literal translation: extra to numbers; actual translation: spare part) by Jill Crocker (Cabin 514). Jill was accompanying lecturer Steve Ragnall
I'm looking forward to this trip, never having been away for six weeks before. Feeling very humble (and lucky), tagging along on Steve's talents. We spent a long time queuing for registration at Tilbury, only to find that those like us, flying from Gatwick to Amsterdam, didn't need to. I spoke to a few passengers in the lounge and we left on the coach to Gatwick. It seems our cabins are still occupied by Dutch passengers who will be disembarking in Amsterdam. That solves a problem. We'd been knitting a story in our heads as to why we could leave our luggage at Tilbury but not get onto the ship until Amsterdam. The best scenario was that the ship was being overhauled in Amsterdam dock, so all the luggage was going by ferry. All wrong.

Tony Rice [another lecturer] and his wife Chris went missing for a short time at Schiphol Airport. They emerged from baggage claim later than the rest of us, but we soon found them. It was stressful for them, illustrative of Tony's persona of absent-minded professor. They are a lovely couple. The Mövenpick Hotel was very pleasant. Minimalist, even down to the toilet paper.

Garbage maybe, but what about obstreperous passengers? (Clive Leatherdale)

DAY 2. AMSTERDAM, NETHERLANDS

'Amsterdam is derived from Amstellerdam, which is indicative of the city's origin: a dam in the river Amstel. Settled as a small fishing village in the late 12th century, Amsterdam became one of the most important ports in the world.'

by Mave Eaton (Cabin 616)

Why am I writing this – an ageing woman travelling with a strong, silent husband? Answer: because I was flattered by Clive. I am lazy and gain my mental exercise by watching others and know I have limited ability – but I am charmed by him.

My first impressions of the ship – better than we had feared. The cabin is compact but with adequate storage. Such a pity that the selling point of a window is a disappointment with its crazed perspex pane. I must learn to look beyond.

We went to our first dinner. We are eight. I am fearful of being with these six strangers every evening for six weeks. We sat down and had our first drama. One couple had been shown to this table by mistake. The correct couple arrived and had already ordered their wine. The cuckoos refused to move: are we so attractive? The wine and the other couple were reluctantly placed at a nearby table. We smiled at them and I knew they would have been my soulmates. It was noisy, so we made polite conversation at the top of our voices. Have you cruised before? Where are you from? And other middle-class pleasantries.

After we left I asked my husband's opinion. 'The male cuckoo is boring,' he replies succinctly.

Today we arrived at Amsterdam. It is freezing with horizontal rain. We wander the streets looking for something but we know not what. It is a relief to return to our warm, womb-like cabin.

by Marion Cox (Cabin 619)

We promised to have *The Times* and a red buttonhole prominently displayed so our friend could recognise us in Amsterdam. As it was, the rain was heavy and we shared a blue 'China Tours' umbrella. No problem. As we jumped off the tram in Dam Square, there she was, in cherry red coat (as promised) and waving like mad. Kisses all round and we headed off to the coffee shop. We picked up the conversation after a twenty-year pause! It was laughter all the way in the horse-drawn carriage. Over cobbled streets and bridges we clattered to our friend's favourite Chinese restaurant in the 'red light' district – such bottoms on display at mid-day! Several beers later and all too soon, we had to say goodbye to our kindred spirit.

by Lizzie Mayes (Cabin 494)

Awoke to find we were alongside in Amsterdam. I was amazed at the options for breakfast on board – full English, cold meats, cheeses, fish, fruit, porridge, cereals, yoghurt, boiled eggs, rolls, Danish pastries, toast, dried and fresh fruit. Only thing missing was Marmite – but who cares, we had brought our own. The weather forecast was for freezing temperatures and rain.

We bravely sallied forth, having acquired a map of the city, and promptly got lost. We fortified ourselves with a good strong cup of coffee and spent a few hours shivering our way round the city. Back on board we thought initially we'd try the late dinner instead, after listening to the wonderful violinist Olga, accompanied by Liliya on piano. Dick had been captivated by Olga and her violin playing the previous night. She is a lovely looking girl, and she and Liliya play beautifully together – maybe they will save the day. Only a few people were listening to them. We went into dinner and were shown to a table for eight. The 'gentleman' sitting next to me was an ex-pat living in Spain. He systematically ate his way though the entire menu – every choice of every section, washed down with copious amounts of red wine. He was clearly not in the least interested in me, and I have to say the feeling was soon reciprocated. Can it get any worse?

The rest of the table also had little to say. Dick was sitting next to an elegant lady in a wheelchair. After several failed attempts at conversation (I could see there was a problem and immediately thought it was Dick's bad hearing) I realised, sadly, she was in another world. Her husband said he had to cope with her Alzheimers, and also a fall on the ship resulting in a hairline fracture in her leg. A nice couple – she had been a bridal-gown designer before this terrible illness struck her down. We decided to revert to the first sitting, with John and Sue. The show team were doing 'Around the World', but after a few minutes we decided to give it a miss and go and listen to the lovely Olga again. At least that put a smile on Dick's face. I went to bed feeling homesick (only six weeks to go) and wondering how Jack (our rescue terrier) had coped with his first days without us. I understand we picked up 150 Dutch passengers today.

'Tired and Frustrated of Clitheroe' by Jill Crocker (Cabin 514)

Bitterly cold in Amsterdam. We were among a large number of British and Dutch embarkees trying to crowd into what felt like a two-man tent before getting on board. It was not too well organised. There was a scrum of passengers disembarking, or visiting the city, or dropping off luggage, or embarking – plus a Dutch school party waiting for a tour of the ship and off-duty crew all passing to and fro through this haven of white plastic, frilled awning. Smile and be grateful, I tell myself, you are just a supernumerary.

One queue leads to another, this next one is to register our 'yellow fever' cards, only to find when we reach the head of the queue that our no-man's-land status (as lecturer and his friend, we are neither passengers nor staff) means that we register at Reception.

There is a very irate gentleman ahead of us in this queue, furious that his cabin doesn't have a double bed, and he won't take no for an answer. Despite the number of passengers on board, I saw him later changing cabins – I think he's anticipating an active cruise.

At least we're warm now, although Saga would have provided a hot drink. We go off to the cabin but can't get in. Rhys from the shore excursion staff (we later find out) has nothing to do with keys but is collared to help us. He does his best to find the housekeeper, who is female, though she could be in drag.

The said lady arrives and is confused by the situation. She opens the cabin door with the master key, only to find the cabin's already occupied. I wait a bit longer, me 'tired and frustrated of Clitheroe'. It seems that cabin numbers have been transposed, we're in 514 not 415.

We wonder where all our luggage might be going, but all's well that ends well (eventually). I take a tour of the ship to remind myself where everything is – I was on board two years ago – but fail miserably.

by Margaret Atkinson (Cabin 504)

It was raining heavily when we arrived in Amsterdam. We stayed on board, as others wrapped themselves against the cold and wet and ventured out.

At 10am an announcement was made: 'The ship is taking on fuel. No smoking until further notice.' The imagination took over. Would some idiot desperate for a fag light up?

Dinner time. Ours is a table for two. To the right, pleasantries were being exchanged on a table for eight. Then, above the buzz, a slightly shrill female voice demanded: 'Yes, there!' Was it the fair-headed lady dressed in a green blouse?

by Piet Pieterse (Cabin 127)

'Please, be on time!' And we were. 'Embarkation time will be 12.00 sharp for the green-labelled group.' And we were the green couple, waiting one hour before 12.00 at the quay in Amsterdam. I sang softly a shanty when I got out of the taxi, the song called 'Piet Hein'. This was because the *Marco Polo* would depart from the 'Piet Heinkade'.

In 1628 the Dutch admiral Piet Hein had captured a Spanish treasure fleet loaded with silver somewhere in the Caribbean. By piracy, of course. Silver was very welcome to the warlords of the Dutch Republic. They fought the Spanish superpower and finally the Dutch won the 80 years' war. When you mention the name 'Piet Hein' nowadays, every Dutch boy and girl will know the shanty that bears his name. It translates in English as follows: 'His name is short / his deeds are big / he won the silver fleet.'

And now, almost 400 years after Piet Hein, I sailed away on the *Marco Polo* to the same regions. I had no silver with me, and no guilders either. Euros, yes.

by Clive Leatherdale (Cabin 725)

Not the best of nights. I was aware in my narrow bunk that the boat was rocking, but without any external reference points I had no idea if the sea was normal or rough. It was rough. We have just had an announcement that, because of the weather overnight, the ship had to cut its speed, which means we will arrive 45 minutes late into Amsterdam.

Now, considering we left Tilbury 80 minutes late, I wonder if the ship is blaming the weather for the fact we have only made up 35 minutes. This is one of the joys of cruising. Listening to the announcements and trying to work out what mischief lies behind them.

I've just discovered why the *Marco Polo* sailed to Amsterdam, northeast of Tilbury, when we're ultimately headed south to the equator. We're going to pick up Dutch passengers. And I thought it was just another place to visit. The ship's previous cruise, to the Caribbean, also stopped off here, so some passengers are actually disembarking as I write. Their cruise started one day later than Tilbury's embarkees.

I'd never been to Amsterdam before. I walked the mile from the ship terminal to the central station in light rain which turned to drizzle. Bloody miserable. Amsterdam is small as cities go, and by counting the number of canals I crossed, it was easy enough to find Anne Frank's house unaided. There was only a small queue in front of me. For some reason, the security man asked me to wear my small blue knapsack hanging round my neck to the front, like a nose bag, which felt a bit odd. The house was unrecognisable from the outside, being modern, straight, and glass. From the inside, much had been preserved, including the steep wooden stairs which led up to the attic. What was striking was the mood of the visitors. Only in churches and cemeteries have I observed more reverence or hushed voices. It was as if this is a sacred place, which in a sense it is.

The most striking memory was the tiny room Anne Frank had to share with the dentist – Fritz Pfeffer – in which she wrote most of her diary and short stories and grew irritated by his stern, overbearing presence. I felt for him as much as for her, and thought back to that searing 1995 TV documentary *Anne Frank Remembered* narrated by Kenneth Branagh. All his life, Pfeffer's son, Werner, had suffered Anne's relentless diary criticism of his late father. Now Miep Gies, the family's main helper in hiding, meets Werner to confide what a fine man his father had been. A reputation unjustly sullied, now restored. This had reduced Werner to tears, as it had me. Werner died soon afterwards.

I had time for a Mars bar and one of the ship's red apples before I took off eastwards. My route took me past a posse of policemen guarding a fancy museum of Islamic art. I then found myself in the red light district (from the sacred to the profane). The bodies on display ranged from youthful divine to those ravaged by drugs. Is it considered rude to stop and stare (gawk), when window-shopping in such places? I never saw anyone do so, so I didn't either.

At dinner, Jack and Dinah had switched to the opposite side of the table, so Dinah was now on my left. She confirmed that she was deaf in her left ear and had heard nothing I said last night. Jack, almost 86, apologised for having a terrible cold and then told me of his wonderful life – at sea for many years and then employed in 'tiles'. Dinah was once a semi-professional artist.

The ship's weather forecast could be terrifying (see page 282)

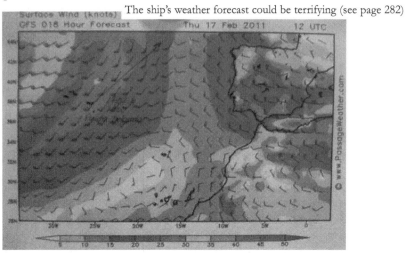

DAY 3. AT SEA

'A day at sea is a perfect opportunity to discover the ship at your leisure. It also includes the first formal evening of our cruise, and our Captain's Reception. You could spend some time on the open decks, in the jacuzzi pools, at the spa, browsing the shops . . .'

by Mave Eaton (Cabin 616)

The third dinner. We are only six, but the cuckoos have returned. The noise in the dining room grows louder and louder. The male cuckoo enjoys dominating the conversation with his great intellect and experience. He is an ardent Rotarian (or Lion) so we learn of his contribution. He informs us he does not like to read books in translation and is currently reading one in the original Spanish (or Italian). Conversation moves away from him, so he sulks. At the end of our third dinner my strong, silent husband says – enough!

We search for the maitre d' but find only his deputy. We ask for a table for two – impossible, he says – but we can share with one other couple on a table for four. We await our next dinner with interest.

by Lizzie Mayes (Cabin 494)

I took time to have a good look around the ship – saw the various lounges, gym, table tennis area, shops, and different decks. It was a bit warmer today but grey skies – I spent some time looking at the sea – I love to watch its constant movement. I saw dozens of dolphins and had a brisk walk five times round the deck. I started talking to an Australian couple desperately trying to contact their family in Brisbane, where there are terrible floods. They were also anxious about the extortionate costs of using the onboard internet, which didn't appear to be working. They had flown from Oz to do this cruise, as it was the only affordable way to see the Amazon.

I sat outside on the aft deck but was shocked by how many smokers there were and that they had the whole of one outside deck (the 'puffin deck') and half of the outside eating deck. The wind made it difficult to escape the smell of smoke. I also spoke to some fellow cruisers but found all they talked about was how many cruises they had been on and which company was best, so they soon lost interest in us – virgin cruisers. The name Fred Olsen kept being mentioned – I thought he must be a very seasoned traveller.

We attended a shore excursion presentation which was dreary beyond description. Descriptions of Lisbon read out by two young men, one of whom had huge problems pronouncing many words and kept apologising. We could have got more information off the internet and decided we would make our own arrangements.

We went to our first lecture – Tony Rice talking about the sea. Most of it went right over my head, and I was relieved that Dick had the same problem.

Oh, there was a formal night tonight, preceded by a reception to meet the captain. We got our glad rags on and joined the line to have our photo taken with him. He had a permanently fixed smile – I wonder what he was really thinking as this army of grey old people approached him. We filed into the Marco Polo Lounge where we were introduced to all the officers on board, lined up on the stage as if facing a firing squad.

We were offered a complimentary glass of cava (the couple next to us announcing that Fred Olsen gives you much better cocktails). He must be a very generous man, this Fred Olsen.

We had fillet steak for dinner and splashed out on a bottle of house wine for £13.50 (deciding we would treat ourselves every other night). I'm still coming to terms with the complete lack of animation on so many faces, and am beginning to understand why the cruise director employs 'Hi de Hi' tactics to try and get some response. We went and listened to Olga and Liliya again – unquestionably the highlight of Dick's day. Slept like the dead again.

by Jill Crocker (Cabin 514)
Steve [Ragnall] goes to his first official meeting to establish the lecture pattern. The plan has been changed already, and his first lecture is now tomorrow. Tony Rice was on today, and the theatre was absolutely packed for him. Follow that, Steve.

I try a bit more ship orientation, but I'm not quite there yet. Tonight is the first formal evening and I see more sequins than on *Strictly Come Dancing*.

Steve is always getting at me for my wine consumption raising the total of his onboard account. He won't have any problems on this trip, as I can't stand to drink the house wine and can't afford to drink much of the rest.

by Dinah Read (Cabin 422)

We dressed up for the Captain's Reception, which must have been a miserable chore for Captain Zhukov – having to shake hands with about 800 people and look pleasant throughout. Not only that, but he had to be photographed with each one, too. What a bore for him – and for us, too, for that matter. The whole range of officers were introduced by name and by function. Twenty nationalities were represented. That, I find impressive. Jack was wearing his dress suit. I must say I think men look fantastic in formal dress. We were glad to retire to our cabin afterwards.

'The Art of Cruise Upmanship' by Dick Mayes (Cabin 494)

As a passenger on my maiden cruise, I was fascinated to learn of a new game. Not for the shy or retiring passenger, the game is akin to chess or bridge, where an ability to plan several moves ahead is mandatory if one is to achieve success at the highest level.

'Cruise Upmanship' is normally played two-a-side, and for a successful game competitors must have completed a minimum of five cruises. The number of cruises, however, should never be disclosed to the opposition.

The winners will eventually, gradually and sometimes brutally, destroy their opponents by driving them into submission by carefully planned release of information.

The game begins with the opening gambit in the form of an introductory remark intended to provoke a reply. The choice of this remark can often decide the end result and should therefore be very carefully considered. Typical opening remarks are:

    (a) Warm, isn't it!

    (b) What a beautiful colour the sea is!

    (c) The natives seem very friendly!

    (d) Weren't you on a recent P&O or Fred Olsen cruise?

The aim of the remark is tactfully to assess the strength of the opposition and also to test their game plan: i.e. are they going to play a careful tactical game or go for a quick kill. Typical opening replies to the above:

    (a) This remark, for instance, could be answered by: 'You obviously haven't been to the Red Sea.' This is known as a provocation. That might be answered directly, but it could disclose a strong card. If left (un)answered by changing tack, it could produce nervousness and uncertainty in the opposition and put you back in the driving seat.

    (b) This could be answered in the affirmative but it gives you the opportunity of stretching your attack by saying something like 'but not as beautiful as the Barrier Reef'.

(c) This is a difficult one for the opposition as they will be concerned about revealing their own social ineptitude and temperament in what would be a very subjective opinion. An answer in the affirmative could indicate weakness and a willingness to agree.

(d) This is a masterstroke. Could they have been the couple on an earlier cruise who had upset fellow passengers with very aggressive power-walking or by vomiting in the swimming pool? Whether you had shared that cruise or not is of no consequence, as they are immediately on the back foot.

So the game progresses with carefully worded release of information and probing questions, building up to a point when the trump card can be played. Obviously, the joker in the pack is the world cruise. This could soon be replaced by a Richard Branson space cruise.

From what I've seen on my maiden cruise, cruise upmanship (CU for short) is an exciting and thought-provoking game which is here to stay and could even be upgraded to a cruise knockout competition. The winners would then become 'Cruise Upmanship Nautical Trophy' holders.

by Clive Leatherdale (Cabin 725)
Can I write 1,000 words on today? That is the daily target I've set myself, but it will be hard. I breakfasted in the Waldorf before most of the other passengers were up. My fried egg was custom-made in a one-egg frying pan while I waited. Bespoke eggs, off-the-peg everything else. Figure that! I tried my best to smile at those on my table and elsewhere, a chore I will try to maintain.

I couldn't miss the 'Sailing Solo' meeting, even though wealthy widows are more likely to opt for Cunard than the *Marco Polo*. I might have missed it, however, had Richard Sykes not announced it late this morning. I was the last to turn up in Scott's Bar. About eighteen people had pulled their chairs into an elongated circle. Most were women, all looked very old, and the only two I reckoned to be younger than me I put down to that scary species, schoolteachers. I sat next to Herman from Belgium. He had lived in Brazil in the 1970s, wore a blue and white striped shirt and had an eye-catching gut. He complained that Germans insisted on spelling his name with two r's and two n's. We were offered (free) champaign, Buck's Fizz, or orange juice and then asked to introduce ourselves, name only, not profession. It was a bit like auditioning for *The Weakest Link*. An elderly dear kept checking my name – Colin? We supplied our cabin numbers and will all be invited to lunch once we have left Lisbon.

Richard Sykes had warned us that it was blowing a Force 7 outside, and that once we passed into the Bay of Biscay around 8 this evening it would rise to Force 8. I will soon discover if I am susceptible to being seasick. Women are wandering around complaining of feeling sick. I was glad I'm on the first sitting for dinner – 5.45 rather than 8.15 – as it will get rougher later on. Dinah, bless her, said I was good company, as we had our table of eight to ourselves, just three, with Jack. Many other tables near us were empty or part-empty, too.

The show team are putting on 'Venetian Nights' in the theatre this evening. I shall give it a miss. Ditto the 'Carpenters Cabaret' and 'Who Wants to Be a Millionaire' in Scott's Bar.

To many female passengers, the *Marco Polo*'s Greek staff captain, 'Nick', was a bit of a hunk. Here he is buying a whopping big fish somewhere up the Amazon (Margit Latter)

DAY 4. AT SEA

'Born in 1952 in Crimea, Captain Valentyn Zhukov graduated from the Odessa High Engineering Marine School. He has since taken the Master's role on many cruise ships working all over the globe, but his favourite port of call is probably the lovely city of Venice.'

by Judy Chapman (Cabin 419)

Our dining table companions are beginning to loosen up a bit. They're not a bad bunch really, but I still cannot foresee either of us seeking out their company.

Then we hit the Bay of Biscay. The least said about that the better. Not that I can remember much as I was drugged up on strong sea-sickness tablets. Fancy holding the Captain's Reception in the Bay of Biscay! I am afraid he was deprived of my presence, although I did manage to drag along my posh green frock (£35 from British Home Stores and worn at every Captain's Reception on the past five cruises). I even staggered down to the Waldorf restaurant to toy with a dry bread roll and piece of fruit before heading for bed.

by Mave Eaton (Cabin 616)

Our cabin is no longer a silent haven. Above us the joggers pound the walking track, below we hear the entertainment revving up. The walls are paper thin. One side has rhythmic snores, but the other side has two elderly ladies. Is one a little deaf? They chatter unceasingly. Perhaps they each live alone. At 1am my silent husband thumps the wall and the girls' dormitory falls silent. But what are the noises we make?

Our new dinner companions provide a refreshing change from the middle class. Husband is a retired miner from Doncaster (or steelworker from Sheffield). Wife was manager of a betting shop. They tell us of the sunbed wars on the top deck. If beds are left for more than 30 minutes, belongings are removed, but the original occupants are not amused on their return.

Fellow diners feel that when one occupies a bed it should be for life: we make polite disagreeing noises.

by Lizzie Mayes (Cabin 494)

I'm still coming to terms with fellow passengers. On reaching 65, I decided I wouldn't waste the precious years I have left with people I didn't really like and had nothing in common with, and here I am imprisoned in the middle of the ocean with some of the most boring and boorish people I have ever met in my life. Conversation revolves around how many cruises they have been on, the merits of the different cruise lines and complaints about just about everything on this ship – I have realised now that Fred Olsen is not a person but a fleet of 'superior' cruise ships, though 'of course' not 5-star. I haven't a clue what they're talking about – Queens, Countesses, Princesses.

The daily programme announced choir club, to be run by none other than Mr Hi de Hi this morning. Well, I thought, I might as well give it a whirl – got to do something to stop me from going mad. After five minutes I was a convert – what a brilliant and charismatic man this Richard Sykes is. He had us all eating out of his hands. I went and fetched Dick and told him it was too good to miss. During the next 45 minutes we found our diaphragms, and sirened and hummed our way into singing *The Carnival Is Over* in four parts, with the help of showteam singers Christian and Adina, and Megan and Cait the cabaret singers. It was a totally absorbing and entertaining 40 minutes. I wondered about Richard's sexuality. Can't wait for the next session. I chatted to Robert from Winchelsea, or Rye – perhaps there are some kindred spirits here after all. I went to an 'abs class' – something about trimming, tightening and firming bits of my body I didn't know existed.

Great excitement – there is a comedian to entertain us. But it was cancelled due to his seasickness. It seemed a bit choppy, but nothing an early night won't sort. So we contented ourselves with the lovely Olga before getting a good night's sleep in preparation for our four hours in Lisbon. I took aspirin by mistake, thinking it was stugeron, but it worked a treat.

by Dinah Read (Cabin 422)

Jack came with me to a lecture by Steve Ragnall on the Confederate warship *Alabama* and her history. It was quite excellent. I had heard her name in shanties and sea-songs about her, but really knew nothing else. She was built in this country, secretly fitted out for war and had unbelievable success raiding US shipping, burning her prizes and their cargoes, though always taking their crews off first. Her captain was a heroic figure. I would not have missed this very effective presentation for anything. Later in the afternoon Jack [85] and I [80] retired to our cabin for what he calls 'rest and recreation'.

by Jill Crocker (Cabin 514)

Steve's first lecture today was about the American Civil War ship *Alabama*. My job (which is absolutely vital) is to make sure there's a glass of water handy.

There weren't as many attendees as Tony Rice had and I hope that this is because of the large number lying prone in cabins due to weather conditions, not a general reduction of interest. I, more than Steve, am fiercely competitive, and want everyone on board to see and hear his talents.

I heard later that some passengers thought his lecture was about cowboys and therefore not really of interest to them.

Note to self: when returning to cabin on Deck 7 go left, left at the lift.

by Clive Leatherdale (Cabin 725)

Welcome to the Bay of Biscay. The bloody Bay of Biscay. I have never before been on a ship across these waters, and on this evidence I never want to again. I have not yet actually been sick, but that could change at any second, even as I write.

While lying flat on my bed, either on my back or on my side, I seemed fine, but the moment I got to my feet I lost my sea-legs and came over all queasy. I wobbled down to the Waldorf for breakfast and was directed to a space at a table nearly full. The waiter brought me tea and orange juice, but trying to traverse the floor to the buffet was a challenge I was in no mood to attempt, so I swallowed my drinks and retired gingerly to my cabin.

The crashing motion of the ship's pitch and fall was most unsettling. I dreaded going over to Marco's Bistro for lunch and postponed doing so as long as I could. But once I knew it was about to close, I went along, served myself soup and dessert, took them outside by the empty swimming pool, and felt slightly better at once. I went back for seconds, and by 3pm the sun had actually emerged for the first time since leaving Tilbury.

Since writing those last words I have indeed been sick. Too late, I took a Boots Travel Calm tablet and feel much better. Richard Sykes came on the intercom at noon to tell us that the sea state was 6 and the Beaufort windspeed 7. While sitting outside I watched as we overtook a number of cargo ships, and saw their bows rise and crash, just like ours.

Richard has just been on the intercom again to say that, because of the 'challenging' conditions in the Bay of Biscay, we will arrive at Lisbon two hours late, 2pm instead of noon. He added that we were now leaving the Bay of Biscay, and it is no coincidence that the motion of the ship is a little smoother.

by Kay Rainsley (Cabin 543)
We hoped we'd see Richard
   We'd seen him before
And each time he sings
   The audience wants more.

Today we saw Richard
   He's awfully good
He was cruise director
   Now he's Victoria Wood.

Curious murals seen in Tenerife, above, and Cape Verde, below (Clive Leatherdale)

DAY 5. LISBON, PORTUGAL

'Portugal's capital, Lisbon, is a large sprawling city with many reminders of its colourful history peopled by Visigoths, Moors, Romans, Phoenicians, Carthaginians and even a few warring Celts. Alfama and Barrio Alto are its charming historic districts . . .'

by Judy Chapman (Cabin 419)

I've always wanted to see Portugal. But not in the cold grey mist such as we had today. We're still wearing our winter clothes, but have shed one layer of pullovers.

Back home, my 94-year-old mother is settled into her temporary care home but is not a happy bunny. In her medically induced state it's doubtful she can appreciate that its only for a few weeks while we are away, and the respite is as much for her overworked children's benefit (all three of us in our 60s) as it is for her own.

We didn't see much of Lisbon. We took a trip on a red tourist bus but time ashore was limited, so we were unable to hop on and off to look at the sights. Coincidentally, sitting next to us were people we knew from Spalding 40-odd years ago. Has my appearance changed in four decades? I like to think not, but I know it's not true. My hair has turned grey and there's two stone more of me now than there was then. There'll be even more if I continue to eat three meals a day in the Waldorf.

Sailing away from cool, overcast Lisbon, there is still the niggling feeling at the back of my mind that, given the chance, I'd jump on the next plane home. Potential enjoyment of things to come has not been helped by several horror stories heard from fellow passengers about dangers to be faced in Brazil from thieves and muggers. What kind of holiday is this, when I'll be looking over my shoulder all the time watching for attackers?

by Marion Cox (Cabin 619)

'Where do those steps go?'

'No idea, let's take a look.'

What a gem of a square, a fountain in the middle, pink-washed church to one side, enclosed by high-storey houses covered in ornate coloured tiles. Washing flapping from the shuttered windows.

'Watch out!' A rickety old tram came swinging round the corner and swayed down the hill, bell ringing a late warning.

'Not seen the likes of that in the UK since the 1950s.'

The nearby antiques museum was in total contrast to its ultra-modern cafe. A glass cube perched over the harbour like an aerie. We moved along its edge, like mime-artists, arms spread out feeling for the door. On the other side a waiter opened the invisible door: 'Sorry, no handle – broken.'

by Jean McGinley (Cabin 229)

At my first dinner in the Waldorf I found myself sitting next to Hermann, shortly to be known as 'H' to everyone. He had a foreign accent that I could not place, but with a hint of Yorkshire. I discovered that he was from Hamburg but had lived in Hull for the past 40 years. His partner Yvonne was a great Yorkshire lass, and we got along famously those first few nights. Sadly, Yvonne became unwell and spent the two days before Lisbon in the ship's hospital. It was with real regret and sadness that we had to say goodbye to them in Lisbon. I learned that this cruise was 'H's' 70th birthday treat, so it was very sad that they had to leave the ship. The one consolation was that the medical care in Lisbon would be preferable to, say, Cape Verde or some of the Amazonian ports.

by Jill Crocker (Cabin 514)

As we disembarked in Lisbon, I was immediately behind the lady who fell and broke her ankle on the first day (how disappointing for her). We were walking, she was not. She was in a wheelchair. We turned left for a red tourist bus and views of Lisbon; she turned right for an ambulance and the pages of forms in her insurance claim [she never returned to the ship]. An early general observation: prices charged in the ship's hospital must increase the cruise company's profits by 50 per cent.

I have often thought I'd like to spend a few days in Lisbon, but I am not so sure, now that I've seen it. This is the main drawback about cruising for me, the brief stays at destinations which put back a longer visit.

by Dinah Read (Cabin 422)

We went early to our cabin. Jack, having been separated from me for half a day, was most affectionate. I like it.

by Caroline Clifford (Cabin 468)

Why have I decided to keep a diary? It's very time-consuming and I'm certainly not a Samuel Pepys, an Adrian Mole, or even a Bridget Jones. The only thing I've in common with Bridget is the size of my knickers.

I've been travelling with James for twelve years now and I've always been content with my photographic record of our expeditions. I've got some lovely pictures of him. Of course, he's not exactly eye-candy – he's built for strength not speed. He can keep me amused for hours reciting railway timetables – not! And he instinctively knows which will be our check-in desk before we even reach the airport. He knows every road-number in Britain – very useful when you want to clear the *Marco Polo* table at breakfast.

Today is Friday, so it must be Portugal – the world's largest cork producer. The rain has cleared but the sea is still delightfully choppy. The Bay of Biscay lived up to its reputation and passengers mysteriously disappeared from dinner, some re-emerging with straps, slings, sticks and bandages. As the sun appeared, fashion sense went out of the portholes. Why do men (and women) with short, fat, hairy legs feel they have to show them off? Suddenly we're all dressed for Magaluf.

My ideal day in Lisbon would be a day on the trams – perhaps No 28 going up to the fort. So why did I book a tour? I hate that whole coach experience. I hate waiting in the ship's lounge until the scheduled tour is called – or not! I hate joining in the stampede, everyone pushing and falling over each other to get the front seat. And when you do get to the coach, some allegedly disabled person is already snuggly installed, ready to cause maximum disruption and delay at every scheduled stop. Funny how the sticks disappear as soon as the buffet is opened. James, who is particularly resourceful, is currently working on a design for a coach with 48 front seats. Patent pending.

I managed to bag the seat behind the toilets. James was pleased (when he caught up with me) but his idea of gratitude is, at the top of his voice, 'You've got a great pair of tits!' My idea of flattery would be to praise him for his latest, ingenious, DIY cabin improvement scheme.

The tour was a relaxed drive through Estoril, Cascais and Sintra. Whilst we couldn't find any gin in Amsterdam, we did manage to track down a wonderful bottle of late-bottled vintage port in a tiny local shop in Cascais. This was during one of those compulsory tour stops where you are forced to amuse yourself for an hour in a location that for all intents and purposes appears 'closed'.

Sintra was lovely, high up in the hills. Show me a 'Noddy train' and I'm happy. Of course, James commented that we could have done Sintra on our own, taking the train from Rossio, Lisbon; or from Cascais: 'There is the commuter service passing by the port every twenty minutes.'

Now, three hours out of Lisbon, we didn't have enough small change for both of us to go to the loo – so we opted for 'scissors, paper, stone'.

I was left crossing my legs till we got back to the ship. Nobody can accuse James of being a chauvinist.

The fog set in with a vengeance on our return, so we saw little of Lisbon. At least it gave something new for the passengers to moan about at dinner.

by Clive Leatherdale (Cabin 725)

I woke to find the sea as calm as if I had waved a wand over it. To the discerning eye there was still the faintest of swells, which caused the ship ever so slightly to list to port, then starboard, but so slowly as to leave no effect on your balance.

After four days I'm having doubts about trying to write this book on my own. Too many people to observe and interview, too much to see, to do, all a bit overwhelming. It will all end up rather superficial. I've collared a few passengers and tried to enrol them, but time is flying and I think I'd better come up with Plan 'B'. Or even 'Plan 'C'. I could pass the word around, hoping the jungle telegraph will spread the message to all corners of the ship. But would that work? And how could it be kept secret from the crew? And what would Richard Sykes say if he knew?

I went to Reception and left a message asking Richard to contact me as soon as possible. He's a busy man, he will be expecting a complaint – for why else would someone demand to speak to the chief? – and will probably give me the brush off for a few days. Yet I don't have a few days to spare.

Five minutes later Richard rang. 'Shall I come up?' He was soon sitting in a space I hastily made among papers and underwear strewn across the opposite bed. Richard swung his legs back and forth as we revisited shared encounters on the *Marco Polo*. He had no recollection of me from three previous cruises, mainly because he naturally remembers the complainers, and I wasn't a complainer.

At length I got to the point. Richard couldn't stop me going ahead, of course, but the best I could hope for was detachment, something like this: 'Well, Clive, please feel free to continue, but you understand that this is not an official publication, we have no idea what will be in it, so it will not be possible to offer you any official backing.'

What he actually said was: 'What a great idea. Why hasn't anyone thought of that before? I'll put something in the day sheet for tomorrow and call a meeting for those interested.' Richard reckoned maybe ten serious contributors would turn up, alongside twice that number of exuberant wannabes who would be more trouble than they are worth. We shall see.

And when I ventured that Richard might want to contribute himself, his face lit up even more than usual: 'Of course I will. I'd be a fool not to. How any pieces do you want?' And so 'Murder on the Marco Polo' was born, although the title was not yet conceived.

We arrived late. Lisbon, quickly buried in fog, was not at her best.

Top: Callhau, Cape Verde. Mighty waves but deserted, apart from this lone fisherman.
Bottom: The road north from Callhau, smooth, new and empty.
Where are you, Jeremy Clarkson and your *Top Gear* racers? (both Clive Leatherdale)

DAY 6. AT SEA

"Cruise Book Contributors' Meeting."
The owner of Desert Island Books has requested a
meeting with diarists, aspiring travel writers,
experienced sea-goers and budding travel photographers.
Today at 11.30 in Scott's Bar.'

by Clive Leatherdale (Cabin 725)

The sky is blue, the sea calm – sea state 2, windspeed 3. Oh that it would remain like this for the duration. The weather was balmy enough at 16 degrees to venture outside.

Just before the appointed time, 11.30, I presented myself at Scott's Bar and waited for Richard Sykes to finish his piano talk on 'how chord structures work'. I wondered where he was going to put me, but he pulled two chairs into the centre of the dance floor, shoved a microphone into my hand and asked me to introduce myself. It was clear he intended an upbeat, joint presentation, passing the mike from one to another, with me the Wise to his Morecambe. This was not what I had in mind at all. Richard Sykes does not do 'low key'. Mr Hi de Hi is turbo-charged at all times.

Around 30 passengers had turned up, more than either of us expected, and the response was quiet but positive. Richard rounded off, suggested meeting again in a week, and went round with a scrap of paper to take cabin numbers of those wanting to actively contribute.

Three of the audience came up to ask me questions afterwards. One woman said she was a poet and asked if contributing poems was acceptable. I gulped hard and said yes. The second was an ex-headmaster writing his memoirs and seeking guidance on how to publish them 'as they were humorous'. The third was guest lecturer Tony Rice, who wanted to know how Amazon could sell his paperback book at less than the discounted price he was paying for it.

Dinner at table 14 was dramatic on account of two new faces. Angela and Bernadine, sisters, were ex-teachers. Bernadine had recently decamped to Cyprus and had a no-nonsense steel behind her generous laugh. Angela had taught in Gateshead but lived in Newcastle. Whereas, for me, yesterday's visit to Lisbon had been a 'fog out', for the sisters it had provided an unwelcome adrenaline rush. As anyone who observed them on deck would notice, the sisters don't walk side by side. Bernadine leads, Angela follows. Irrespective of their formation, they lost their bearings on the way back to the ship, which had docked a considerable distance from the city centre. Finding no helpful landmarks, they rang the 'emergency contact' for the ship's agent. This vital piece of information is provided on the day sheet for every port of call.

All the sisters got was someone who didn't speak English. (This was anything but a one-off. Throughout the cruise desperate passengers forced to ring the emergency number often found no helpful response.) For Bernadine and Angela, without passports, money, or any essentials, and with the clock running down, they were beginning to panic.

Then they saw a stationary police car. Bernadine ran over, and presumably the urgency on her face transcended her lack of Portuguese, for the police said 'get in'. Sirens wailing and blue light flashing, the police car shot off in the direction of *Marco Polo*. The distance was much greater than they thought, confirming that on foot they could never have reached her in time. They arrived at 6.31pm, a minute after the ship was intended to sail. Bernadine kissed the surprised officers on the cheek in gratitude before the sisters dashed up the gangway. She laughed when telling the story, but one sensed her stomach was still in knots.

Out on deck I waylaid Mark and Sue Edwards, both rowing coaches. They detailed the contrasts between real rowing and the Concept2 indoor rowing machine. 'Ergs don't float,' said Sue, a little obviously. Mark explained how each of the four who won British gold in Sydney in 2000 brought something distinctive to the boat – Tim Foster, for example, being a supreme technician. 'Put him in any boat and it simply went faster.'

by Mark Edwards (Cabin 423)
Passengers with camcorders have become fair game to interrupt. As a user of a big camera who attempts to take better pictures than just snaps, I am used to lots of passengers who snap away and then move on. The trick to getting the shots you really want is to be at the back of the group. I might miss some of the commentary from the guide, but Sue [wife] will catch me up on that later, and will often point to pictures she wants me to take.

The camcorder-users, however, plant themselves down and then start recording, muttering away for a couple of minutes whilst filming to give a commentary. Invariably, where I want to stand is in their shot. If they take too long, I walk in front of them onto camera and then turn to them and apologise. And as they only walk slowly, never quite catching up the group, they are always in the back – in my way.

by Sue Edwards (Cabin 423)

A good night's sleep. Breakfast today was just fruit and yoghurt for me. Mark added a Danish and a bread roll. Up to the pool deck to catch some rays, as this is the first day it has not been solid cloud.

I made a comment to Mark at breakfast. The last words we will ever want to hear again are 'thank you'. We all say it dozens of times a day. The boat is so full of staff, crew – call them what you will – serving you, dispensing hand sanitiser, clearing up after you, etc.

Mark struggles to carry books and chairs while navigating a way past the old Dutch ladies – a regular trip hazard. He has now voted them the first candidates for the 'man (woman) overboard contest'.

It is wonderful to arrive in the Waldorf dining room first. To sit at your own table – a well-worn path, and to be greeted by the lovely waiters, especially their concern that the 'gentleman' is missing.

by Judy Chapman (Cabin 419)

The sun's shining. The temperature's rising. The sea is calm and passengers are wearing t-shirts and shorts. There's a world of travel in all those t-shirts – Sri Lanka, Vietnam, Sydney, Las Vegas. Our fellow passengers have, between them, covered the globe. And the nice thing is, they're ordinary people like us. Like Mike, some worked in local government. Others are retired engineers, teachers or administrators. All right, some are more highly paid professionals, but all are relaxed and easy going. A cruise to an unusual destination such as Brazil is not for the snobbish. It is for those like Mike who prefer to go off the beaten tourist trail.

by Dinah Read (Cabin 422)

After lunch I went to a lecture on whales by Tony Rice, which was both informative and entertaining. It was amusing to be told how some people apparently come on cruises in order to play cards, and that reduced their chances of seeing a whale considerably! I caught up with Jack again on deck and we went down to our cabin for an hour before dinner. I never felt more appreciated in my life.

by Steve Ragnall (Cabin 514) Steve was the ship's maritime lecturer

It's day six on board MV Marco Polo. Day six of a six-week cruise to South America and we are bowling along at 17.7 knots towards Tenerife in a moderate sea. After two bumpy days in the Bay of Biscay (well, what do you expect in winter?) things have now settled down and we've been sitting out 'catching a few rays'. The paper sick-bags that have adorned the handrails throughout the ship for the use of poor sailors have disappeared and everyone is beginning to relax.

I wonder how many of Christopher Columbus' crew were seasick as they sailed down to the Canary Islands in 1492. No paper bags for them, just find the lee-side of the ship.

On such a ship as *Marco Polo*, how can you begin to equate their passage to ours? We're travelling in luxury – excellent food, comfy cabins with all mod cons. There was only a single cabin on *Santa Maria* (which Columbus claimed for himself, of course) and no berth deck. The only full-length deck was open to the elements, except for sheltered areas under the quarterdeck, which covered the rear third, and the forecastle, which covered a smaller area in the bows. The strongest of the crew no doubt managed to find a corner of these sheltered areas to sleep in, but the rest would have slept in the open, whether rain or storm. There were no hammocks, so it was either bare wooden deck or, if you were lucky, a coil of rope or a sail. Hammocks were an invention that the Spanish later brought back to Europe from the indigenous peoples of the Caribbean. Thank goodness for en-suite staterooms, I say.

The voyage from Spain to landing in the West Indies took Columbus and his men 69 days, including a repair stop of over a week in the Canaries. It will take us ten days from Lisbon to Brazil.

It's interesting that we're on a ship called *Marco Polo* when the Venetian traveller that the vessel is named after had a substantial role in Columbus' thinking. Columbus was searching for the Orient, and the published book of Marco Polo's travels was the main account of the Far East available to him at that time. The fact that it was written some 150 years before would suggest that it might be ever so slightly out of date. And we throw out our *Lonely Planet* guides if they are just a couple of years old.

Calculations made from Marco Polo's travels suggested that Asia was far broader than it is and, coupled with the view that the world was only 18,000 miles in circumference (instead of the actual measurement of 24,901 miles), Columbus thought Japan was just 2,500 miles to the west of Spain. It was a good job that he hit his 'New World' instead.

This vessel that we're on isn't the first to carry the name 'Marco Polo'. There was a very famous clipper ship of that name built in St John, New Brunswick, Canada, in 1851. Launched on 17 April, it didn't have the most auspicious start, hitting a mud bank and falling on its side as the tide went out. No real damage was done and it was soon on its way to Liverpool with a cargo of timber.

It was always a flyer, and some people think that its launching accident bent the keel in such a way as to increase its speed. Quickly purchased by the Black Ball Line of Liverpool, she was converted for passenger service to take emigrants to Australia. After being copper-bottomed, it did the voyage from Liverpool to Sydney harbour in 76 days, spent three weeks in port, and then returned home in another 76 days, the first recorded return voyage to the colony in under six months. People now clamoured to travel on her and there's an oft-quoted saying that one in every twenty Australians can trace their roots to a passage on *Marco Polo*.

Such a long passage was always a hazardous affair in the 19th century and, powered just by sail, there was no guarantee of a fast voyage, but under two famous clipper captains, James Nicol Forbes and Charles McDonald, *Marco Polo* was the most consistent on the route. Incidentally, James Forbes' nickname was 'Bully' Forbes – these were hard men.

That earlier *Marco Polo* was 184ft 1in long, 36ft 3in beam, 29ft 4in draught, had three tall masts and a huge spread of sail. Steam propulsion was already starting to enter the shipping industry, usually as auxiliary power, but it was expensive and needed specialist shipyards, so at least 90 per cent of all ships were still powered by sail alone.

Our *Marco Polo* is powered by two huge diesel engines coupled to four generators to run this highly complicated vessel and, with a cruising speed of 16.5 knots and a maximum speed of 22 knots, we can reach speeds unheard of in the times of the clipper ship. We are three times longer than the clipper at 578ft 5in, twice as wide at 77ft 3in, but slightly shallower draught at 27ft. In a clipper, the deep draught is needed not just to increase the size of its carrying capacity but to give it stability and ability to hold a steady course. We have ten decks (eight passenger decks) against the clipper's three. Our vessel was built in 1965 in an East German shipyard as a liner and delivered to a Soviet company to inaugurate a passenger service from Leningrad (now St Petersburg) to Montreal. Launched as the *Alexandr Pushkin*, she was renamed *Marco Polo* after sale to, and refit by, Orient Lines in the early 1990s for some US$60 million.

MV Marco Polo can carry a maximum of 820 passengers in 425 staterooms. I don't know how many passengers the clipper carried, but you can bet that conditions were very cramped aboard her. There were few private cabins, most of the passengers being berthed in dormitories with partitions made of canvas.

Every voyage had its own triumphs and tragedies, its own births and deaths, mostly unrecorded except as a note in the captain's log. Burial at sea was a routine occurrence. Many brought their own food aboard and would have to queue at the ship's galley to have it cooked. Provisions would often run low and water was always at a premium. Waste disposal facilities were non-existent. In journals kept by some on passage to Australia, you often see references to 'a brown sea' as, when in the light or negligible winds of the doldrums, all the detritus from the vessel would stay around the ship as it floated along.

Our cruise liner has not only a huge store of quality foodstuffs (and many chefs to prepare them) but also, at the other end of the spectrum, has environmentally friendly disposal equipment. We will not experience the 'brown sea'.

The clipper's hull had to balance the need for speed, for time was definitely money, with a good carrying capacity. The hull shape was developed over many years and would result in even faster vessels, the so-called 'extreme clippers' such as the *Cutty Sark*.

Our *MV Marco Polo* has traditional liner styling to its hull, making her a thing of beauty, rather than the blunter bow and slab-sided look of a modern cruise ship, and this adds to her charm. There is a thought that, with her ice-strengthened hull, high freeboard and built-in extra stability, she was built to double as a troopship. She was not an ice-breaker *per se*, though she did need to be able to navigate the icy Baltic Sea.

The clipper was built of pine and fir and in 1861 collided with an iceberg south of Cape Horn. Leaking badly, she limped into Valparaiso for repairs. Her career continued, however, until she finally failed passenger safety regulations in 1867, was sold and converted back to cargo carrying. By then she had also been hailed as heroic, after saving the passengers and crew of an emigrant ship, *Eastern City*, which had caught fire off the Cape of Good Hope in 1858.

Clipper *Marco Polo* was finally driven ashore on Prince Edward Island in Canada in 1883 after springing a leak. Its wreck site is listed as a National Historic Site. All ships have their day, and even *MV Marco Polo* will eventually come to the end of her operating life, but here's hoping that she continues to roam the seven seas for a good few years to come.

This sunshine feels good after the ice and snow at home. I think I'll order a cocktail from one of the ever-attentive stewards and drink a toast to all the vessels that have carried the proud name of 'Marco Polo'. Here is a lyric I composed about the clipper.

'The Marco Polo' lyrics by Steve Ragnall (Cabin 514)
In St John's fair harbour a long time ago
    She was slid down the skids, she made a fine show
On a high Fundy tide they loaded her low
    And set sail on a course for England

And carrying timber to Liverpool town
　　Crossing the ocean in leaps and in bounds
She proved her construction was better than sound
　　And they named her the great *Marco Polo*

Chorus: A clipper she was like not seen before
　　The fastest square-rigger from Canada's shore
Her home was the Ocean, on trade winds she tore
　　And they named her the great *Marco Polo*

Black Ball converted her for a new trade
　　For a life in Australia people would pay
A new life for families who proudly would say
　　We came by the great *Marco Polo*

Old 'Bully' Forbes, he drove her along
　　Hard man of renown with curse or with song
With him in command naught would go wrong
　　With the flyer they called *Marco Polo*

Chorus: A clipper she was like not seen before
　　The fastest square-rigger from Canada's shore
Her home was the Ocean, on trade winds she tore
　　And they named her the great *Marco Polo*

A fine ship to voyage in, on the high seas
　　Where others just follow, she always leads
There's no other place I'd rather be
　　Than travelling on *Marco Polo*

Now the ship *Marco Polo*'s still here to this day
　　Though that fastest square-rigger's long faded away
There goes a fine looking vessel they say
　　Her name? The great *Marco Polo*

Chorus: A clipper or cruise ship, it's all the same
　　A vessel of fortune, a vessel of fame
Her character clear from her proud name
　　They called her the great *Marco Polo*.

Comparative sizes of
the clipper and the
cruise ship *Marco Polo*
(Steve Ragnall)

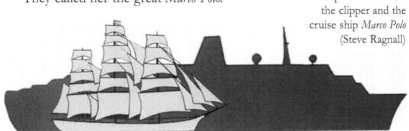

DAY 7. SANTA CRUZ, TENERIFE

Tenerife is the largest of the Canary Islands and has the highest elevation in Spain. It's a World Heritage Site that is the third largest volcano from its base, El Teide. The name Tenerife is derived from the words "Tene" (mountain) and "Ife" (white)'

by Sue Edwards (Cabin 423)

The tannoy delivers a constant supply of ambient music. Some might complain that there is no escape from the evil musack even in the Atlantic. It matters little as the wind carries off the melodies long before they reach my ears. The music that is constant is that of the bass throbbing of the funnel. Sharp notes are provided by the regular, if not orchestrated pings of china and cutlery tidied by our ever-vigilant stewards. Then there are the harmonies of human voices, in all their variance of tone – the gasps, the giggles of joy and surprise, and certainly pleasure – for who could not be experiencing pleasure at this moment?

I look two decks up to people hugging the rail. Are they looking to sea or to the swimming pool below? Who will take the first plunge into the pool? Is the fishing net over its surface a deterrent?

The voices are predominantly English, of many regions, and some Dutch, and are interspersed with what I presume to be Russian, from the crew portraits, as they move off with their buckets and rollers to tart up another section of railings. Mark is interested to know how the painters will deal with the rusty hole! I fear he may be immovable until his curiosity is satisfied. Ten minutes later that rusty blemish on an otherwise pristine white wall still engages our curiosity.

by Lizzie Mayes (Cabin 494)

The temperature is rising as we head south and sun-loungers are festooned with towels from early in the morning. The [top] 'broiler deck' is gradually filled with translucent white bodies basted in oil, glistening in the sun – all shapes and sizes in the briefest of bikinis and proud cockerels strutting their stuff amongst the geriatric hens. I found a nice quiet place on the shady side. Very peaceful, just watching the sea. No other ships anywhere – just miles of ocean. Met someone called Clive who noticed that I was scribbling and asked if I was keeping a diary. He is planning a book about the cruise (didn't totally understand what he had in mind) but he talked me into attending his next meeting as I had missed the first one.

Richard Sykes wandered by and told a story about scraping noises from a cabin: on investigation it emerged that someone had dragged her lounger into her cabin last thing each night and out first thing each morning. A fellow passenger happily told me Fred Olsen had more loungers. I am beginning to get better at avoiding some people.

We disembarked at Santa Cruz to see another passenger bite the dust – sitting in the back of an ambulance on a drip. We are beginning to see the odd injured passenger – arms in slings, and hearing how expensive a visit to the doctor is. I must keep fit!

We walked to the bus station to get a bus to Puerto Cruz. We were amazed to see the island development since we were last here about seventeen years ago. We bought a bottle of gin to take on board – (if we buy drinks on the ship we will be bankrupt at the end of six weeks) and decanted it into two water bottles in the bus station before furtively binning the glass gin bottle. Felt like naughty teenagers – next step drinking cider in the park.

We went back on board to the deck party and discovered that other passengers had cabins full of illicit booze, which made our two water bottles seem very pathetic.

At dinner tonight the menu offered 'fillet of pugnacious fish'. Whatever is that? Decided not to risk it and ate the Moroccan Lamb – delicious. I found somewhere quiet to sit and scribble this, and am getting adept at finding quiet spots on the ship away from the 'parrot house'.

I thought it might be interesting to rewrite the Ten Commandments, but could only come up with one. Love the Planet and Everything Still Left on It. Then we could do away with all the god stuff. It must be because it's Sunday and those called are filing out from morning service.

Don't start Liz. I have to write a song for Richard's class.

I have been wondering if the snowdrops are emerging back home; are the daffodils being brave enough to look up; and what will I plant in the garden this year? Are the chickens laying again? Will there be more baby ducks on our return, are the first lambs born? But I am going to see the rainforest!

by Judy Chapman (Cabin 419)
This is more like it! Church service [inter-denominational] in the morning in the main theatre – something we rarely do at home. To our surprise

the chaplain turned out to be a fascinating medical man and TA officer with whom we shared breakfast the other morning.

An afternoon ashore in Tenerife. We must be some of the few people on the ship who've never been here before. Some fellow passengers even live here. Off the ship with 'Bill Gates' and his German lady travelling companion Margit ('Think of Margate and you'll remember my name'). Incredibly, they'd only returned from a holiday on the island two days before we sailed, so they knew the best places to visit. They took us by local bus to a mountainside village with a sandy man-made beach.

We came back on board to a lively pool-side party hosted by Richard Sykes. Exhausted, we fell into bed at midnight.

'I wonder what they're doing at home,' says Mike.

'Home?' I murmur contentedly. 'This is our home for the next five weeks.'

by Marion Cox (Cabin 619)

The Sunday market was in full swing. Our quest for the day was swimming trunks (we had forgotten to bring them).

'It looks as if they only have women's.'

I simulate the breast-stroke and point at husband. A big shake of the head from the stall-holder.

At another stall we find some. 'Look at bit small to me.' Gesticulate a bigger size. The lady stretches them bigger. 'Elastic,' she says, 'all sizes.'

'I'm not sure they'll hold everything in.' More explicit gesticulations. Even more laughter – our lady says they stretch even more.

'I'll take that as a compliment.'

'Euros?'

'Five.' 'A bargain.' Back on board, the try-on.

'Not really you. The stripes make you look like Captain Webb on the old match-boxes.'

by Dinah Read (Cabin 422)

She is beautiful, the old girl (I am, of course, referring to the ship and not to myself). She is a ship-shaped ship, not a rectangular hotel-block clapped on top of a shoebox. Her lines are classical, elegant, satisfying. I am enchanted by her. This cruise is all that I had dreamed of. The crew are multinational, willing and polite, and happy to be here. The waiters glide around smiling as though they take pleasure in their work, and the cabin staff never stop cleaning the ship, from handrails to stair-treads, to door handles. Passing into the dining room your hands are sprayed for you. Everywhere, decor and furnishings are coordinated and tasteful in a somewhat retro style. I have never seen so many mirrors, which give a sense of space and brightness.

I popped down for a quiz at 10am but am not likely to bother with that again. I know nothing about pop musicians anyway. Afterwards I came back to Jack for half an hour. On the way I stepped aside to make way for a passing power-walker and tripped on an iron bulwark fixing and went flying down onto the deck. It hurt a bit but no real harm done. The power-walker did not seem to be aware that anything had happened.

We went into the Captain's Club and listened to the piano player. She played quietly and dreamily – not as a concert pianist does – more as though she were practising. The way my mother used to.

'My Tenerife Adventure' by Vivian Walsh (Cabin 609)
I was happy when we reached the port of Santa Cruz; I really needed a break from the ship. My travelling companion had been ill from the start and we were quarantined in our cabin. There was nothing wrong with me, but I had to stay there for four days. Jim was still unfit when we arrived in Tenerife so I was off on my adventure.

A long time ago I owned a hairdressing salon. Today, on impulse, I was going to find Jean, who once worked for me. Jean had moved over to live in San Miguel eighteen months earlier. I had no phone number, but I did have an address at a golf course. Jean was unaware that I was coming, so fingers crossed I left the ship.

I had no idea where San Miguel was, or how far it was, so I ran the gauntlet of the waiting taxis. A nice-looking young man, Antonio, approached me and asked, 'Where would you like to go?'

I told him.

'€200,' he said.

'That's much too much,' I replied. 'I'm going to see a friend and she may not be in. It's a surprise.'

Five minutes later we had made a deal. He would drive me to San Miguel and wait two hours, and then bring me back to the ship for €100. I was happy with that. I just hoped she would be in.

It was a long way to San Miguel, down south in the direction of the airport, but up in the hills. It was when we arrived that the fun began. Situated way back from the beach and the main road were three golf courses. As we could not find the right one, we visited all three. At each golf club Antonio would say, looking at his watch, 'I will see you here in two hours.' Each time I would come back and say, 'It's the wrong one.'

Third time I was lucky. This time I came back with a map to the lanes where the houses were. He said for the third time, 'See you in two hours.'

I walked down the lane until I found the right number, then said to myself, 'Please be in.' I knocked on the door, waited, then tried the bell. The door opened. It was David, Jean's husband.

'Hi David. Do you remember me?'

'Well I know the face, but not the name.' David had not seen me for 25 years!

'My name is Vivian.' He stepped out to grab me for a hug, and at the same time, was calling for Jean. 'Vivian's here!'

'I'll be down in one minute,' I heard from within. Jean came rushing out, still wet from the shower, and was dressing while running to greet me. She was crying with excitement, which made me cry, too.

I had not seen Jean for seven years, but we always sent cards with long letters and every year we would ask, 'Where has that year gone?'

Jean and David were feeling homesick. They missed their schildren and friends. And they had just become grandparents. 'I am going to sell the house and go back home,' Jean said. 'What are we doing here? I feel I have one foot in my coffin, every one is so old.'

The time had passed so quickly but I had to get back. Jean and David walked me to the taxi. We said goodbye and hugged each other. David thanked Antonio for bringing me.

When I arrived back to the ship, I paid him his fare with a tip. He gave me a kiss on both cheeks and said it had been a pleasure to drive me. This made my day complete.

by Clive Leatherdale (Cabin 725)

Conversationally, the richest day so far. The sky was blue, the sea blessedly meek, and the only obstacle to working on deck was the wind and occasional spray. I did not need the sun, so moved round to starboard in the lee of the bridge. And there I continued to type up my notes. Before long an old couple came to join me. How redundant to describe them as old. With an average age of 65, almost everyone on board is 'old' or 'getting old' or 'very old'. The lady sat next to me and her husband next to her. He was a retired academic working in development studies, or something like that.

But it was she who took the eye, or rather the ear. What a tongue the lady has. She has already asked to move from her dining table because she can't bear the company of the pompous, white-haired old chap who reads Garcia Marquez in the Spanish original.

I was now joined on the other side by Lizzie, who for the first three days had wondered what on earth she was doing on this trip. At reception in Tilbury she was surrounded by old fogies debating whether Fred

Olsen cruises were better than others – the first woman, incidentally, had put in a good word for the poshest of the lot, Swan Hellenic. Disaster had befallen Lizzie and her husband Dick in Lisbon. They had taken tram 15 into the city, there was a commotion, and the chap causing it dashed off. It was then that Dick realised all his euros were missing from his back pocket. I asked how much. Too much, she replied.

We arrived in Tenerife ahead of the 2pm schedule. It is mountainous and arid, and brown rather than green even in winter. The first shock was the size of the capital, Santa Cruz. It is a city, not a small provincial town. The second shock was finding no one who could speak English to supplement my long-forgotten Spanish. Normally, late teens are the ones to ask because they have either just left school or are at university, and will have some English somewhere. Not here. At the modern, spacious bus station I was unable to easily follow the logic of the timetable. I also had no serviceable map, so was badly underprepared. Apparently, they started giving out maps to passengers disembarking the ship, but only after I had gone ashore. There was, of course, a tourist info office at the bus station, but it was closed.

With the help of a gesticulating bus driver – their pin-striped uniforms and badges give them a degree of social status – I figured I would take a bus to Puerto Cruz on the north coast. It was perhaps twelve miles away. It was an illuminating 40-minute journey, climbing up and across the mountain ridge and down the other side. Tenerife is so Spanish it might be in Spain itself. It is prosperous and built-up, full of gee-whizz tunnels and bridges in ornamental and exotic shapes. A modern form of hell, some might say.

At Puerto Cruz I picked up a map from a hotel and wandered through narrow streets and seaside knick-knackery, past rocky coves which put me in mind of Jersey's *Bergerac*.

I had taken bus No 103 out to Puerto Cruz but caught No 101 back. The driver took my 'Ida y Vuelta' (there and back) ticket, then printed out a fresh 'Vuelta' (back) ticket. Odd.

I was momentarily confused when the bus climbed out of Puerto Cruz and headed west rather than east. If it took hours to reach Santa Cruz, I might be in trouble. But this was simply the local bus, taking twice as long to get back as I had to get out. It avoided the mountain highway and stopped at every hamlet.

Angela came alive at dinner this evening. Dinah mentioned farming in Manitoba. 'Ooh, I like the sound of that place,' quipped Angela.

'Where don't you like the sound of?' I asked.

Angela thought for a moment. 'Huddersfield,' she said.

'Huddersfield?' I enquired. 'But Huddersfield contains "udder" and "field", lovely bucolic images.'

'All right then, Scunthorpe,' said Angela, quickly changing the subject.

Sauntering around the deck at dusk I espied Eugene Terre'Blanche, the late South African white supremacist – or rather the passenger masquerading as him, complete with glued on white beard. I gave him a wide berth, even though he's dead.

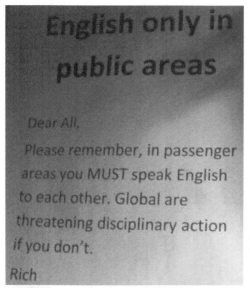

These posters were discovered away from public areas. Cruise director Richard Sykes cracks the whip against staff nattering in their own language. What does disciplinary action mean? Walking the plank?
(Clive Leatherdale)

Marco Polo passengers possibly thought these children in Mindelo, Cape Verde, were actually living in cardboard boxes
(Clive Leatherdale)

DAY 8. AT SEA

'"Cruise Book Contributors"
Can we remind our contributors to keep detailed diaries
and travelogues. Those who would like advice or would
like to join in please come along to meet with
Clive Leatherdale today at 14.30 in Scott's Bar.'

by Lizzie Mayes (Cabin 494)

I am beginning to lose track of dates. Another lovely warm day. The 'broiler deck' occupants were in position early. It's a different world up there – I won't be visiting it too often. The briefest of bikinis and bathing trunks appear in all shapes and sizes. I noticed three jacuzzis. We went to choir practice and did *Swing Low, Sweet Chariot*. The alto next to me resolutely sang soprano very beautifully, but she really buggered my efforts. I must make sure not to sit near her next time. Another enthusiastic lady appears to be totally tone deaf and totally unaware of it. Stand next to Cait, the cabaret singer, in future Lizzie, and keep your head down.

I am finding the crew, mostly eastern Europeans and Indians, really kind and helpful, but of course the crew on Fred Olsen are much better – 'mostly Filipinos you know'. I felt like asking if they actually licked the passengers' arses for them. Maria, our cabin stewardess, is from Bulgaria and told us today that she is a chemistry teacher but can only earn €200 a month at home and she has a fourteen-year-old son. She is delightful and works so hard. We have clean towels every day (even though we don't throw them on the floor, to be changed as suggested) and our beds are always beautifully made and changed regularly. I feel sorry for her. Although we are trying to be tidy, our dressing-table top is already covered with detritus. I told her not to worry about cleaning it. I finished reading *Any Human Heart* – and wept at the end, especially when he found his dog Bowser had died – beautiful writing. Don't be silly, it's only a novel. The author described someone as a CAUC – a 'complete and utter …' Which might also apply to some of those on board.

I'm fascinated to see a gathering of masons is planned this afternoon – what sign do you have to give to get admitted? I meant to walk past and have a look but forgot – damn. Richard commented that the intellectual quality on this cruise was superior to any other because of the Amazon interest. How does he survive the banality of it all – it drives me completely crazy.

We noticed more casualties on board – the hospital must be making a fortune.

I am sitting on the top deck as I write this, almost alone. There is the wonderful sound of the ocean, inky blue all around as far as you can see. I have just seen porpoises jumping close to the ship. I feel like a small speck in a little world, floating in this vast watery universe. Still no other ships in sight. I somehow thought we'd see lots wending their way south. I now begin to understand why people sail solo around the world (not for me, I'd be terrified). I have just been to get a cup of tea – those in the 'parrot house' are crammed like ants and the noise is deafening. Some people cannot bear to be alone. Does it reflect their lives at home?

I yearn for peace. Dick is practising his violin – he never misses a day. Thank goodness for the silent violin – I think it's keeping him sane. We're just not used to doing nothing.

We went to the 'Andrew Lloyd Webber' show after dinner. The costumes are amazing – and are never repeated. Having once again been invited, in Richard's catch-phrase, to 'go through those doors', or 'go through those doors', we played a silly parlour game where he sang one set of words to a different tune and we had to guess the tune – very clever and fun. Is there no end to this man's talents?

After the show we sat on deck – sea so calm, soft air and stars in the sky. There is hardly anyone about – where do they all go?

by Jill Crocker (Cabin 514)
Steve Ragnall's second lecture today, on Columbus' world. I thought this might be a bit dry for some, when Steve first ran through it for me, but it was very well received by those who managed to stay awake after lunch. It was a good example of what he can do, and his illustrations look really good.

My shipboard orientation is now much improved – remember, left at the lift.

by Dinah Read (Cabin 422)
Eight hundred passengers. So many people. 'Ships that pass in the night,' most of them. There is a man of Indian origin, born in British Guiana, 92 years old, here with his second wife and his daughter Chandra. He engaged Jack in conversation, saying that he thought he had seen him somewhere before. I think not, but he, they, are so charming and gentle. Then there were a couple at breakfast who had sailed the Atlantic (and I

mean sailed!) on more than one occasion and were planning to do it again. They looked the part, lean and fit.

A palpable change is coming over the whole ship – passengers and crew. We are getting to know each other, relaxing, laughing, becoming friendly. We like Ar Kar, the Burmese waiter at our table in the Waldorf, and the Ukrainian girl who brings the wine, and Yuriy who is our cabin steward. I asked him if he was happy working on this ship and he replied 'Is my dream!' with great sincerity.

At our dining table we are five – Jack and I, sisters Bernadine and Angela, and Clive. I am happy to go along with whatever interesting opportunities come my way. Maybe even Clive's book project.

Well, even Jack just came along in my life when I was not looking for a partner. Even this cruise came out of the blue without any prompting on my part. Dear Jack, he is so in love. Our interaction and conversation, our deep affection and kindness to each other are quite beautiful. Nobody knows what passes between us.

by Sue Edwards (Cabin 423)
I just had to pop into the shop to buy the stuffed bear (avec suitcase) that has had my name on since I first saw it a week ago. Back in my cabin I unpacked my purchase as he is 'mit coffin', and a slightly lopsided endearing smile looks up at me. Plus two glassy black eyes. Who could resist? But what is this? His label proclaims his name – Fynn. There is no way this fluffy beige ball in the faux travelling trunk is ever a Fynn – such a disreputable name and not at all suitable. Is it unlucky to rename a bear (as it is a boat)? A more suitable name would be Marco (not very original, but apposite). We shall have to pay a visit to Asquith's when we go to Henley and buy him a swanky boater, and I shall knit him a nautical sweater. How sad to be planning a wardrobe for a Teddy, but he must be smart enough to join the crowd back home.

by Clive Leatherdale (Cabin 725)
I led another session of the 'book club', though Richard Sykes introduced me over the tannoy as Clive 'Leatherhead'.

Word seems to have got around, for the numbers were up. Quite a few newcomers meant I had to repeat everything I said last time. Having no idea what kind of response I'm going to attract, I said I was looking for four different kinds of input – first, daily diaries, recording the minutiae of life on board, the gossip and frolics; second, literary travel features about the places we visit; third, anything nautical about the bits and bobs of *Marco Polo*; fourth, high-quality photographs. There are any number of serious snappers on this ship, judging by the size of camera cases and telephoto lenses. My own camera is the size of a matchbox, point and click. I need someone and something better than that.

I told them that contributors can submit anything they liked, provided it was relevant to *this* cruise, *this* ship, *these* people, *these* places. This was shorthand for saying: 'Don't bother writing about Fred Olsen's fantastic trip to bongo-bongo land ten years ago.' And I added the dread words every writer fears: 'The editor's decision is final.'

I added something I had omitted last time. That is, we all tend to embellish our words, blurring fact and fiction, so if anyone present found it easier to write fiction dressed up as fact – imaginary romances with imaginary passengers, for example – then who was I to object?

Richard excused himself immediately I was done, saying those with questions should stay to direct them to me. Smart bugger. I was left with retired accountants and local government officials queuing to tell me they had lived extraordinary lives and asking for a few moments to enlighten me. Richard must have sensed that was coming, hence his rapid getaway. Last in the queue was a desperately old woman with a faded professional air about her. She told me she knew 'all about ships' and gave me a ticking off. I had mistakenly called the *Marco Polo* a boat. 'It is a ship!' Could she have my cabin number so she could correct me about other things.

God, I hate formal dinners. All that silly dressing up. I only own one tie, brown, or it was when I bought it for a friend's wedding in 1972. Dinah told me she had four children and eight grandchildren; her parents had been Jehovah's Witnesses. Bernie and Angela were both unmarried and childless. They had both been at my talk, sitting quietly in the corner.

'High Spirits' by Sue MacPherson (Cabin 714)
High spirits take to the skies to fare
   On finer things than mortals dare
To consume.
   Thus zephyrs play on invisible thermals
Airborne ethereals
   Landing with a bump in the morning
Their staunch constitutions quail
   But once they quaff
that first ale of the day,
   Up rise the spirits
borne aloft,
   And so to play. [see linked artwork on page 86]

DAY 9. AT SEA

'Ladies and Gentlemen, this is Richard Sykes speaking from the Bridge on behalf of the Captain. There has been a power failure affecting all circuits. While this is being repaired please stay exactly where you are. I can assure you we are perfectly safe for now.'

by Clive Leatherdale (Cabin 725)

Richard continued: 'If only I'd stopped two syllables earlier. The senior officers put their heads in their hands as I tried desperately to backtrack.'

This is one of Richard's favourite self-deprecating stories, his biggest verbal cock-up, which happily happened long ago, early on in his cruise director career. He related it on the front page of the day sheet, alias daily programme, alias hymn book, and various other unprintables. Every day Richard composes a four-page sheet – actually a sheet of A3 folded in half. These are distributed round the ship by cabin stewards and tucked under every door in the early evening. Passengers returning to their cabins from the theatre or weighed down by debt from the bar can therefore cheer themselves up by planning their events for the morrow.

Print quality is not one of *Marco Polo's* strengths. These sheets reminded me of the stencils I mastered in my childhood, or what became known as roneo machines which, to my knowledge, became obsolete at the time of the Beverley Sisters. I had visions of a tiny darkened room attached to Richard's opulent suite (linked by a feeding hatch), in which some poorly paid dwarf cranked the handles to meet pressing deadlines. I felt sure that, to a keen sleuth, a blackened trail of ink stains would lead to the hub of this Rupert Murdoch-type operation, and in idle moments I would curse myself for not having the foresight to bring along my huge magnifying glass to see if I was up to the challenge.

Print quality is measured not just by clarity, but also by the range of colours. To this extent the day sheet excelled, if that is the right word, for while text and photos appeared in smudged black, it boasted a crisp navy masthead and spine, fetching salmon-pink horizontal stripes adorned pages one, two, and three, and to my eyes a wishy-washy blue-grey slab was dumped at the foot of page four. This particular pigment lightened or darkened on a daily basis according to the amount of ink left in the pot. Grey shading was accomplished by resorting to dots, which had an effect rather like sprinkling a vacuum cleaner over the page.

It is important for cabin design that the gap beneath the foot of the door be high enough for items to easily pass to and fro. It is big enough for day sheets and periodic accounting bills to be slipped underneath, for otherwise the only methods of delivery would be the knock at the door or cabin mail-boxes. These would have attracted unwarranted noise or minor theft to compare bills. Hence the gap, which is big only because cabin doors open inwards against airless corridors, and therefore have no need of draught excluders. Even so, but for a curtain of bristles they would provide a temptation for Peeping Toms. Whether Gideon's bibles could be safely exchanged from cabin to cabin was not put to the test.

Richard's day sheets have a simple, helpful format. Page one tells you where you are, what day it is, and lists the onboard highlights under 'Don't Miss' banners. These range from the daily lectures, to 'Muddled Melody' gameshows, to Megan Fox's 'Live and Luscious' cabaret. On trans-Atlantic cruises like this, involving multiple time zones, the need to change clocks also merits front-page treatment. Unfortunately, confusion reigns because day sheet time-changes refer to the following night, not tonight. Passengers note, for example, on Sunday the instruction to put their watches back on Monday night, by which time most have forgotten, particularly as the day sheet for Tuesday appears on Monday and makes no mention of any time-change. With Manaus four hours behind UK, that's a lot of time changes going out and coming back, and bleary eyed passengers prowling the pre-dawn deck or, conversely, grumpily missing breakfast because they got up too late, were a regular feature of life on board.

Page two reflects the eclectic mind of its editor. It provides restaurant opening times, the daily dress code for the Waldorf, warnings against power-walking before the official start time and against hogging sunbeds, and bizarrely offers a 'Quote of the Day'. These are an art form in themselves. How many of us will remember Publilius Syrus as the author of 'Anyone can hold the helm when the sea is calm', or that Jon Hammond penned the pun, 'The early bird gets the worm, but the second mouse gets the cheese?'

Page three is the *Marco Polo* equivalent of the *Radio Times*, providing detailed listings for cabin televisions. Channels 1 and 2 offer satellite news, but only when close to Europe, which means hardly at all. Channel 3 provides classic British TV, mostly comedy like *Blackadder* or *Only Fools and Horses*, but occasionally an epic like Bronowski's *The Ascent of Man*. Channels 4, 5, and 6 show feature films on a rolling basis so passengers have no idea when they started or finished. Channel 8 is the nautical equivalent of the moving map on aircraft, giving speed, distance, direction, and most exiting of all, a view over the bows from a tiny camera. Much fun was had on breezy but boring days watching from the comfort of your snug cabin as obstreperous passengers lost their hats in view of a jeering armchair audience. Channel 8 is the only one to stay on 24 hours.

There is a lucrative trade in official cruise DVDs, particularly on long exotic trips like this. Channel 7 offered constant showings of what was already in the can, short at the beginning, interminably long by the end. Channel 9 tried to tempt you to splash out on forthcoming excursions at the next destination. The tone was Judith Chalmers on *Holiday*.

The rest of page 3 gave an itemised itinerary of 'what, where, when' for the day in question. Page 4 tempted you with, 'Your evening at a glance.'

by Mave Eaton (Cabin 616)
Today we are at sea – our third consecutive day. Husband and I play a familiar game. He goes to find seats – where we sat yesterday – I then seek for him. After an hour I admit defeat and acquire two chairs where we sat yesterday. The search for him was interesting and provided exercise. I saw mountains of reddened flesh and one elderly Dutchman lying uncomfortably on his lounger, wearing very large black boots. Still no lost husband. He returns to tell me he had a wonderful place on the sundeck with two loungers. He hates lying on a lounger, so it was the only place I did not search. He reappears almost apologetically.

by Lizzie Mayes (Cabin 494)
There is a guy who is on his own and walks the deck continuously and has affectionately become known as 'David Niven'. According to the grapevine, he has worked on ships for 40 years. He has announced he has no intention of eating off plastic trays in a cafeteria and takes every meal in the Waldorf.

We hadn't seen the woman I call the Limpet for a few days, but she is back in circulation with a rich tan and an exhausted-looking other half. The mind boggles. I was sitting with the immaculately shod Mr Clarke (he was 'in shoes' in his working life, hence the nickname) when the Limpet came over to our table. She proceeded to talk about herself for fifteen minutes without a break, going on to say she had been diagnosed bipolar/manic depressive three years before at 67, and since then has been on the pills and is fine. Must get some, if they give you that much energy.

I saw my first flying fish at 12 noon today.

Dick has just met someone who can out-cruise the whole ship – he must surely be the record holder at 27 cruises. I have just realised that it's cheaper than an old people's home. So there you are kids, when the time comes just wheel me up the gangplank, wave goodbye and leave me to the mercies of the ship's crew. With the availability of two five-course meals a day, buffet breakfast, afternoon tea and a night-time buffet at 11pm, a full entertainment programme day and night – not just bingo and singalong – what more could an old girl ask? Mind you, I was informed by a well-meaning passenger that you get prawns on Fred Olsen.

While I take it easy on the shady upper deck, enjoying my solitude, Dick is being much more proactive and attending lectures. I had thought they would be specialist lectures about the Amazon – but one of them is still going on about the ocean and the two others lecture on a miscellany of irrelevant subjects, ranging from comic songs to Columbus. A great disappointment, as I had hoped to learn a lot about the Amazon, as had many of us choosing this cruise. I must remember to write to the management about that.

My lunchtime companions regaled me with stories about their previous cruises, complaints about just about everything on this ship – the food, the staff, and the chipped mugs. I am learning the 'push button to off' technique, but did take on board that Fred Olsen would have given me a complimentary Bucks Fizz for breakfast.

The 'broiler deck' basters are taking on a healthy glow. I decided to give the bingo session a miss – £5 for three games. The dreaded comedian is on again tonight – will give him a miss and listen to the lovely Olga and Liliya before going for our nightly stroll on deck and star-gazing. It is magical and so peaceful on the fo'c'sle, especially as the air is warm late into the evening now.

by Mark Edwards (Cabin 423)

One of the memorable phrases on this ship is 'good morning'. Because the ratio of staff to passengers is high and because the staff will get the shit kicked out of them by three layers of management if they don't say good morning to everyone all the time, you end up saying good morning twenty times just getting to breakfast. Aaaaah! A few 'hi's' and similar would be nice.

Mind you, I'm sure you could take out at least two layers of management directly above the staff. Just give the staff the trust that is needed to do the job properly and effectively. Employ the right staff and empower them.

by Sue Edwards (Cabin 423)

I am reminded by Clive that we have to do 'people watching' and write up descriptive cameos for our diaries. Typical of Brits abroad, I take in the various degrees of grilling – the pink of the first sun for months on pale skin, the lobster red of too much exposure without any tanning product, and the brown of the veteran exposure. There are going to be some sore bodies tomorrow. Sunburn is an experience similar to a hangover – at the time you swear you won't be so silly next time. But by the time 'next time' comes along – which, let's face it, living in Britain could be years – you have forgotten the resolution and also the dire outcome of not behaving sensibly. Whether it is just one more drink or just ten more minutes, they are always fatal, their consequences far outweighing the minimal quantity absorbed.

Ooh, just look at him. Those large ears rising defiantly up the sides of a tightly pulled-down cap – just asking to be frazzled. Bless him, he also has sandals and no socks, and the sun beats down hard on all his delicate parts.

We head up another deck, out of the sun. Luckily we find a table and chairs in the shade. Others find it more reliable to take their chairs with them. There are a handful of intrepid souls who are quite content to carry their chairs (once acquired, never let go) up decks and down decks to be assured of a seat.

Earlier, Richard Sykes was at the piano for the song-writing group. The lyrics were written by passengers and Richard puts them to appropriate music (tempo, key, etc). The best of the songs was 'Insanitise', which should be made into a cruise CD. [and here it is]

'Insanitisity' by David Mackenzie-Crooks (Cabin 641)
VERSE 1: Just as you wake at early dawn
   Before you even rise
Repeat the mantra of the cruise
   It's time to sanitise
CHORUS:
Sanitise your hands my lad
   Sanitise your hands
To hell with all the other bits
   Like tonsils, toes and glands
Let dirt fly free, let germs abound
   Let cobwebs hang in strands
Let muddied boots walk in and out
   But sanitise your hands

Verse 2: Before you drink, before you eat
     Before you taste those pies
Before you even smell the food
     It's time to sanitise
Chorus:
Verse 3: And when you climb into bed
     Before you close your eyes
The last thought in your mind must be
     It's time to sanitise
Chorus:
     Written with a sanitised hand.

by Clive Leatherdale (Cabin 725)

Two slots from me today, sorry about that. The clocks went back another hour, which does not really constitute jet-lag, but then what is jet-lag if not the changing of the time according to time-zones? There you are, I'm jet-lagged.

At lunchtime Richard announced a table-tennis competition at 2.45, so along I went. Cait the singer took down names as she went round. She then paired them off, so the first name played the second, and so on. This meant you would be playing your wife or whoever you turned up with. None of this pulling numbered balls out of a black bag malarkey. Each game was the first to eleven points, the serve alternating after every two points. Would you believe I won my first match. My victim, what a lovely word, told me a chap by the name of Neville [Singh] had won an earlier competition and was 'the man to beat'. I looked forward to a classic final in which I would strain every sinew in search of *Marco Polo* glory and the pride of 'Sarfend-on-Sea'.

Before I faced Neville, however, I had to play Dutchman Hans, handicapped to the extent that he had a metal knee, if not a wooden leg. Nor was he exactly agile on his good leg, which meant he took root like an oak at the far end of the table and refused to budge an inch. Easy peasy, I thought. Alas, Hans edged through 11-0. Neville would have to wait.

I did not wait to see if Neville or Hans triumphed in the Clash of the Titans as I espied a pleasant-faced women leaning over the rail who might have been as young as 55, pretty but with a little too much puppy-fat. She had come on the cruise in company with a 70-year-old windbag who was pretty ill. He had been so poorly one day that she phoned the ship's doctor. An ECG and blood tests, all of which came back normal, cost him £1,400. She was so desperate to escape her unwanted companion that she had gone to Reception and asked to change rooms – only to be told that yes she could, but at a hefty price. So she is staying put for the time being. Apparently she has three past husbands in her locker, four according to accounts given to other passengers, and her latest beau was planning their luxurious marriage in the spring. He was the stuff of fantasy and, according to some accounts, was planning a helicopter landing on the *Marco Polo* in mid-Atlantic to whisk her away.

At dinner this evening I told my table I had a birthday coming and asked them to guess my age. Angela (whom I've nicknamed 'Purity') tactfully suggested 58; her sister Bernie ('Bravura') said 66. Gawd almighty. I'll only be 62.

Dinah told us how she had met Jack the Eyebrows. Their families had known each other for decades. Their children had even dated. Dinah had been a widow for twenty years and, after Jack's wife died, they slowly got in touch. They have been together since last April.

'Divisions on Board' by Kay Rainsley (Cabin 543)
Unable to mix, suspicion will reign supreme. Forced to co-exist. We are split into two:
British – English, Welsh, Scottish and Irish.
Dutch – English speaking and non-English speaking.
Passengers – split into decks, travelling with family or friends, travelling alone.
Crew – split into nationalities, positions and job titles.
Keep fitters.
Keep out of the gym.
Card players – bridge, whist, hearts.
Card makers – birthday, valentine, get well, greetings.
Readers – fact, fiction, news.
Readers – seeking escape, seeking a truth.
Dancers – professionals, amateurs.
Dancers – those who like to dance but can't.
Wet – diving, snorkelling, swimming and those who got wet when they wanted to stay dry.
Dry – don't want to swim and swimmers who wanted to get wet but no pool.
Smokers – united on the starboard deck – some recreational, some heavy.
Non-smokers – united against the smokers.
Retired – recently retired, semi-retired, long-term retired.
Non-retired – working their way towards retirement.
Carnivores – some avoid red meat, special diet.
Vegetarians – some eat fish, vegans.

Photographers – photograph everything that moves, photograph every
    thing that doesn't move and everything in-between.
Selective photographers.
Non-photographers – leave it to the professionals, hide from the camera.
Male – tend to mix easily with the second group.
Female – tend to mix easily with the first group.
Bug lovers – only the winged and antennae variety.
Bug haters – indiscriminate hatred of all bugs.
Sailors – love the 'wave' of the ocean life.
Cruisers – love the 'life' without the waves.
Sun worshippers – top deckers.
Shade worshippers – lower or even below deckers.
Quiz-meisters – answer the questions, question the answers.
Quiz-sheisters – question the point of it all.
Writers – poets, jotters and scribblers – recording their thoughts.
Non-writers – say it's not for them.
Complainers – complain about the non-complainers not complaining.
Non-complainers – complain about the complainers complaining.
Like the two rivers, we live beside each other, until we all blend.

The first sight that greets passengers on touching land in Brazil – in Icoaraci.
Four policemen weighed down by weapons. This suggests they are needed,
and that ladies should not go ashore draped in gold (Clive Leatherdale)

Day 10. Mindelo, Cape Verde

'Cape Verde is an archipelago made up of ten islands and eight islets. It is remote, mountainous and unspoilt, 400 miles off the west coast of Senegal. Mindelo on São Vicente is the largest port, where you will find beautiful Portuguese colonial buildings.'

by Mave Eaton (Cabin 616)

Mindelo, Cape Verde Islands. We reject the official excursions and set off to explore. It is hot. The women have beautiful faces and walk like queens, and often carry fruit baskets on their heads. Our impression of Mindelo is of attractive Portuguese buildings, groups of unemployed youths, and poorly stocked shops, surrounded by inhospitable, jagged, barren mountains. We are unlikely to return.

by Lizzie Mayes (Cabin 494)

Woke up to find we were alongside – surrounded by misty volcanic islands rising up from the sea like velvet cushions. Ate breakfast on deck to the sound of sort-of Brazilian music – the band on the quay come to welcome us. A helpful breakfast companion announced he had been to Mindelo on a cruise three years ago and 'there's nothing there, I'm not bothering to go ashore'. Undaunted, we made our way on shore and wandered around the town taking in the sights and smells – a pavement strip of people sitting gutting fish in small bowls to sell, stalls with just bunches of parsley, or some fruits, mostly the size of a coffee table and manned by two people. There were grand old buildings in various states of disrepair, lots of cars and motorbikes, and lots of people going about their daily business, whatever that was. We went into the beautiful covered market crammed with fruits, vegetables, honey and strange vats of extraordinary meat – huge knucklebones and gristle. I bought a bottle of a local alcoholic concoction with honey, spices limes and lemons, and some goat's cheese.

I also bought a strange little purse for €1 from a 'lookie-lookie' man, much to the disgust of our party, while we sat in a bar having a cold drink. We then set off to find a bus to go round the island, but failed miserably to find anything going anywhere outside the town. We ended up in Eric's taxi with Lyn and Paul from Bovey Tracey. They were going to the beach at Baia das Gatas. It is earmarked for a tourist destination but at present it's a long way off that, with some scattered villas, a small bar-restaurant and a festival site for the annual festival in August. We had a little picnic, paddled in the warm water, and found some coral and a sea urchin. The island has little rainfall so there is always a chronic water shortage.

Eric gave us a wonderful guided tour – he understood not a word of English – which was at times hair-raising as he gesticulated with both hands off the wheel. This got even worse. Eric became even more animated when Dick mentioned football and discovered that Manchester United's Nani was from Mindelo. They threw footballers' names at each other for the entire homeward journey which pleased them both greatly. The island is barren – a few goats, some brown maize, a donkey or two. Eric pointed out the hill on the island in the shape of a man looking up to the heavens, and which obviously has great spiritual meaning for the islanders. We noticed small fishing boats (little more than canoes) coming in and out of the harbour with up to eight men on each with a fishing net. This is how they eke a living.

by Dinah Read (Cabin 422)
I was up early. The Cape Verde islands were in silhouette against the dawn sky. The line of volcanic peaks was fantastic. We circled around them. There was another brightly lit ship on our quarter. I find it all so enchanting. I was born a girl, albeit in a busy seaport, but in the days when girls stayed at home caring for the family while the menfolk went to sea. If I had been a boy I feel sure that I would have done that too.

I left Jack still at rest and went to breakfast, as I had booked to go ashore at Mindelo where we were tied up. It was a fascinating excursion, first of all to the town centre, where the houses were almost all in Portuguese colonial style. I loved the views from the harbourside with brightly painted boats of all sizes. When we left, our minibus climbed higher by twisting roads, the tarmac changing to cobblestones, up to the heights of the old volcanoes covered in dry scrub with scorched strips of maize and barely recognisable crops. The painted villas of the town gave place to decrepit or abandoned concrete shells of houses. Here and there was a well where a man might be seen drawing water and we passed a few lean figures carrying lumpy sacks of unknown content on their backs.

Oh! but the glory lay in the distant views of town and harbour and other islands from the high shoulder of the mountain. We could see Catfish Bay on one hand and Mindelo on the other. I felt elated to be there and I longed to have Jack with me.

We went back down to the town with its oleanders and hibiscus and jacaranda trees and a scrap of a museum and an uninspiring church and a dusty vegetable market. There we had refreshments in a smart hotel with a band and three dark-skinned people posing for us in carnival costume. But I was glad to get back to the ship and Jack. Walking back to the gangway I had a good view of *Marco Polo* and realised just how big she was compared to the little tramp steamers of my childhood.

There is curious graffiti on the dock walls – mostly in Russian or Greek script – the names and dates I think of ships that have tied up there. Several ships are at anchor offshore. One of them is painted bright green and yellow, which would be considered very unlucky where I come from! Jack and I went straight to lunch and then came back to our cabin where we lay close in each others arms until we slept for a while in deep content.

We are getting to know people more and more and are very much at ease with those we know best. There are only one or two that we avoid. Jack can't stand the man with the rictus grin. I find him odd myself. He is in the power-walking train, half a dozen times round Deck 10. I walk that way myself but I don't feel the need to join the chain-gang to do it. There is a woman who always seems to be seated behind me somewhere and has a laugh just like a machine gun. Ha-a-a-a-a-a-a-a-a! Just like that, in repeated bursts. One might get used to it, but if not it would drive you insane.

'A Short Cut in Mindelo' by Kay Rainsley (Cabin 543)

We decided to take a short cut in Mindelo through the cobbled back streets. The temperature was rising and shadows were already falling across the large, patched, wooden doors which punctuated the peeling walls. Les, my husband, was five paces ahead when I glanced to one side and peered into the gloom of a dimly lit shop. A man was poised, arms raised, head to one side, holding something shiny.

'I've found a barber.' I gesticulated towards the open door. Inside we could make out a client seated in one of two old hairdressing chairs. Luckily for us the client spoke French. A deal was quickly made, two centimetres, three euros and a free pee. Les was ecstatic, as was the interpreter and the barber. Our translator, newly shorn, left us to it.

A well-worn circular piece of cotton cloth was passed over Les's head, it having only a hole in the middle. Scissors in hand and sporting a pair of old blue tracksuit bottoms, a pair of trainers and a French football shirt, our man set to work. He was balding with a long, thin, grey, pigtail which rested on his back. I sat quietly on a tired seat flanked by cream walls showing remnants of dark blue and, below that, pale blue paint. The design on the tiled floor was reminiscent of old linoleum, being brown and beige criss-crossed with angular lines. Most of the decoration was provided by tattered posters depicting football teams, save for the biggest one, which featured a young, attractive, black girl. She stood, ankle deep, in the sea wearing a wide smile and a white topless swimsuit.

Behind me three identical mirrors reflected the back of clients' heads. On the floor beside me was a small, painted, wooden stool which had seen better days. A few shoddy wooden drawers and shelves housed the meagre selection of combs, scissors, clippers, a brush and an electric razor. There were no basins or water – a fact which Les confirmed later, after having stepped behind a grubby, flimsy curtain to use the loo. Standard toilet and wash hand-basin but no visible signs of water.

The guy worked methodically, snipping and revisiting bits which he had already cut with standard scissors. When he was satisfied he selected another pair of scissors, this time with a fine end, and set to work on eyebrows, ears, and nose hair. A young girl aged about five and wearing a pink t-shirt with 'Adorable' written on it was as fascinated as I was. With a final flourish the barber selected an electric razor and ran it over Les's neck. This was followed by a quick brushing to remove any loose hair and he was finished. Perfect – another short cut in Mindelo.

by Clive Leatherdale (Cabin 725)
I breakfasted on deck on my usual 'one fried egg, melon and porridge', then returned for muesli and tinned fruit, with a carton of yoghurt for both. They don't provide trays on board, presumably because passengers would pile up too much food if they did.

While eating, I was button-holed by Jill, partner of Steve Ragnall, the onboard lecturer on maritime themes. Apparently he is an authority on James King, Captain Cook's second-in-command, who completed Cook's log after Cook was killed. Steve says no serious biography of King has ever been published, and Jill wonders if I'll have a look at Steve's manuscript. Sounds intriguing.

The Cape Verde islands are not clustered in a neighbourly pile, like say the Channel Islands, where you can pop across from one to another without too much fuss. The distance from Mindelo on São Vicente to the capital Praia on Santiago is 167 miles, the same as separates Canvey Island in Essex and Barry Island in south Wales. São Vicente and Santiago, however, have the open ocean separating them. This realisation transformed my understanding of what it must be like to be a Cape Verdean. Identity is felt not so much with Cape Verde, the state, as with one's own island, for few inhabitants had ever been to many, if any, of the other islands. Nor is there any reason for them to go. The distances are so huge that most inter-island transport is by plane, and ferries between neighbouring islands often run to erratic timetables.

There is one exception, however, and a rush of blood to the head might have landed me in a spot of bother. The only daily, round-the-year ferry – the *Armas* – runs from Mindelo across the strait to Santa Antão and back. My guidebook made heavy play of Cape Verdeans' Olympian capacity for being seasick, implying that the seas separating the islands can be terribly wobbly. It even gave tips on how to avoid being 'showered' by afflicted passengers. Nevertheless, I knew the daily ferry to Santa Antão left at 8am and that there was a fair chance the *Marco Polo* would dock in time for me to catch it.

In the event, it did not, and for that I am grateful. It was a bright cheerful day and the wind was on its best behaviour. I watched from on deck as the *Armas* ventured out of the bay towards the open sea. Even before she got there, however, she began to pitch and rear. It was like having a ringside seat at a rodeo, and was almost enough to induce seasickness in itself. I turned away, counting my blessings.

I asked Purity and Bravura, my sisterly table-mates, if they fancied sharing a taxi to the other side of São Vicente. We arranged to meet at the 'presidential palace' at 10. By then I was already enchanted with Mindelo, its absence of street threat, the smiles of its people, their willingness to be photographed in all circumstances, the girls with their tight shorts and ample innocent flesh.

A woman and her young daughter 'manning' a kiosk showed me printed taxi fares. All taxis were cream Mercedes. It was no more than €10 to get to Callhau on the other side of the island. It was eleven miles away on an empty cobbled road, Roman in sentiment if nothing else, passing through arid, barren terrain flanked by bricked-coloured mountains. Neither I nor the sisters had ever seen anything like it. Callhau itself seemed deserted, no shops, a chap fishing in the surf, dogs, endless dogs curled up sleeping in the sun.

Cape Verde and I got along nicely. This was my kind of place. We negotiated a fare to take us to Baia das Gatas, then up Monte Verde, and down to São Pedro, more or less a circumnavigation of São Vicente. The coast road up to Baia das Gatas was paved, smooth and offered immense vistas of dunes and deserted bays. So empty was the road and so perfect its surface that it was obvious foreign investment had poured in – though for what future desecration it was not clear to see – and these idyllic miles would not remain unspoiled for long. Jeremy Clarkson and his *Top Gear* gang had better get here quickly if they want to race these dreamy empty roads.

Baia das Gatas was no more peopled than Callhau. It was largely shut up. Many houses were more like villas, offering so many architectural styles it was impossible to work out where you were, if you did not know.

The winding road – now cobbled again – to the top of Monte Verde offered postcard views of Mindelo below and the *Marco Polo*, so tiny from this range. At the very top was a gate, beyond which military or satellite dishes pierced the sky. We ignored the gate and strolled past it. A boyish soldier emerged from a concrete hut, weighed down by a huge gun. In most places in the world this would be the time to take a deep breath, mumble apologies, genuflect and scarper. But the soldier seemed more scared of us that we of him. We even posed for photographs, which I hope won't land him in trouble.

Walking back to the ship, I watched the *Marco Polo*'s inflatable zodiac drag what looked like a body out of the sea with a hook. Only when the zodiac pulled alongside could I see that the 'body' was in fact a headless mannequin.

A pretty sight on the road from Mindelo to Callhau in the Cape Verde Islands
(Clive Leatherdale)

DAY 11. AT SEA

'May we remind passengers that reserving sunbeds for over half an hour is prohibited onboard Marco Polo. If you find a bed that has been unoccupied for over 30 minutes please inform a deck steward or hand any left items to Lost Property at Reception.'

by Mave Eaton (Cabin 616)

The captain is a small, spare man with an air of authority. He is from the Ukraine. On arrival, we had the compulsory lifeboat drill. It was unusual because we assembled in our groups, put on our life-jackets, and were then marched up to our lifeboat by our leader, one of the entertainment staff. We stood in three lines with hands on the shoulders of the person in front. The captain inspected the members of each lifeboat. Oh, the pride we felt when he dismissed us first as we were the best.

He regularly walks the decks to see the never-ending cleaning and painting. He never gives the noon daily address [which is undertaken by Richard Sykes] so remains a distant figure. But I heard today from a fellow passenger how the captain challenged all-comers at table-tennis and beat almost all of them. Perhaps he is human.

by Margit Latter (Cabin 335)

Lucky me, I got a sunbed. Pen poised, I tried to write a poem for the Valentine's Day poetry competition. On the next sunbed lay a very corpulent lady, fast asleep, snoring and her mouth wide open, dribbling. She wore big red shorts and her legs were parted.

Then, suddenly, a very large cicada, about five inches long, landed on her thigh. My instant reaction was to take a photo, but my camera was in my cabin. The cicada, a stowaway, must have been hidden on board ship since we left Cape Verde. I saw many of them there. The green alien started to crawl towards the gap in her trouser leg. Why, oh why, did I not have my camera?

What should I do? I grinned and hoped. Should I wake her or let the cicada crawl up and wait for her to scream: 'Stop it Henry!' Or, if I put my hand on her to shoo away the predator, she might scream too, and I would be in trouble.

The dilemma solved itself. The insect flew off, probably to its hiding place to disembark somewhere on the Amazon, and nobody but me would have known about the little stowaway on the *Marco Polo*.

by Lizzie Mayes (Cabin 494)

I still haven't seen any other ships, apart from those in Mindelo harbour – and I am completely overawed by the size of the ocean. Scores and scores of flying fish now – all fleeing from the big fish that is the *Marco Polo*. I did a few fitness spins round the deck. There is one woman (not very affectionately known as the Belfast Sink) who barges her way round every day elbowing anyone in her way – haven't seen her smile yet. We went to Tony Rice's lecture on the Amazon but I am none the wiser as to what we will and will not see. He kept saying that he was no expert and that probably the audience knew more about it than he did. Just what you need to hear from your lecturer. He is a very affable, absent-minded professor type, and knows a lot about oceans.

Went to choir practice – *Some Enchanted Evening*. Richard has certainly gauged the age of the inmates. Inertia is setting in with a vengeance. One day merges into another and I truly have no idea what day of the week it is. If it weren't for writing this journal I would have no idea how long we've been away. It's like living in a bubble. I am amused how everyone queues up for the daily newspaper of what's happening at home and around the world. I really don't know and don't care. I chatted on deck with a mother and daughter. Mother a painter and daughter running her own organic fashion business in Dublin. Mother kindly lent me a paintbrush as I have brought some watercolour pencils with me, but I can't get on with them and can't concentrate enough to draw.

People are getting more aggressive about guarding their sun-loungers, and I have been bounced out of the buffet queue a few times. The thing is not to rise to these people but make a mental note to keep out of their way.

Delicious lentil and samosa dish for dinner. I wish we could have more of the chef's delicious curries – he is Indian, after all, and that's what he does best.

We went to Richard and James' 1960s singalong, which must have been good as even we danced the night away. I slept well. My little bed is really comfortable. The small cabin isn't proving to be such a problem and having no window has the advantage of no early-morning light to wake us up. I spend very little time in it, other than to sleep, and Dick seems perfectly happy practising his 'silent' violin there every day. It's getting untidier by the day, but we do try to put our clothes away.

by Sue Edwards (Cabin 423)

Our Dutch neighbour rings Reception to ask if there is anything wrong with the air con, as her cabin is very warm. This may have been the result of her crashing several of her drawers – in, out – working up a lather. Though she would probably not appreciate the noise she made half an hour ago, as only 'other people' make a noise. Yesterday she had Richard Sykes in her cabin and was complaining to him about the noise from the main lounge upstairs. He assured her that he would not program anything there for after 11pm. We could barely hear it anyway.

Watching the sea is compulsive – following a wave until it breaks, white-topped, and the accompanying swoosh. I imagine this is similar to the feelings of a baby in utero, the gentle rocking and swooshing of fluid and the reassuring beat of maternal blood going through their blood vessels.

It is so tempting to dive in – if I was guaranteed a speedy rescue I may well have a go. Mother Nature is luring me into her womb. Do cetaceans have any realisation of this environment? If so, how lucky they are. They really are the most privileged of creatures on this blue planet, living as they do in the most sensuous, interesting and varied environment – and humans seem bent on despoiling it all – what sacrilege. I don't blame them for popping their noses – or fins – over the parapet for our delight. We don't deserve it. Humankind and its activities fill them with toxins and strange bits of plastic. We deafen them with our noise at sea, snare them in nets made for their species, and still hunt them. How barbaric to kill another intelligent species.

Must stop now – all this thought, with the sun scorching my head and squinting up my eyes. The sun-worshippers have gathered, the smokers amongst them to one side, seemingly unknowing of the double whammy of cigarettes and sun's rays ageing their skin ten times faster than if they imbibed neither.

by Clive Leatherdale (Cabin 725)

Each evening when my cabin steward slips the next day's programme under my door or leaves it on my bed, I immediately rush to inspect the predicted sea conditions printed on page 2. I did it just now and it says 'calm', which makes me 'calm', and will bring about another peaceful night.

My, how time flies. It was so hot today that when I went down for lunch they had erected huge parasols on the pool deck. While queuing for lunch I met Neville, the table-tennis supremo. Did you win again, I asked? But no, he had been beaten by the same peg-legged Dutchman who had thrashed me. Apparently he was at one time a Dutch badminton champion of some kind.

Anyway, I saw a gap at a table and sat with two northerners of limited imagination. They had gone into Mindelo yesterday purely for the purpose of having a beer, and then wanted to pay for it in dollars, which understandably caused confusion.

I eat so well, fish every day, and lashings of salad and fruit, that I am eating better than I do at home. So much fresh air leaves me fatigued. Tonight's menu offered the gloriously named 'Fussily' pasta. At table, Angela opened up a bit. She has been an arkela and brown owl for many years, and talking about cubs and girl guides made her more animated than anything we've discussed so far. Hers is the 25th Newcastle group.

Although I had offered brownie points to anyone in the book club who could come up with a snappy title, it came to me this afternoon: 'Murder on Marco Polo'. I shall sleep on it and not divulge it to anyone.

by Richard Sykes (Cruise Director)
Death is a serious subject. It's also one of the few certainties in life. Deaths happen on cruise ships, but in my experience, only one has happened as a consequence of cruising (on a previous ship, a tragic case of a tender boat crushing an able seaman in bad weather). The rest just happen to have taken place onboard.

I remember reading a news story about a teenager who fell from a third-storey window whilst mooning. This is appalling, of course, but it's made worse by there being an element of humour to it. It's a ridiculous thing to do and it's certainly not worth dying for. So your reaction as a reader to the following stories will either be sympathy or schadenfreude.

A young couple had enjoyed their cruise very much. They were the 'gameshow' players and could be relied on for good humour, often at each other's expense. It worked particularly well in the traditional 'Mr & Mrs' gameshow, which they won at a canter. The morning afterwards I happened upon the gentleman walking, a little dazed, around the corridor close to his cabin. We chatted about the night before and I thanked him for taking part. I asked casually how his wife was this morning and whether she'd got him back for a particularly barbed comment. He replied that he thought she'd died.

We walked back to his cabin and checked. Sure enough, his wife lay there. Utterly cold. She'd clearly been dead for a few hours. The business of removing the body, the arranging of her repatriation and the endless paperwork, I won't go into here. One thing that I will say, though, is that the gentleman was asked if he'd like to accompany his wife home. He declined and said he would stay on board as 'it's what she would have wanted'.

It was a phrase that he would use again. A dedicated quiz player, he would collect his prizes with his new catchphrase: 'It's what she would have wanted.' He even won the comedy quiz – I read out a joke and if you guess the punchline you score a point – and his new catchphrase was so entrenched that the audience joined in. To be brutally frank, I'm not sure it's what she would have wanted at all.

There is a story which is so well-known that I assume it's an urban myth. It involves a rotating gun platform, a coffin draped in a flag, an over-exuberant cleaner and a sack of potatoes. It's a little too convenient to be true so I'll leave you to make that one up for yourselves. I'll stick to the ones that have happened to me personally.

Like the awful death of a lady who expired on the gangway. Often deaths can be kept secret, but this was as a ship excursion was returning from Cairo. She was among the first to return and so was followed by about 300 people queuing to get back on the ship. She collapsed in full view of the ship's 1,200 passenger complement. A terrible way to go, under such public scrutiny – everyone watching (and even videoing) agreed. Her body was never returned to the ship and was, once again, repatriated.

Coincidentally, there was also a burial at sea being performed on the cruise. A gentleman had brought on the ashes of his father to be scattered. It was done privately by the captain the next day. This led to some extraordinary comments, including the following: 'I was very impressed by the ceremony held for the lady who passed away on the gangway. Did you cremate her in the ship's funnel?'

On my very first ship we had a wife whose husband died during the course of their two-week cruise. She stayed onboard while the body was being repatriated and she casually asked on the penultimate day whether she was entitled to his duty-free allowance.

There is often an attitude with deaths that implies that dying on a cruise ship is 'actually quite a nice way to go'. I would agree with this, in some cases. Again, on my first ship, I saw a gentleman laugh so hard at a comedian that he died in the show lounge.

But, for me, the nicest death was that of a regular passenger on one of the Thomson ships. He would cruise three times each year. His arrival would be greeted by an enormous clamour, as he would bring two suitcases, one of which was filled with chocolate and crisps for the show team and hosts, who hadn't seen 'pickled onion Monster Munch' in a few months. He would invite the dancers for a meal and buy drinks for everyone. He knew every answer to every quiz because he'd seen them all before – many, many times.

I last met him on one of his jaunts. He wore slippers around the ship and would need assistance getting from lounge to lounge, but he was a great conversationalist and had had an extraordinary life. He mentioned that he never felt more at home as he did when he walked up the gangway. So I had mixed emotions when a report came through that he had died whilst on the ship. It really is 'what he would have wanted'.

But the final story for this, somewhat morbid section, is of a gentleman who passed away during an intimate act on a ship on which I was cruise director between Lisbon and Brest. Heart failure was the cause. His next of kin was contacted using the satellite phone and a lady answered in Hampshire. It turned out to be his wife – who was somewhat surprised to hear that her husband had died on a cruise ship when he had said that he was at a conference. Suddenly, dying whilst mooning seems like the preferable option.

Outdoor toilets at a school in Almeirim on the Amazon.
Segregated between teachers and pupils (Clive Leatherdale)

Day 12. At Sea

'On the night of 21st January, all passengers will receive a preliminary bill in order to check their onboard account. If you have any queries, please report to Reception. For those passengers who have not yet registered their debit/credit cards, please go to Reception.'

by Margit Latter (Cabin 335)

I had a strange dream last night. The weight of millions of cicadas made the *Marco Polo* unstable. She tilted. She must have hit a rock, as the port side was left with only a few planks. She did not sink. The incredibly competent captain managed to put the *Marco Polo* onto a railway line, so we could continue our wonderful cruise. The journey led through a jungle, where thousands of flowers, snowdrops, covered the ground. I was picking snowdrops through a port-hole window when my alarm-clock woke me and ended my dream.

by Caroline Clifford (Cabin 468)

Not a good start. I had had this sinking feeling in my stomach that something was going to happen today. I had tossed and turned most of the night, 'listening' to James sleeping in the other bed. Perhaps it was just seasickness again. The people next door announced sunrise, he with his 'man sneezes' while his poor wife was still hacking away. She has had that cough for ten days now.

Anyway, 'Stalin' was on the restaurant door and I just knew there would be another fight to get a table for two instead of eight. And then less successful passengers stare at us as if we thought we were special or something. I thought that if I had to share my meal with another bore, I shall top myself.

My order of prosciutto ham was forgotten – I thought it had been too good to be true – so I opted for poached eggs. They were good, but were the ones James always describes as 'old man's testicles'. Lucky the chef will never read my diary.

I caught a glimpse of my reflection in the lift door. How did I become so fat? I thought perhaps a power-walk might be a good idea – I had read about it in the daily programme – but after half a lap I got distracted by some stunning flying fish – after all, Tony Rice had said we should look out for them.

I joined the rush to the Marco Polo Lounge for a shore excursions lecture. Just as I feared, the theatre was heaving. James was in a shocking mood, something to do with the tallest guy on the ship arriving late and plonking himself in his view, and muttered that these bastards should get there on time.

There was rather a dull period after the lecture, so I thought I'd pick up a sudoku sheet from the rack at Reception, and wished I hadn't. I always mess up just before the end. I looked around the deck for someone who looked intelligent and might have the time and inclination to do mindless puzzles. I spoke to 'Madge' from *Benidorm* fame – well, that's what I call her. It's much easier not to ask for a name – it saves causing offence when you forget it. Then there's 'Harold Bishop' from *Neighbours* – he must know that people are thinking the same as me. I always did fancy Harold – he got swept out to sea and reappeared several years later.

Lunchtime at last. I persuaded myself that there were passengers fatter than me – lots of them, a lot fatter – so I headed to the buffet, or coffee shop as I call it. I was met by a sea of walking sticks and power-driven zimmer frames and not a free table in sight.

Perhaps another confrontation with Stalin in the Waldorf would be preferable, so I went there, although I found it difficult to get excited about couscous salad. Our waiter was the Bulgarian 'Robson Green'. His hair is a little darker but he is short and theatrical looking. The risotto was the best I have ever tasted – I hope the chef reads my diary. James said the fish was nice, such as it was. He wasn't quite so polite about the fellow diners – said something about them being 'golf-club types' and a few other descriptions that I shouldn't really repeat.

Today's lecture on the Amazon by Tony Rice was the highlight of my day – it was a pity the old gentleman next to me slept through it all. He would probably still be there now if he had not got caught up in the stampede of beards and shorts when tea-time arrived. I tried to persuade James not to go in case he voiced his observations again. He did suggest that all lectures should start fifteen minutes later than advertised, and then everyone would be there on time.

As dinner time came I changed into something a little smarter. I vowed that tomorrow I would lose weight and James said his trousers 'used to fit with a load of slack'.

Turning off *The Darling Buds of May* [channel 3 on TV], I asked myself what sort of sad and presumptive person keeps a diary? And the answer was 'me'.

by Lizzie Mayes (Cabin 494)

Still no ships anywhere in sight but we have hundreds of flying fish for company, shining irridescently in the sunlight for the few seconds they are out of the water. The temperature is rising daily and it's becoming more humid. The 'broilers' only come down to grab some food – they can't risk losing their sunbeds. People are now employing tactics to ensure they have the same spot all day. Luckily the shady spots aren't so popular so I manage to find somewhere quiet most days. I will have to venture into the swimming pool soon.

We haven't been away two weeks yet, but I feel totally disconnected. We went to a presentation about Santarem, one of our stops on the Amazon. We got cold feet and decided we should book excursions, as our leaders implied it was difficult to go it alone on the Amazon. We were so afraid we would not make the most of this opportunity that we booked several excursions. But we were again appalled at the presentation – lack of any real knowledge and having four goes at pronouncing 'arboretum' doesn't bode well.

I thought I should exercise the grey matter a bit, so did the quiz. We scored 13/20. I was ashamed not to remember Charlie Dimmock, as she was forever etched in male gardeners' brains. I also tried a craft session and made a little bag. A bit too WI for me. We watched a block of ice being carved into a swan (of course, someone told us they do much better ice carvings on Fred Olsen).

The wonderful Olga and Liliya gave a classical concert in the Marco Polo Lounge, which was much appreciated by Dick, firmly planted in the middle of the front row. I tried to send a text message back home, but no luck – we're out of range. We finished the day with our second 'Elvis' cabaret. It is incredible that this 6ft-plus, curly-haired, blond, blue-eyed Richard Sykes can morph into Elvis from the first note. I can understand why everyone says he is the best in the business and we haven't heard any complaints about him – yet.

'The end of the day' by Mark Edwards (Cabin 423)

Being an outdoor person, one of the joys is the tranquillity that comes at the end of the day. That lovely time when there is time to reflect on the day, think about nature in all its forms of good and bad. Sunshine equals good, mosquitoes equals bad, and so on. Pondering the shape and form of life, from people to animals and plants.

Then why the hell is it so difficult to achieve on this ship? I can accept the constant drone of the engines and generators whilst we are at sea, but why are that same group of eight making so much noise, especially when we are either anchored or docked? And it is always the same group. Oblivious to the rest of us. The regulars at the end of the day, couples sat quietly, not interfering with anyone. And this same group, with their loud voices, and that screech of that woman's laughter. Go and get changed for dinner, you rowdy rabble, and leave the rest of us to our contemplations.

The one thing about the rowdies is that they can't get going in the mornings, it would seem. That does mean that it is quite possible to start the day enjoying the world. Just as it ends in tranquillity, it also starts in the same fashion. So it is possible to grab it early doors. The only people up and out at that time are of like mind. Being English, we don't need to speak, just a nod of good morning, and a recognition of being in a fantastic world. For good or for bad, it doesn't matter. Good weather means less clothes, bad weather means more clothes, that's all. Just follow the maxim: be cold or be wet, but don't be cold and wet.

by Dinah Read (Cabin 422)

It is really a delight the way topics of conversation can be carried over from one mealtime to the next with a different set of people. One can seek confirmation or added light, or differing views on any matter of interest.

It is afternoon and I have had a short nap. I had a glass of cider at lunchtime. I had been fancying one for several days. Today is noticeably hotter. Jack is asleep on his bunk. He looks so innocent, almost cherubic, and I do love him. How can a bearded man in his mid-80s look cherubic? But he does.

The evening was pleasant. At table we are still building on shared experiences and different viewpoints. Bernadine and Angela were both convent school girls. Clive turns out to be an atheist, but with interesting friends among the priesthood in Peru among other places! There are so many well-travelled and knowledgeable people on this ship. The entertainment this evening was a concert of classical music, the violinist Olga playing solo. Magnificent.

We started the night on Jack's bed, but I so much wanted to sleep and there really isn't room to turn over without waking, so I went to my own bed and rejoined him at 4.30. Dear Jack. He is so full of love for me. We still can hardly believe it.

by Clive Leatherdale (Cabin 725)

I've met my first twat. It was this afternoon when I went to reclaim the only available sun-lounger in the shaded, lee side of Deck 10, which I have come to consider my outdoor office. I busied myself tapping up my notes on my laptop, oblivious to the fact that the man on my left obviously wanted to talk.

It was some time later, when I closed my computer and struggled to my feet, that he said: 'Before you go ...' He asked to know how to contact me after we got back home, but would not elaborate, speaking in ways which sounded more cussed than quirky. He said he was an engineer and had asked Richard Sykes if the first officer would give a talk about the specifications of *Marco Polo* and what made her behave the way she did. He suggested that as the ship had been 'stretched', it was therefore too thin, and that made her wobble in the water more than she might otherwise have done. He escorted me to the rear of the ship to observe how – even in these calm conditions – the boat was zigzagging as the autopilot kicked in to correct tiny changes of directions, eating up masses of fuel for each realignment of the rudders. He had an off-putting, know-it-all manner and I was glad to escape. I must try to avoid eye contact for the rest of the cruise.

For the second successive night, ours was the last dining table to finish, with waiters fussing around, obviously wanting us to go so they could prepare for second sitting. Last night it was the revelation that Angela and Bernadine were bigwigs in the cubs and girl-guide movements; today the discussion turned to Catholicism. Angela takes it seriously. She knows the names of all the churches (and presumably all the saints) and comes over all gooey at anything called 'Our Lady of Immaculate Conception'. I teased her about this. I earned a brownie point, if not a reduced sentence in purgatory, for having dined with Cardinal Keith O'Brien, although it was more than twenty years ago when he was mere head of Blairs College in Aberdeen. Anyone taking supper with a cardinal has a certain chutzpah in Angela's eyes. I could have walked on water.

'Murder on the Marco Polo' is at present a title without a book. Dozens of passengers say they are interested, but how will this translate into hard copy? One obvious problem is paper. Some contributors have laptops with them, and presumably we can find ways to exchange files. Some have brought along exercise books to serve as journals, often at the demand of relatives back home: 'Mum, dad, you can't go off to the Amazon without keeping a diary!' The rest have nothing to write on, except what they can scrounge from Reception. At our last book meeting a small pile of A4 paper sitting innocently on top of the piano disappeared within seconds, like sharks gobbling sardines. To paraphrase, it was like 'five leaves and two folios' having to feed a whole ship. Those left without will have to improvise or starve for want of paper.

But even if they find paper, what if they write tosh? The whole project stands or falls on the quality of the contributors. I am taking a leap in the dark here, but something tells me it will work out. The ship is full of educated, affluent, retired people from every walk of life. It's a cruising Encyclopaedia Britannica (if not Wikipedia), if only I can tap into it. I have purposefully given everyone *carte blanche*, so that if anyone asks me 'What sort of thing are you looking for in the book?' I can answer, 'I'm sorry, I haven't a clue. It's up to you.'

Until today I hadn't actually received anything by anyone else. Some diarists have asked to show me their entries only at the end of the cruise. Others are too shy, fearful of criticism or rejection. This could be a real problem, no matter how much encouragement I give.

Some time during the night two contributions were shoved under my cabin door. One of them was written on pink card, perhaps nicked from the craft room. At lunch a lady nervously pushed an envelope into my hand. Inside was 500 words of delicious bile. Things are looking up.

A striking image from Parintins, Amazon (Clive Leatherdale)

DAY 13. AT SEA

'There has been some confusion about the location of the Marko Zero Monument. This is found between the port of Santana and the city centre of Macapá. For those of you booked on "Macapá on Your Own" or "Macapá Transfer Service" it is a 20-minute taxi journey.'

by Caroline Clifford (Cabin 468)

Day 13, my lucky number? Perhaps not – I'm guessing that James forgot to take his miracle tablet again last night. 'Snoring?' I thought we'd hit an iceberg. He woke up in a terrible mood again. He calls it 'cachalote syndrome'. The Cachalote was a tiny, cramped boat that we took around the Galapagos Islands. The cabin was so small that we drank our pre-dinner cocktails in the shower room – me on the sink, James on the toilet.

I felt a 'power walk' calling, so I climbed up to Deck 10 – by which time I was rather short of breath and took some time to watch aspiring, or do I mean perspiring, passengers exercising in the gym. And, reading the daily programme, I thought perhaps I could just watch the 'ab blast' at two o'clock and the yoga at four, and at least I could learn 'how' to exercise. No point in rushing into it. In fact, I was not the only voyeur at the ab blast. A doting husband was watching his wife and explained that she would be telling him what to do later. I asked whether she was the plump, clearly struggling, lady in red. 'God no,' he said. His wife was the drop-dead gorgeous blonde who looked like she had never done a day's work in her life. Retiring meekly, I decided to write a letter to mummy:

'Dear mummy, do you remember that Alan Sherman song, "Hello Mother, Hello Father, here I am at Camp Grenada"?'

Of course, reference to Grenada is unfortunate. But then would mummy know where Puerto Ordaz, or even the Orinoco, is? The Amazon, yes. I know she travelled there years ago when head-hunters were still a threat. Or was that Africa? Piranhas were considered deadly and pygmies were famous for blow-jobs, or, I think that was what James said. Of course, the song ends on a happy note – the sun comes out and he doesn't want to go home any more. James was in Grenada in 2004 at the time of Hurricane Ivan. Despite the efforts of the elements and the local people, James survived.

'Dear mummy,' I continued. 'I met this nice man on deck yesterday. His name was Clive. He promised to read my manuscript, 'World Through the Windscreen,' if I did him a small favour. No change there, then. I was hoping I could tell James without a fuss – and I know you never approve of anyone I meet, but I shall soon be a pensioner like you, so perhaps you can let me make my own mistakes.

We still have no satellite news service, but the ship provides a daily news bulletin, a precis of the important stuff. James reacted predictably to the earth-shattering news that P Diddy was making himself available for William and Kate's wedding, saying, 'Should I know who he is?' I finished my sudoku today, so perhaps 13 is still my lucky number. Lots of love, from 04 degrees, 30.63 minutes N, 041 degrees 40.15 minutes W.'

by Lizzie Mayes (Cabin 494)

The temperature is really going up now – 29 degrees by midday. Really calm sea and some mackerel cloud. I love these days at sea – just this ship and nothing to see on any horizon. I am awed by the shear size of the ocean. You don't appreciate it when flying over it for several hours.

We had a great choir session, basically recapping. Richard wants us to be more animated in *Swing Low* and asked us to give him the 'click' not the 'clap'! There is lots of innuendo in his humour but it seems to go over most people's heads. As he announced he didn't do drugs, drink or women, I am in no doubt about his sexuality now. I asked Cait [one of the singers] if he was always the same or if it was an act for the punters. It appears he is always upbeat, bouncy and positive and they all love him. I suppose it's what I expected to hear but it's good to know it's true.

I went to the latest book session, where Clive read some funny contributions. More people are turning up now as word is getting around. Every time I see Clive he nags me to keep writing and show him what I've written. He'll have to wait.

I sat outside in the shade most of the day, yet managed to get sunburnt. I have a bright red and shiny face. This is not so good, as it is another formal night and I look like a dressed lobster. There is lots of glamour around – some people obviously take their cruise wardrobes very seriously. In the evening we went to the jazz concert and actually quite enjoyed it. And, in 'Richard-speak', we went 'through those doors' or was it 'those doors' to the rest of the evening's entertainment.

by Clive Leatherdale (Cabin 725)

Would you believe it's raining? I had grabbed my computer and gone to the back of the boat to stretch out, only to find the decks soaking wet, so

I am having to take refuge under an overhang, but the spray is splashing onto the screen.

Now, let me try to recover today's conversations. From time to time I pass a Dutch woman with her hair tied back. She must be about 60, with a vital face, and must have been gorgeous when she was younger. Each time we pass I ask her to speak to me in Dutch, which she does, and I look heavenwards and tell her how wonderful it sounds.

Earlier I had got talking to an even older lady who said she had a chest infection when she got on at Tilbury. She went down to the wonderfully equipped doctor's surgery. There was room for two patients in the waiting room and she did not like having to say what was wrong with her in the presence of someone else. She was given intravenous antibiotics and tablets, had a blood test, and was presented with a bill for £1,100. Heaven hopes she can get her money back through her insurance.

This afternoon the sun emerged and I espied a spare lounger. There was no one to my right and a sleeping woman to my left. Before I knew it she was awake and leaning over my computer. At first I thought she was interested in my grammatical imperfections. But no, she was man-hunting and I was the nearest fodder. She told me about her unbelievable life. I asked her what was most unbelievable about it, to which she replied that she had once been on a cruise where she was introduced to a VIP – a Saudi prince! I suggested that she might have married him, or even been carted off to a harem, but no, she had simply been, er, introduced and allowed to get off the ship before the other plebs. She was sharing a cabin with an untidy lady friend who was, apparently, 'desperate for a man.'

For those readers not yet familiar with the layout of *Marco Polo*, there are two places to eat. The Waldorf restaurant pretends to be posh, you get seated, wined and dined, and turn up at appointed hours. The ship's 'greasy spoon' is out at the back. Named Marco's Bistro, it offers buffet food, too few chairs, too few cups, and presents 'a diner's challenge'.

'The Diner's Challenge, Marco's Bistro', by James Coleman (Cabin 468)
They said we should go to Marco's
    And there's no real need to book
We're happy with the Waldorf
    But thought we'd have a look.

We've been around the world a lot
    And dined out here and there
Been in the finest places
    But for some we didn't care.

In Singapore we dined in Raffles
    And at the Peninsula in Hong Kong
We tried the Ukrainia when in Moscow
    But we didn't stay there long.

The George the Fifth in Paris
    Just takes your breath away
At the Four Seasons down in Sydney
    We ate kangaroo all day.

We stayed at the La Paz Hilton
    The food there was divine
We dined at the President's Table
    And he paid for all the wine.

The King Zog Hotel in Tirana
    Was indeed extremely rare
While the King Minos in ancient Athens
    Is now no longer there.

The Sheraton in Nairobi
    Is a well-known social trap
While the Holiday Inn in Llasa
    Served up a load of crap.

We've not yet mentioned London
    We dined there at the Ritz
The Savoy was somewhat pricey
    But they played the latest hits.

The Top Kapi Palace Restaurant
    Is a Turkish takeaway
You'll find it deep in Hackney
    Where all the villains stay.

Near the Taj Mahal in India
    We enjoyed some great cuisine
But the Taj Mahal in Bradford
    Was a different kind of scene.

Some countries were a challenge
 Like Zimbabwe, Chad and Togo
The Seven Stans and Wolverhampton
 All these places are just 'no-go'.

The Head Shrinkers Grill in Borneo
 Had a worrying sort of name
And we once ate a load of rubbish
 On an Indonesian train.

At all these places mentioned
 We were seated straight away
But here at Marco's Bistro
 Was not a seat today.

The tables there are taken
 From sunrise every day
There are gangs in shifts that guard them
 And insist you go away.

We'd love to dine at Marco's
 And perhaps we will one day
We've been brave enough to go there
 But weren't brave enough to stay.

On leaving the Amazon, deck crew went through the ship with buckets and brooms to
rid the vessel of thousands of invading creepy crawlies (Clive Leatherdale)

DAY 14. AT SEA

'Enjoy another relaxing day at sea, and witness yet another beautiful sunset. Watch the ship's information channel as we nudge closer to the "big zero" or join us on deck for a fantastic deck party. We're due to cross the equator between 22.30 & 23.00.'

by Caroline Clifford (Hutch 468)
The morning after the night before, and I picked up my discarded clothes scattered around the cabin. I was hoping I hadn't offended anyone at the formal dinner – who knows, and do I really care? Not a good attitude, but I'm sure James will put me right later, when I'm least expecting it. The French say the English say 'please' and 'thank you' too much. I'm not sure I agree but if another passenger drops that heavy door (starboard in Marco's Bistro) in my face one more time, I shall not be responsible for my actions.

No coughing, sneezing, or snoring last night – perhaps next door have died – or perhaps it's an omen for a good day.

Stalin [the head waiter] had the morning off and my breakfast experience was heightened by the 'Macedonian Adonis'. 'Table for two – no problem.' Shirley Valentine, eat your heart out. I am so in love. I hope James doesn't find out.

At the next table all was not well. 'My cup is dirty, give me a clean one – and this one is chipped!' Then the poor waiter brought poached eggs instead of porridge. James said that was just about what she deserved. I think it was just the way she spoke – a sort of demeaning, queen-like accent. I've called her Betsy. Then Private Godfrey [of *Dad's Army*] related tales of traffic jams on the M25 and some Woody Woodpecker impersonator drove everyone up the wall with her laugh. I'm amazed her husband didn't put her right. I had to leave.

James had wandered off with the daily programme. He said to meet him at the 'topless limbo dancing' in Scott's Bar. I was a little confused and when I met him he was characteristically evasive – made some joke about dentures.

Then, queuing up for the Barbados lecture with all the ungodly passengers (those not attending Sunday service), I had a *déjà vu* experience.

On a previous voyage on *Marco Polo* to Spitsbergen I had got trapped in the ladies' loo. Now, someone had shouted out 'Beluga whale' and the queue waiting to get into the theatre all surged forward to the window to get a view, leaving me no space to escape. I was stuck there for twenty minutes and never got to see the whale.

Our cabin, or 'the hutch' as we affectionately call it, was still not made up, so I decided it was time for a showdown with Patrik. As soon as I put the green ['make up my room now'] sign outside the door he seems to develop an 'avoidance tactic', or else he is colour blind. I don't mind that he doesn't create jungle creature shapes with the towels or leave chocolates on my pillow, but I wish he would make the bed so I can get in without remaking it. The ice bucket is a nice touch, but why are there no sanitary bags?

Patrik says there is not much call for them on *Marco Polo* – most people use them for putting their money in. James said they would be just about as much use as a climbing wall on the 'Saga Rose', where the gangway is considered just as strenuous. I can only imagine what it must be like to have a cabin at sea level where the poor people stay. Do they have to slop out before retiring, does the daylight ever reach there, and is it just like Pentonville? I asked James – he should know.

I hardly dare write about the climax of the day – the equator crossing. What a beautiful evening, a wonderful crimson moon, and Richard Sykes strutting his stuff. What would we do without him?

James, however, persuaded a few elderly ladies to hold tightly on to the handrail as we went over 'the bump', and then he told 'Madge from *Benidorm*' that once we crossed the equator the moon would appear upside down. And I can't believe she fell for it. I worry about James.

by Marion Cox (Cabin 619)

A red-faced Englishman and an equally red-faced Dutchman took turns to shout and kick each other's sun loungers. It was becoming very territorial. At this rate we will have our first murder on the *Marco Polo*.

Oh dear. After three days at sea the 800 middle-aged (er, geriatric) 'happy cruisers' were like ants in an overcrowded nest, agitated and ready to swarm.

The pheromone trail directed everyone to the tea bar [outside by the swimming pool], but confusion reigned – no cups – things were brewing! As the post-lunch lecture finished late and 'afternoon tea' had already been cleared away, the culprits surrounded a bunch of bananas and carried them away. They sulked when told 'only one each, not two'.

'Staff keep them hidden under the counter,' someone whispered.

Matters worsened by the evening. As soon as the late show finished, like the Charge of the Light Brigade zimmer frames were cast aside and the audience raced along Deck 9 (ignoring 'Do Not Disturb' signs) to commandeer chairs in Scott's Bar for the late cabaret – only to find when arriving, gasping and breathless, that all the seats were occupied by first-sitting diners with smug expressions on their faces.

On our return journey, 'six days' at sea might prove interesting for people watchers.

by Lizzie Mayes (Cabin 494)
Tonight we will cross the equator. It is still very hot, over 30 degrees. I spent most of the day in the shade with 50 factor on, chatting to different people. The deck party to celebrate crossing the equator was great fun. Richard did *Great Balls of Fire*, which made Dick's night.

It is interesting watching tensions rising on the boat – mostly regarding chairs and loungers being secreted away and the reactions of the secreted to the secretors. I saw a large lady chase a man across the deck after he removed a chair from her table without asking and grab it back from him. Not a word passed between them, but if looks could kill. Of course, this wouldn't happen on Fred Olsen as they have plenty of chairs!

We saw another ship's lights for the first time for days tonight – the moon rose yellow-gold on the horizon, flashes of lightning lit up the sky and we crossed the equator at 22.12 local time. Tomorrow we will get our first glimpse of Brazil and the adventure will really begin.

'The Sun Lovers' by Mark Edwards (Cabin 423)
Have you noticed how you can tell the true sun-worshippers from the outdoor types, and those that just sit in the sun to read? The true sun worshippers are tanned everywhere, all over. How do they get their armpits tanned? I don't want to go up to the jacuzzi deck to find out.

And then there are the older ladies who have been sun-worshippers for years, in their bikinis. Their very dark brown skin has lost all its elasticity and hangs in wrinkles over their bodies. When they walk, the skin moves up and down their bodies in waves; absolutely disgusting, but I bet that they don't know what it looks like.

Those that read out in the sun have white stripes across their throats, where the sun doesn't get into the folds of their necks as they read with their heads down.

And then the outdoor types have only parts of their bodies bronzed, faces, forearms, and necklines, but then they are used to being outside, and knowing the power of the sun keep most of their bodies covered.

by Kay Rainsley (Cabin 543)

Everything is tacky today. Not in the sense of 'cheap and nasty' but in the sticky sense, including us – we are all sticky. Condensation is pouring down the windows of the gym in indignation at the hot air outside. The wooden rails were rubbed down and varnished yesterday by the bow, so they are tacky. The pool was emptied – boo – in readiness for Brazil – can't have water in the pool in port. We will be at anchorage and will go ashore via tender.

Went to aerobics – good. Did the quiz – Jill sat with us, 15/20. Had a 'crossing the equator' party on deck. Music, singing, dancing. Moon amazing – like an orange bonfire in the sky. We see the first lights outside of our ship since we left Cape Verde. We haven't seen a ship for four days. Water – blue, blue, blue, beautiful and clear, laced with froth from our ship. Azure, turquoise, waves, edged in white foaming bubbles, we melt in the heat.

by Jill Crocker (Cabin 514)

Steve's [Ragnall's] lectures are going well but he can't beat Tony Rice's attendance record. That's my observation, not Steve's. He gets into a bit of a flap from time to time. He forgot his notes for one lecture and sent me to get them. I'm Debbie McGee to his Paul Daniels, he tells the audience. Kay insists on calling me Debbie for the rest of the day.

I always sit at the back for Steve's lectures. I don't take up a better seat, but I can see the audience reaction. It is not particularly animated on this trip but it might improve. There was, for example, no reaction when Steve said the *Orellana* was 'emasculated' instead of 'emaciated'. Shame.

Pam the craft lecturer has certainly earned her passage. Two sessions a day, every sea-day.

by Dinah Read (Cabin 422)

We went to the Marco Polo Theatre to watch a dreadful old black and white Cary Grant film – all shouting and too American for words. I sat through it for Jack's sake as I thought he must like it, but as we got up to go afterwards I discovered that his reaction to it had been identical to mine. We went to our cabin and lay down on his bed and mine alternately, from one to the next, with breaks for cold showers and intervals for contented sleep in between. We do love each other.

by Clive Leatherdale (Cabin 725)

There is some concern on board about getting sunburn despite sitting in the shade. Some attribute this to reflection from the surface of the ocean, but whatever the cause I am told my face is red and so is the gap between the top buttons on my shirt. The stinging from my exposed insteps was enough for Dinah to go her cabin to fetch her aloe vera skin cream.

On one of my morning walkabouts I came upon a lady who asked me to sit down next to her. She told me that she had been wooed by her future husband when she was 23 but decided to emigrate to New Zealand instead. She then changed her mind and went back to marry him, even though, as he pointed out, they were complete opposites intellectually and every other way. They have three children and she is particularly proud of her youngest daughter, a former shares trader who gave it all up to live in Cornwall to be closer to nature. She is gay and wrote to her mother to 'come out'. For a year her mother could not handle it, but then she got used to it. Her husband was much more understanding, saying he could not understand what women see in ghastly men in the first place, and if he was a woman he would prefer women too.

The long-awaited first Waldorf lunch for solo passengers was held today. Incidentally, 'solo' does not mean being a single occupant in a cabin. Two friends travelling together are eligible, too. In fact, that probably accounted for most of those present. Everyone was allocated a name badge on a circular table – boy, girl, boy, girl (I would never say gaga man, dribbling woman, incontinent man, botox woman) – as far as possible, but that still left several ladies flanked by other damsels.

The woman to my right asked what I did before I retired. Answer, I'm not retired. And what's the favourite place I've ever been. Answer, North Korea, but that didn't spark any response.

Later I stood near the bow chatting to a chap who ran a digital television business. He remarked on how – apart from flying fish – we had seen no other airborne life. And just then we saw our first birds, first a small thing ducking around the bows, then a larger one, which he provisionally identified as a boobie, or gooby, or something like that.

I ventured to the equator party about 8-ish. It had stopped raining. The pool deck was packed, so I stood and looked down over the railings from Deck 9. Richard Sykes (a distant relative of Eric, he says, of the comedian family) announced that we crossed the equator about 10.10. Beforehand passengers were entertained with quizzes. Whoever got the most consecutive answers right had to wear a silly Viking hat. Afterwards there was live music, dating more from the 1950s than 60s – the Drifters, that kind of thing. Richard, Cait, Megan and Sarah, took turns to lead the vocals. Richard never fails to amaze, this time with his singing and dancing routines. I was in bed by 11, leaving them all to it, knowing that I had a busy day tomorrow and probably an early start.

'The Complement' by Sue MacPherson (Cabin 714)

A boatful: yes, a boatful of people … well mostly,
    For there are a few
Whose views, if you can call them that
    Curdle the bile
Complainers by profession are a dreary lot,
    But here comes the crunch;
Age with gin conspire
    A meaner creature to make
Giving forth with venom and spite
    Where others see nothing but contentment and good service,
Peace and solicitude.
    To encounter these monoliths
Take a moment to reflect
    upon the average soul to inhabit our ship
In holiday mode, regardless of age
    to make the most of their time
with bon homie and grace
    monoliths notwithstanding.

The name *Marco Polo* adorns the back of this bus in Alter do Chao. But it was not an occasion to advertise, as the local driver put passengers' lives at risk – see pages 110-11 (Alan Smith)

'Flying Dutchmen' reproduced by kind permission of artist Sue MacPherson
[see linked poem on page 48]

DAY 15. ICOARACI, BELEM

'Belem, Brazil, is the capital of the state of Pará and chief port of the Amazon. With a population of 1.3 million, it makes the city the largest of the Amazon region, after Manaus. Located 90 miles from the sea, the origins of Belem date back to 1616.'

by Caroline Clifford (Cabin 468)

Early morning and the whole ship was galvanised into action, and by 7.15am breakfast was a sell-out. Rucksacks and walking shoes were once more the fashion 'must haves'. I was looking forward to Icoaraci [the port for Belem] – like Clive said: 'Mix with the people, talk, dine and stay with them.' Well, obviously not stay with them. After some queuing and some pushing I had a tender ticket 'A' in my hand [which meant first off the ship onto the tenders to take us ashore]. I was confident of an exciting day. Hot, cold, wet or dry; I didn't care.

Tendering – there was delay and confusion. Was it caused by the officials who arrived in the stunning little boat 'Sweetheart', or was it pistols at dawn at the landing place? It really didn't matter; there was mud, rubbish, children diving into the murky and dangerous port waters, crumbling buildings and a number of locals looking the worse for wear.

I heard urgent walkie-talkie conversations as our tender rammed itself against another one, which had been strategically tied up to guard our place and act as bridge to the pontoon. *Marco Polo*'s visit had clearly disrupted the everyday workings of the port and the free passage of the ferries crammed with locals, chickens and food for market.

Finally ashore in Icoaraci – wonderful shops full of plastic goods, shoes, knickers and skimpy dresses I could only dream of wearing. Pink, green and spotted tops, all body-hugging. My 'must do' list included changing money, and visiting the market and a supermarket to marvel at the local diet.

The smell of warm meat and fish still unsold easily identified the location of the market. Fruit, gourds and vegetables not found in Tesco's decorated stalls and walls. And for me, a great treat, a species of cockroach I hadn't seen before but unfortunately squashed under feet. Outside the market, the familiar smell of open drains, and what caused great amusement, the challenge of raised pavements, so high as to impede the fittest athlete. And to jump down meant to join the oncoming traffic which drove, apparently oblivious to accepted rules, on the left and on the right.

Shopping was not easy. American dollars were not 'widely accepted' as we had been led to believe on the ship. Not just in the market and the knicker shops, but also in the Bank of Brazil! James was critical in unprintable language. This necessitated a return trip to the ship to collect plastic money.

If you walk straight into Icoaraci from the landing stage you cannot miss 'Boa Companhia', a busy local supermarket with a 'one table' bar at the entrance and a scruffy restaurant at the back. It was while inspecting the specialities of Icoaraci that I spotted a bottle of cachaca, bringing back fond memories of an ambassadorial party in Brazilia when I was barely old enough to drink. Then, I thought, if I could buy limes from the market, steal sugar from the ship's galley, and get some ice from Patrik, I could make myself a caipirinha. It did occur to me that bringing alcohol back on board was probably not allowed, but for 3½ Brazilian reals [about £1.50] I couldn't leave it on the shelf, and hopefully no one would see me. And at that price it would be very poor quality, so surely no one would wish to confiscate it?

I was wrong – leaning unsteadily on the small bar table was a member of the crew, beer in hand. He didn't miss me, and as he backed to let me pass, probably a little ashamed of swigging from the bottle, he stepped into and demolished a free-standing display of baby-milk powder. Without words, just a smile, I think it was understood that 'I wouldn't tell if he didn't'.

Sadly, it was time to tender back to the ship, but not before spotting Tony Rice photographing some vultures who were ignoring the attempts of local drunks to frighten them with bird-scarers – which sounded at first blast like a dynamite charge. On the river, local life floated past; traders, fishermen, ferries, and a flat-bottomed boat moving a few dozen cattle upstream. The animals appeared quite unfussed, just staring at us staring at them. What a magic place.

by Lizzie Mayes (Cabin 494)
So here we are in Icoaraci (which means sunset), the port for the city of Belem. 'DinoRod' [Di and Rod], the Australian couple without visas, are definitely not allowed ashore. I felt so sorry for them but they are amazingly upbeat about it. I really admire them. We are moored off and will have to go ashore by tender. Today we are doing the Guama River Tour.

It was a long drive into Belem in the coach and we passed mile upon mile of graffiti-covered shanty town. It looked dirty and dusty and was very noisy. A really depressing introduction to Brazil. As we approached the city centre I was struck by the number of high-rise buildings painted in bright blues, greens, and peach colours.

We boarded our riverboat and I was so glad to be on the water again, away from the city noise, and I was immediately struck by the vastness of the river system. We went past dozens of rusting riverboats abandoned on the city riverside, others setting off in different directions, and small motorised canoes with two or three people in each, coming and going from their riverbank homes.

We headed for our first walk into the forest about 40 minutes from the city. Our guide showed us brazil nut trees, quinine and countless other trees and palms such as acai, famed for their medicinal uses, purporting to cure everything from the common cold to cancers. We saw a beautiful shiny brown lizard, lots of butterflies and moths, and some strange grey and black hairy tree crickets. There was a small souvenir hut but I didn't feel tempted to buy anything.

On the return journey we passed close by the riverbank, getting our first sight of how the river people live in wooden stilt houses on the river-banks, eating the fruits of the forest and fish caught in the river. Small canoes were moored on the riverside and were their only form of trans-port. There are very few roads. I couldn't help thinking that if this were the upper reach of the Thames they'd all have to be millionaires! Some homes do now have electricity and you could see the pylons knifing their way through the forest.

Back in Belem I found it really depressing to see what progress is for these people, moving from forest to city squalour and a different kind of poverty. The power of modern technology is so strong.

I am always happy to get back on the *Marco Polo* – this ship has such a nice feel to it. The show team put on a rock and roll concert – it was wonderful and I have to admit I went to see it twice. Christian strutting his stuff is a sight to behold – I think if he's not careful he'll be the next casualty for the doctor. We keep hearing horrifying stories that if you go to the doctor you get a whacking big bill. I don't envy him with this aged population, working alone with just with two nurses. He can't afford to make any mistakes.

'To Market in Belem' by Kay Rainsley (Cabin 543)
We hear squealing, raw and urgent, a cry for help. A couple of minutes later there is more squealing – it pierces the already chaotic background

of noises. Again – the scream abates. We hear men shouting. We look at each other. Dare we follow the source of the brouhaha? We dare.

Carefully we pick our way back along the quayside. Past the moored boats with their somnolent crews and scraps of plastic erected as a foil against the piercing rays of the sun, past the piles of rubbish until we reach the source of the scream.

Laid on the ground like so many fallen dominoes were two neat rows of wild boar. Each had its left trotters secured with string, as were its right. Around its neck was a loose necklace of rough sisal. They lay close together, calmly and quietly – 32 in all. In contrast, one pig was being hauled unceremoniously into the air and attached to a large hook beneath a stout pole. This is when the squealing started. Protesting wildly it continued emanating the high-pitched sound as one man, bare-chested and holding one end of a pole, took the weight and another grasped the other end, thereby swinging the animal aloft. A third man quickly adjusted a small scale until the weight was ascertained. He then shouted said weight to a fourth individual, who noted it down. The screaming continued until the pig was laid down again amongst the others, whereupon it fell quiet.

We watched the whole process, along with a group of men, presumably prospective buyers. The boars were smaller and darker in colour than their domestic cousins, with long, hairy snouts and small tusks protruding from their lower jaws.

The next victim is hauled aloft and the squealing starts again. We move away with the sound still ringing in our ears. We are unable to help.

by Dinah Read (Cabin 422)
I was awake and up and dressed very early because I was booked on a trip up the Guama river and we were to leave at 8.30am. Jack was not coming, as we thought (quite rightly) that it would be too taxing for him. So he stayed on board all day, perfectly happy to do that. Later he told me that Captain Zhukov had taken lunch in the Waldorf, dining alone. Richard Sykes had dined there too, and Jack had had a long chat with him during the afternoon. Richard had agreed to arrange a war veterans get-together on the passage back across the Atlantic, and also considered that future cruises in the North Sea might include Heligoland. That pleased Jack who had some remarkable experiences there just after the end of World War One.

As for my day, it was 9.45 before we left the ship in one of the two tenders. Part of the delay was due to the pier being public and very busy. There were more armed police there than I have ever seen. A coach took us from there to another landing, skirting Belem. This was interesting to me and informative. We glimpsed the modern and highly developed city with tower blocks to match Moscow, but mainly we passed by industrial complexes and trading estates with little houses and stores in pastel shades behind ornate grills decorated with palms and brilliantly flowering trees. Everywhere there were heaps of rubbish awaiting collection, reminiscent of Birmingham during a dustman's strike. There was also near-destitution, buildings crumbling into rubble, red beaten earth beyond the tarmac, long straight alleyways leading off into slumlike areas, skinny dogs and appealing children much in evidence. There were quite stylish young women and handsome boys on bicycles – lots of bicycles.

At the end of our excursion we went back to the jetty by a different route, with even more stilt dwellings, through mangrove swamps and back to town, where we reversed the bus journey past the airfield and the army training camp and the naval base and the breakers yards.

There were delays on every part of this trip but I really did not mind as the people were so attractive and polite and the children so beautiful that I felt quite at ease. The scene was picturesque, even in its material poverty, the many boats quaint and curious. The transfer back to the ship in the tender was fun. She took on a fair bit of water and it was quite a performance coming alongside. I loved it.

'The Volga River Boatmen' by Tim Major (Cabin 469)

Our Atlantic crossing reached its conclusion at the village of Icoaraci, our landing place for the city of Belem, state capital of Pará. *Marco Polo* anchored some distance out, the best place having been already occupied by a merchant vessel, so we had a half-hour boat trip to get ashore.

Our orange lifeboats were swung out to be used as tenders to shuttle ashore passengers interested to see their first Amazon town, or just keen for a few hours on dry land after four days of 'water, water, everywhere'.

The first shuttle was ready for boarding and the lucky holders of shuttle pass 'A', urged on by helpful crew members, almost fell over each other in their enthusiasm to vacate their temporary home. I was not on the 'A' list, so I only learned later that in their anxiety to board us quickly, crew members kept passengers so close together that they could hardly see where they were putting their feet. Indeed, one lady fell and was later diagnosed with one broken elbow and torn ligaments in the other, leaving her as walking wounded for the rest of our voyage.

With all aboard at last, the shuttle set off. It pulled up to a jetty where, with some pithy advice from locals, it was discovered that this was not the right one. It seems almanacs for the Amazon ports are a little sketchy on detail.

At length, the shuttle found the correct pier. Having approached fast from downstream, it thudded into local vessels protecting the pier against unwanted visitors. The shuttle bounced clear and recommenced its approach, this time upstream, under better control, and was finally secured. Passengers climbed gratefully over such neighbouring vessels as separated it from the pier, well-meaning assistance from the crew notwithstanding.

With the obstacle course presented by local vessels in various stages of embarking and disembarking their own passengers, our operation lost one tender immediately in order to provide a permanent landing stage. This would allow *Marco Polo* passengers to climb over one of our own tenders, helped by our own crew members, rather than competing with local travellers and having to depend on the help of Brazilian sailors with better things to do.

Throughout the day the cluster of local vessels complicated docking, but served the essential function as fenders. It usually took at least one approach and several jolting contacts with other vessels before our tenders could pass mooring lines to the crew waiting to secure them to the landing stage. News filtered back to the *Marco Polo* that the tendering operation would be slower than anticipated.

My own alphabetically retarded tender pass was finally called and I took my seat, ignoring attempts to assist me by crew members who apparently felt that their supporting hands were more reliable than allowing me to grip the firm handholds offered by the landing stage rail and the tender roof supports.

I found myself a seat and was promptly told to squeeze up. Others looked askance at my not inconsiderable bulk. Firmly wedged, I watched as fellow passengers of varying levels of agility and infirmity were helped down into the boat until at last, in conditions which a dead sardine would have found constricting, we set off.

I was now able to experience at first hand the small-boat handling skills of our tender crews. These were, of course, the very crews who might one day be responsible for transferring 1,200 souls from a sinking *Marco Polo* into its lifeboats in sea conditions bad enough to destroy a 20,000 ton ship. Our good-humoured crew, both those on the ship's entry platform and those managing our tender, brought my nerves to fever pitch as they contrived to drop long rope-tails in the water and then whisk them away in the nick of time from our whirling screws. I nervously eyed the lifejackets tucked under the roof beams of the tender as our skipper applied power, swung the helm over and delivered a resounding thump with our stern to the entry platform by way of farewell to the ship.

At length we approached the pier, whose presence had to be deduced from its popularity with other boats, as they concealed the structure until we were only a few metres away. Even with previous experience, our tender still initially approached downstream, cannoned off a couple of local vessels, the air thick with what may have been helpful advice in a number of languages, before drifting clear downstream and recommencing its approach from there.

Although ropes were passed across to our 'landing stage' tender, a loss of focus by our coxswain allowed our bows to swing out and get caught by the current. The blond sailor on the 'landing stage' had omitted to take a turn around a cleat when receiving the bow line. He now faced the unenviable choice of letting go the hard-won rope, or allowing himself to be dragged from the roof of the 'landing stage' into the water. Fortunately our coxswain noticed the peril in the nick of time. With engines roaring he managed to reposition the boat before the warp reached the bitter end.

We disembarked gratefully, although I had been wedged so firmly that my knee had become stuck to some not-quite-dry paint, so I spent my visit ashore with a blue patch on the right knee of my chinos. Still, it was better than a broken elbow! Once again I carefully avoided the helping hands of free-standing crew members, preferring to put my trust in elements firmly attached to boat or pier.

My first contact with an Amazon city was initially quite enjoyable. The bus was modern, air-conditioned, with seatbelts and a loo, although I declined to inspect the last feature. The escort was more helpful than our excursion desk had suggested we had a right to expect, and she provided maps and helpful advice. Her words, however, had to be repeated more than once, as the bus PA system was not operational.

A longish walk around Belem ended pleasantly at an area of waterside bars where it was possible to sit and have a drink and even a meal while watching the bustling activity at the pier immediately opposite. I resisted the temptation to eat, but a beer and a study of Brazilians displaying their boat handling skills was enjoyable and probably safer.

In the interests of safety, I also resisted the offer of a massage from a female customer at a neighbouring stall, although her conversation was pleasant enough, and it was with some regret that I made my way to catch the shuttle bus back to Icoaraci.

The bus increased that regret considerably because the excursion desk's warnings about the variable quality of tourist transportation were now borne out. The bus was not air-conditioned and its seats were threadbare and seatbelt-free. There was no loo, although from the smell of the upholstery it seemed to have spent a good deal of its off-duty time parked next to a sewage treatment plant.

Despite its visual and olfactory disadvantages, the bus conveyed us back to the pier, where we were once more assisted over the landing stage tender and packed into our conveyance for our return trip to the distant *Marco Polo*.

With only a couple of mild collisions we were on our way. Our coxswain set a cracking pace across the bay. In this he showed a regrettable insouciance regarding conditions below. Positioned high above his passengers he was unaware that the brisk breeze from our starboard bow, coupled with the waves it had created and our own speedy progress, was delivering bucket-loads of spray through the open side of the boat directly onto passengers unfortunate enough to be sitting at the rear. Even where I was, in the closed bow, water flying up over the bow periodically poured down the strut to which the davit attaches, leading me to wonder whether a better seal might be desirable in the event of having to endure a storm at sea in the lifeboat. One would not wish to use too much fuel just running the pumps!

Eventually the sailors sitting comfortably in the dry, forward of the open side, could no longer ignore the protests from those being soaked. They themselves got wet letting down the side cover, so that although already very wet, the hapless victims were at least spared further Amazon water full in the face.

Arriving back at the ship, our coxswain managed to get us alongside after only one futile, but mercifully brief, attempt to work the bow between the ship and the boarding platform. Secure alongside, we were assisted out of the tender with an urgency on the part of the crew which was unnecessary, as no one wanted to spend longer in it, particularly those who were dripping and needed to get a towel to both themselves and their cameras.

Comparing notes later with others who had been ashore, I discovered that one tender had not docked quite so swiftly. Just as it was about to tie up alongside the ship's entry port, a crackle of static announced a walkie-talkie message to the coxswain. The tender sheered away on an urgent mission. Apparently the painter for the inflatable had not been properly secured, and the zodiac was drifting away in the wind and current. The passengers were none the worse for their diversion.

by Clive Leatherdale (Cabin 725)
We did not get ashore at Icoaraci until 9.45, three quarters of an hour late. Our tender set off, then had to return to the ship so a sailor could

retrieve the zodiac. Heading upstream, it then took 35 minutes to land, a journey made more unpleasant by being stuck in the back by the exhaust, which was belching toxic fumes. It was bad enough for me, but worse for the couple opposite, as the black fog, with nowhere to escape, enveloped them. They had to cover noses and mouths with hankies.

Some indication of public safety awaited us as we disembarked at Icoaraci, for the jetty was lined with the poor, the young and the male. Armed police were everywhere, four in a line when we got to the main road. I had reluctantly paid £15 for a waiting 'special' bus to Belem, normally preferring public transport, but though the distance was not great – twelve miles – I had no knowledge of local bus times or routes, and fear of missing the ship would have demanded an early return.

I took rapid-fire photos out of the window. Gutters were deep and dangerous, the military everywhere. Our US-accented, English-speaking guide had no microphone, so only those at the front could hear him. I was in the back and he might have been reciting the Quran for all I knew.

We pulled up at the Estacio das Docas on the waterside. Our guide had no city maps to distribute, nor had the ship, so most of us had no idea how to get around. My first priority was getting a map, and I knew posh hotels would have them. I popped into one to ask for 'mapa' and one was produced. The woman asked if I was staying there, meaning – I presume – that I would have to pay for it if I was not. I just shrugged and she handed it to me.

I shortly came across the Belem Hilton, where I got another map, but any attempt to find sterling exchange rates met with failure. Across the road the Teatro da Paz was closed. This was the commercial heart of the city. Every other building was a bank or financial house and armed guards were as numerous as customers. Wearing my best gormless expression I passed through a revolving door, just to see what would happen. Rather than sweep me forwards, the doors locked with me inside, unable to go forwards or back. I gave them a shove, and they juddered forward a few inches. It needed repeated shoves before I could gain access. It was only when I came out the same way that I noticed all other customers were depositing metal objects – keys, phones – in a plastic hatch. I had not even seen it, and must have triggered the jamming door. Presumably I did not invite suspicion, otherwise I might have received an unwelcome tap on the shoulder.

I came upon a small demonstration. Two men supported a huge banner with poles at either end. Each time the traffic lights turned red, they would unfurl it across the stationary traffic, then hastily remove it when they turned green.

DAY 16. ON THE AMAZON

"Behind the Scenes:"
Richard Sykes and our showteam members explain how shows are put together before hosting a backstage tour. Costumes, choreography and choruses. Don't miss it!'

by Dinah Read (Cabin 422)

We had a nice lazy morning. Everything outside is grey, a milky pearly grey with just a touch of warmth. We are heading for the Amazon.

We went to Tony Rice's technical presentation on the measurement of sea miles, and longitude and latitude, and wave measurement and the causes of variation according to the configuration of the seabed. His lecture was as good as ever and appealed to both of us.

We then stayed on for an introduction to the show team and its choreographer and director. We had a brief glimpse of the dressing rooms and costume rail. Amazing use of the very minimum of space. And they really do rehearse at night between 11pm and 2am! I am overcome by the talent, enthusiasm and sheer dedication of these people. They alter and mend their own costumes, dress their own hair, everything. As for Richard Sykes, veteran cruisers all declare that they have never known a cruise director to match him, and I am sure that comment is well justified. He has the charm and energy of a young gun-dog. He is a very competent and well-educated musician and is a man of ideas at the same time. Seeing him on the first day of our cruise, I thought, 'Oh yes, Compere!' almost disparagingly, but he is far, far more than that.

We are still moving slowly ahead through water coloured like the Severn. There are six ships of various kinds at anchor here – freighters, container ships, heavy lift vessels. We must be arriving somewhere.

by J Armitage (Cabin 301)

The ship's full of twitchers and snappers
    There's no room for posers and snappers
Look, look there's a whale
    No, no it's a sail
But we power round the deck like the clappers.

by Jenny Liddell (Cabin 496)
I was delighted to hear that a choir would be formed amongst interested passengers. At the first gathering there were quite a number of us, but that number grew rapidly with each rehearsal. Cruise director Richard Sykes proved that everyone had a singing voice. We started by being told the type of voice we had – soprano, alto, tenor etc – and then singing well-known songs in harmony. We soon forgot our inhibitions.

'Rude text messages up the Amazon' *by Marion Cox (Cabin 619)*
Text: 'Where r u?
1st reply: 'Up the Amazon now looking for whales.'
2nd reply: 'Two Irishmen travelling to London to donate at a sperm clinic. One missed the tube and the other came on the bus.'
Reply to above: 'What's this about Paddy at the Opera and looking for sperm whales up the Amazon?'

by Lizzie Mayes (Cabin 494)
Burns Night tonight. Think we'll give that one a miss.
Everyone is hoping to catch a glimpse of pink dolphins, and passengers are hanging over the sides of the boat, cameras at the ready. The river is so wide. I hate to use the word 'awesome', but it is. The muddy river waters now replace the rich ocean blues and no longer mesmerise me.
I had a long chat with someone who had realised she's made a terrible mistake travelling with a companion who was driving her insane.

'The Onboard Boutique' *by James Coleman (Cabin 468)*
Available now in the ship's boutique. Something new, absolutely new and recently successfully tested by Saga Cruises. The Universal Chair Strap with quick-release buckle. Never be without a chair again. Strap the chair of your choice to your back and keep it for the full length of the cruise. It leaves both hands free for carrying two cups of coffee. No need to confuse the deck crew again, wondering where all the bloody chairs are, that have been removed from their correct locations, including smokers' tables. Special low introductory price.
Available soon, recently invented in Germany, the Electronic Sunbed Guard. Protects your empty sunbed for 48 hours. This device will emit a noise like a deranged rottweiller if anybody decides to even touch your prized possession. It is no longer necessary to risk your towel, book or handbag being dumped overboard by an envious and irate sun-worshipper when you are absent. Comes complete with six AA batteries.

Stop Press: Why not get the Super de Luxe model for an extra £9.99. It emits a screeching voice (in a choice of four languages) of a demented old woman.

'Gifts from the Moon' by Piet Pieterse (Cabin 127)

According to Regina Peixoto Vasquez, there are many indigenous legends among the Amazonian peoples. This is one called, 'Gifts from the Moon'.

The Indian tribes think that many plants in the Amazon area are a compensation for suffering. There was a little girl whose name was Naia. She was very beautiful. She fell in love with the moon. In her language the moon is called 'Jaci'. Each night Naia looked at the sky. Maybe the moon was there.

Her deepest wish was to become a star. It was told that Jaci chose the nicest girls and transformed them into stars. But Naia was never chosen. The moon's rejection made her unhappy. One day she became so weak that she fainted. When she awoke she was sitting on the riverside, where she experienced an enormous surprise.

She saw the moon Jaci on the water's surface. She did not understand that it was not the real moon but a reflection. Naia tried to catch the moon but she drowned.

The moon took pity on her and felt guilty that she had not answered Naia's love for her. That's why she did not change Naia into a star but into a very special flower – the Royal Amazon Water Lily, sometimes called Queen Victoria's Water Lily.

'Desert Island Discs' by Clive Leatherdale (Cabin 725)

Apparently the ship's engines stopped in the night. The sudden absence of the throbbing diesels caused one or two nautically minded passengers to stir. Anyway, we were moving when I woke to the now-familiar leaden skies and steady morning rain which has been a feature of the past few days. I shared a breakfast table with a Dutch couple who told me that Dutch youngsters today are ignorant and make so many mistakes in everything they do.

I went to hear Richard Sykes explain what went on backstage for each of the shows. Apparently, last night's 'Rock 'n' Roll' early show earned a standing ovation. Rehearsals start around 11.30pm, after the second show has finished, and can go on for hours. Those cabins directly above the pillars supporting the stage have been known to complain, but not on this cruise, says Richard. We were invited to peep into the cramped changing quarters backstage; one for dancers, one for singers. Funnelling several hundred curious souls in and out of a cubby hole with just one door took some time. The most curious aspect was notices pinned to the wall, not for passengers' eyes. The first was signed 'Rich', stating in bald terms that whenever performers were in public areas they must speak English at all times. Failure to do so would result in serious consequences from the company. The other notice was a form report on a crew member leading a shore excursion. He was judged 'very attentive'.

By mid-afternoon, we were clearly in the north channel of the Amazon, although it had not been clear from my map which was the navigable channel, north or south. My Amazon chart, bought from Stanfords in London, made me instantly popular with mapless passengers. We were approaching what could only be Macapá, the only sizeable town on the north bank. Earlier, through binoculars, we had seen dilapidated motor boats like the *African Queen*. Later, we passed half-a-dozen anchored cargo ships, some of whose names I noted – *Golden Saguenay* (Hong Kong), *Rodon Amarandon*, *Sunrise Serenity*.

Near me on the rail looking out was a distinguished-looking, slightly stooped man who looked vaguely familiar, whether from television or not I could not say. I had seen him from time to time about the ship, more often than not on his own. His pretty pony-tailed wife was standing between us, so I engaged her in conversation before gently asking about her husband. She told me he had recently featured on *Desert Island Discs* and quietly moved round so I could have him to myself.

I was now talking to Lord David Cobbold, strictly speaking the 2nd Baron Cobbold. The title had been created for his father, Governor of the Bank of England from 1949 to 1961, and David is one of 90 surviving hereditary peers in the House of Lords. He's a cross-bencher, in other words an independent, and attends the House about three times a week. I ask if he is related to the gentlemanly Cobbold dynasty who famously oversaw Ipswich Town's glory years under Sir Alf Ramsey and Sir Bobby Robson, and he replies yes.

The reason for the programme with Kirsty Young in August 2010 was his family's ownership of Knebworth House in Hertfordshire, whose grounds for the past 40 years have hosted mighty rock concerts. David is the great-great-grandson of the famous Victorian wordsmith Edward Bulwer-Lytton, credited with coining the proverb, 'The pen is mightier than the sword.'

Weeks later, after I returned home, I found the broadcast on the internet. It had gone out on Sunday 8th and Friday, 13 August. I was puzzled that I had no recollection of it, as I am a regular listener to *Desert Island Discs*. But I had been in Lebanon that week, and on 13 August was driven to Beirut airport, anxiously peering through the windows, for this very route had seen the kidnap that brought years of solitary torment to John McCarthy in the 1980s and early 90s. Had I listened in, I wonder if my Amazonian interest would have flickered, for David and Chrissie were soon to enjoy their golden wedding anniversary, and David announced to the world that they had booked a celebratory cruise to the Amazon. And here they were, admiring the same view as I was.

Naturally enough, Kirsty Wark had raised the question of whether, as is reputed, Knebworth is haunted. 'I hear them [the ghosts of my ancestors] and feel their presence,' answered David, 'but my wife [a former debutante] sees them.'

Over the years, David has enjoyed close-up performances by some of the great names in popular music – including Paul McCartney, Led Zeppelin, Robbie Williams. Is it true, asked Kirsty, that Noel Gallagher of Oasis had taken a bath in the ornate bathroom of Knebworth, and that David had brought him champagne? 'Yes,' replied David. 'He thought I was the butler, and probably still does.'

I was intrigued by the unusual mix of privilege (Eton and Cambridge) and love of rock music, and wondered at David's choice of eight discs. Here they are, in playlist order: 1) Pink Floyd's *Brain Damage* from *Dark Side of the Moon*; 2) Wagner's *Rienzi Overture*; 3) Lennon and McCartney's *Hey Jude*; 4) Mozart's *Now that the Wine has set their Heads Whirling* from *Don Giovanni*; 5) Edith Piaf's *Milord*; 6) Ella Fitzgerald and Louis Armstrong singing *I've got my Love to keep me Warm*; 7) Frank Sinatra's version of *Some Enchanted Evening*; 8) Mary Hopkin's *Those Were the Days*.

In the timeless words of the programme, what disc would David save above all others – he replies Pink Floyd; what would be his book (in addition to the bible and complete works of Shakespeare) – *Zanoni* by Edward Bulwer-Lytton (a novel featuring Rosicrucian occultism); what would be his luxury? David's first choice, a solar-powered something-or-other, Kirsty banned for being too practical, so he settled for a fishing rod instead. This was granted, even though it was no less practical.

Some days before our conversation, I had seen David – though I did not then know his name – poring over a manuscript on the pool deck. The sight of any manuscript, with proper double-spaced type, sends publishers' antennae twitching. What is it? Is it any good? If so, has anybody signed it up? My immediate assumption was that it was Lord Cobbold's autobiography. But no, he was checking what he described as a powerful critique of the use and misuse of drugs, penned by his friend Max Rendell. David confirmed that in the House of Lords he campaigns for the anti-criminalisation of drugs, and I wondered how many other passengers on *Marco Polo* had their own Wikipedia entry.

After dinner I joined Mark and Sue Edwards for Twenty Questions. I mention this piece of trivia only because of Mark's profession and the the nature of one of the questions: 'What is the biggest non-contagious disease in the world.' None of us knew, so we guessed at leprosy. The correct answer was 'tooth decay'. Mark is a dentist.

According to the ship's original itinerary, tomorrow we should have been anchoring at Santana and then been tendered ashore at Macapá. Excursions had been booked. We were then informed that because the ship could not take on enough fresh water in the time available, we were steaming further up-river. That explains why we steamed past Macapá today and will now be stopping at Almeirim tomorrow, one day earlier than planned. We will now be visiting Macapá on the way back.

Some passengers are puzzled by this. Surely water supply is something that would have been known in advance? And suppose passengers had friends and relatives waiting for them in Macapá or Almeirim, who now turn up and find no ship on the appointed day?

Lord David Cobbold discreetly plugs Knebworth,
(site of the great rock festivals) on his jacket.
David featured on *Desert Island Discs* in August 2010
(Clive Leatherdale)

DAY 17. ALMEIRIM

*'Almeirim is the northernmost municipality in the state
of Pará and is crossed by the Equator. It lies on the
north bank of the Amazon near the outlet of the
Xingu River. The population is divided between city
dwellers and those that live in the various villages.'*

by Marion Cox (619)

Our Chinese brolly was needed for both the rain and the sun today. We
wandered up the hillside to the chatter of parrots in the mango trees. At
the top of the village, three curious children peep from behind a glassless
window. A fellow passenger steams up and commands them to smile and
wave. He photographs them and then walks away.

We buy three lollipops from a shack and take them to the kids – obrigado, big smiles and waves.

A gentle-faced man sat at the front of his tiny general store.

'Accident?' I ask, pointing at the plaster cast on his arm. I ascertain by
signs that he slipped on the wet tiles outside his store, hurt his back, cut
his shoulder, and broke his arm. He had to go to hospital to get it fixed.
Still not good. It was difficult to keep dry when he has a shower – not a
bad conversation for no English and no Portuguese.

by Lizzie Mayes (Cabin 494)

We arrived in this little riverside town at midday in blazing hot sunshine.
Only the British go out in the midday sun, so there was a wonderfully soft
atmosphere when we arrived – people sitting around in sheltered bars
watching the world go by. This little town is crossed by the equator and
was founded in 1758. Today, there is a population of 31,500 and only 4
per cent of homes have running water [according to the day sheet]. We
wandered along the dusty waterside street with its little shops and bars.
We saw hammocks made from beautiful woven fabric and bought two for
about £15 (the young shopkeeper had been to England and wanted to
return – he loved Whitstable).

My hammocks will always remind me of the riverboats. Colourful
rows of them were slung from the beams – and served as beds for river
people as they move between towns and villages.

We walked to the end of the boardwalk along the riverside. People gradually emerged from their siestas – children everywhere with pet parakeets on twigs, some shy, looking at us anxiously with enormous brown eyes, others smile in greeting. These often immaculate wooden homes on stilts mostly had just two rooms and glassless windows. Some had back decks with raised beds growing lush vegetables and herbs. Pet parrots eyed us from doorways, and mothers proudly showed off their babies. A man displayed his catch of two large fish.

Schools on the Amazon don't reopen until the end of January. As we were getting back on the tenders for another demonstration of eccentric boatmanship, a small boy asked for the bag of sweets I had in my hand. I gave them but gestured that he should share them with his friends. He immediately stood to attention and an orderly line formed. He solemnly handed a sweet to each child who walked away with a smile and a thank you. The last sweet he kept for himself.

I loved this day and this little town and was sorry to say goodbye when the ship left in the early evening.

Unease is creeping in about the ethics of tourism. The idea of ships off-loading hundreds, often thousands of people into small communities, intrusive clicking with cameras at everything that moves is unsettling. So is the romanticisation of the harsh reality of others' lives and believing that giving the odd dollar here and there, or some sweets, is improving lives. Perhaps I'm just a miserable old fart.

Good news from the ship. Dick will now be able to treat me to eight wooden red roses on Valentine's Day, together with a card chosen by him and a chocolate favour, all for the 'the loveable price of £15'.

'The Wall in Almeirim' by Kay Rainsley (Cabin 543)
Some may call it language, others age, still others culture or even mistrust. Whatever it is, it's there: either in large, glaring letters, like the name 'Almeirim' standing white and glossy against an emerald backdrop as we approach, or in a lesser, subtler form, as in the way we view each other. We cannot see, smell, hear, taste or feel it, yet we have an awareness of it.

Meandering through the town we came across a crude bar. Inside were stood two pool tables, worn by years of use and abuse. Gathered around each table, groups of young men alternately eyed their hand of cards and played them, casting them onto the green baize. What had drawn us to this scene were the strains of Pink Floyd emanating from the CD player. I've heard it hundreds of times, as it is my husband's favourite, and we paused to listen. 'Tear down the wall, tear down the wall.' The proprietor glanced across. I cupped a hand to my ear and put my thumbs up – a useful sign in any country. He smiled and pumped up the volume to the surprise of his customers. Maybe he thought we were deaf.

He came over to us wearing a heavy chain around his neck and a broad grin. We smiled in return. Pink Floyd played on and we watched. Manuel, as he had introduced himself while giving us a hearty handshake, came out with two plastic chairs and placed them in the shade opposite his bar. I'm sure he turned the volume up again as Les sang along to, 'We don't need no education.'

One youth came out. He was wearing a t-shirt with Moto Taxi on it. He climbed astride his motor cycle and sped off to find a customer. The others remained absorbed in their games. There were no raised voices and only a smattering of beer bottles in the odd polystyrene container used to keep drinks cool. A collarless dog daintily nosed the nearby rubbish bin, carefully selecting a bone and proceeded to peel the flesh away, leaving it clean. A second canine appeared, observed the scene and left as quietly as he had arrived.

Manuel approached us bearing two deliciously cold cans of beer – more thumbs up. Brick by brick, we were tearing down the wall.

by Tim Major (Cabin 469)

At Almeirim the tender operation was slightly less complex than at Icoaraci, although disembarking onto a slipway was not ideal for passengers whose footing was not very steady. One coxswain apparently tried to get his tender to mount the slipway, perhaps to try to make disembarkation easier, but he wasn't going fast enough, so the tender slid back and he had to fall back on the same method the others had used. After the demonstration of boat-handling we had seen at Icoaraci, I was concerned for the safety of local children swimming from the slipway with our tenders' threshing screws only a couple of yards away.

It was while sitting at the café on the pier refreshing myself after exploring Almeirim that I witnessed a near collision between two tenders. A departing tender turned away from the slipway to starboard, apparently not having noticed the next tender approaching its starboard quarter. Huge gouts of black diesel smoke gushed from both vessels as they applied full power, the departing tender trying to turn inside the other, and the arriving tender trying to escape. This desperate expedient was fortunately successful, as the consequences of the two tenders colliding under full power could have been serious.

I remained at the café for a further shot of courage-building beer and to watch tender operations for a while before taking the plunge and boarding for a thankfully uneventful return to *Marco Polo*.

by Dinah Read (Cabin 422)

The most exciting thing about this morning was that dozens and dozens of moths, beetles and cicadas had come on board overnight, attracted by the ship's lights. We went about taking photographs of them. Some of them were very large, quite willing to crawl onto your hand, but too exhausted to fly away again, poor things.

There are just three people on board that I try to avoid. One I call 'the Frenchman' (though he isn't), 'Linda Snell' who has me marked down as her friend (and I am not), and a Yorkshire man who constantly complains about the ship, the company, the crew, and everything else. I would like to put him in charge of a concern like this and see if he could do it better. On second thoughts, heaven forbid!

At dinner Clive was full of his adventures today. Bernie and Angela, too, thought it a lovely and unspoiled little town. I am sorry that I missed it. Having finally made the decision to go ashore and walk around the town on my own, the heavens then opened and I thought better of it. This region is not called rainforest for nothing.

by Clive Leatherdale (Cabin 725)

I was up at 6, mainly to see what the Amazon looked like at dawn. The delta fingers had merged, and we were now in the main channel, perhaps two miles wide, steaming up its brown waters. From time to time, we could make out clearings with low-roofed houses or open-sided pillars. White local ferryboats hugged the riverbanks.

Almeirim loomed ahead. We could see letters spelling it out against a grassy bank, a mini 'Hollywood' on the skyline of Los Angeles. I had time to kill while waiting for my allocated tender. There are huge moths all over the ship, in frozen postures on the deck, walls and doors. These unexpected stowaways attracted admirers with cameras, and provoked a spat between an obese man who insists on sitting on the same lounger, in the same space, every day and Tony Rice, the environmental professor, who was an eager snapper.

'Leave the bloody thing alone,' yelled the obese man as a moth took wing. 'Now look what you've done with your constant pestering.'

'I assure you sir, that if you knew as much about environmental issues as I do . . .' I forget Tony's explanation, but it was fun while it lasted.

Once ashore I wandered the waterfront. My eyes were assailed by pool tables, motor cycles, and lack of drainage, for huge brown puddles covered the roads from recent downpours. It was hard to tell if anyone had a job, for no one appeared to be working. Every house seemed to have a gaggle of poorly dressed children in glassless windows.

Today had the potential to be a corker. All the ingredients were in place. Small town, enough hours to get to know it, nothing touristy to ruin it – it wasn't even mentioned in either of the guidebooks I had brought – and if all goes to plan, I'll get under Almeirim's skin.

I tried to roll back the years to set myself targets as I would once have done. Not for me churches, museums, that kind of thing. I generally favoured lower orders of existence – cemeteries, prisons, brothels (window-shopping only) – for these would tell me more about how any community functioned and what values it held dear. And to achieve this, I needed to interact.

Level 1 interaction is simple; conversation with locals. Ask them anything, even if you don't care about the answer, and then go and ask someone else the same question to see if their answers matched.

Level 2 is getting an invite into homes. That's not so hard, and gives you a chance to look around, to see what they've got and what they haven't.

If level 2 goes well, I might get an upgrade to level 3, the offer to eat or drink. This both fills the stomach and teaches me the local diet.

Level 4 would have been precious to my younger self, short of money, but the offer to 'stay the night' no longer applied when I had my cosy cabin awaiting me.

My simple target for Almeirim was to find the school and, once I had found it, announce myself to the head teacher. If he or she could not speak English, it should not be too hard to find a teacher who did. And then I would ask if I might possibly address a class, hijack a lesson for ten minutes by introducing myself and engaging in a little English conversation as a native speaker.

Such a project would be futile even to attempt in any city. But in small, out of the way places like Almeirim, such a variation in the daily routine was more likely to be welcomed than obstructed. We would see.

I had ticked off several 'level 1s' before the latest deluge forced me to take shelter under an overhang. Just feet away from me a smiling family eyed me through the window (which I call a 'window' for want of a better word, because like all other windows nearby it had no glass, so technically it was just a huge square open hole).

A man in his twenties beckoned me, and within a matter of moments I discovered he was a teacher. A few minutes more and he was pointing to show the direction of the school.

I shall 'fast forward' now. The town itself lay up a long flight of steps away from the river, which I might have missed but for my guide. When, hours later, I eventually returned to the ship, my mental logbook was full of ticks. The oldest observable date in the sandy graveyard was 1912. Countless baby-sized graves competed for space with imposing mausoleums, whose cost must have been considerable.

Next stop the municipal offices and the court-house. The public hospital surprised me by having guards at the entrance, but all seemed so still it might have served as a cemetery waiting-room, which perhaps it was. Almeirim's prison had six cells, I was told, but was empty at present. Its walls were built of latticed white bricks, and when I put my ear to them, I heard what I thought were wails within. Not so empty, perhaps.

Local ice cream in the smart apartment of my guide's parents – shoes off at the door, every available mod-con within – concluded my tour of Almeirim. It was hard to know what to make of the 'facts' given me by my host – only one doctor in the whole town, just twenty policeman, and the same number hooked up to the internet, of which my guide was one.

Did I speak to the local school? Sadly no, it was closed for holidays.

Bernadine and Angela had enjoyed themselves, too, although they weren't impressed by *Marco Polo*'s cribsheet. For each port of call a loose page is inserted in the day sheet offering a brief guide and practical information. Richard Sykes is not responsible for the cribsheet, which is prepared in head office. 'There are no banking facilities in Almeirim,' it said.

'Oh yes there are,' retorted Bernie. 'A lovely bank and lovely cashiers who showed us what to do.'

The letters 'Almeirim' are so small, but they could be seen from way down the Amazon
(Clive Leatherdale)

Day 18. Alter do Chao

'Rustic Alter do Chao lies on the right bank of the Tapajos River, upstream from Santarem, 20 miles away. The bay, overlooked by two hills, is very beautiful and serene. It is a small fishing village, whose population of 2,500 depends on fishing . . . and tourism.'

by Mave Eaton (Cabin 616)

Another Amazonian landing at Alter do Chao. A small river village separated from a lagoon by a sandbank. Today is wet and this dampens the spirits of many passengers. The tender trip has a tense start as we are all crammed in by a grimly smiling girl (is she in the entertainment group?). An angry Scotsman shouts and shouts about the dangers of overcrowding the lifeboat, but she smiles and finds more space for the large bottoms which keep arriving.

We arrive safely, and suddenly there is an internet cafe. As we check emails, the rain becomes torrential. Dripping passengers shuffle past, and we feel snug and dry. If the shopkeepers had umbrellas and plastic macs, they would have become rich very quickly.

After eighteen days on board, the passengers are starting to form groups. Twenty per cent of passengers are Dutch [who embarked at Amsterdam]. One of them has the book *Birds of Brazil,* which is much lusted after. The English divide into tribes according to their social classes. The upper middle class honk happily at each other and are scrupulously polite to everyone, especially the staff. The lower middle class enjoy moaning about the ship's shortcomings and telling how it is not what they expected: they are used to better things. Some of us vacillate between tribes.

by Lizzie Mayes (Cabin 494)

This is the next of our booked excursions. We went to get on our bus for a long drive to the Santa Lucia arboretum. After about a mile or two, the bus broke down and, after much poking and prodding at the engine and mutterings, a second bus was summoned. Thank goodness for mobile phones. The second bus arrived but it wasn't a tour bus – just a local service one. Our guide was very pleased with himself, a Brazilian of German descent. Dick took an instant dislike to him, recalling the German involvement in Brazil.

Soon after this the rain began to fall and we arrived at our destination. There, we were met by a tall American who, we were told, had purchased 100 hectares of forest and turned it into an eco-forest tourist destination. There was a small hut with some samples of wood in it, but he made no move to tell us about it or any of the animal skulls adorning the veranda. We then set off, through well-walked muddy trails through the 'eco forest' with a commentary all the way.

We certainly learnt the meaning of the word 'rain' in rainforest. It came down in sheets. We were once again introduced to countless forest trees and told of their value to society in the world of medicine, although it was difficult to hear everything in the torrential rain. Any hopes of seeing any wildlife were dashed by the rain and by all the traffic pounding through. The only things that seemed to like the rain were the countless unseen frogs singing their hearts out.

On return from this short trek, we were not offered any refreshments as promised, so returned to our bus for the long ride back to the *Marco Polo*. We decided that, as our Amazon itinerary had been changed and, as a result, we were destined to do another forest walk the next day, we would ask the shore excursions team if we could change to another excursion. Obviously, I was one of the last in a long stream of people asking the same thing and was categorically told no.

I did lose it a bit and said what I thought about our day out. I was told it wasn't anyone's fault that the bus broke down or that it rained. I said that was not what I was complaining about – these things happen, but I was not at all happy about the actual destination. A glazed look came over his face – total uninterest – and he said we could go on the walk tomorrow or not, as we chose, but there could be no refund as their policy didn't allow cancellation at short notice. In other words, like it or lump it. I went to bed feeling really ratty.

by Dinah Read (Cabin 422)

We decided at midday to go down to the gangway and take the next boat ashore for a walk along the string of sandy beaches that we could see half a mile or so away. We arrived there just as it began to rain again, a real downpour. So we thought better of it and went into the Waldorf instead. I had a glass of cider with my meal. The wine waitress has trouble with my strange request as she plainly doesn't understand what cider is or why anyone would want it. Then we went back to our cabin and lay down together for a nap, Jack being very sweet and considerate.

by Tim Major (Cabin 469)
Our next tender port was Alter do Chao. This delightful, sandy, river beach resort greeted us in a fashion which was to become a predictable feature of our rainforest adventure. It was raining, and its only redeeming characteristic was the relative warmth as compared with the frozen wastes which British seaside resorts become in inclement weather.

Our tender crews had become slightly more proficient in their tasks, although the port and the Tapajos River were less challenging than our previous two stops. Some hard contacts were made, possibly due to skippers being unaware that a tender with almost half a ton of people on board takes longer to stop than an unladen one, but the transfer operation was otherwise uneventful.

'A Tale of Misrepresentation and Incompetence'
by Judith Buckley and Alan Smith (Cabin 447)
Our group of 32 passengers disembarked from the ship's tender onto a landing stage which led to a large sand spit, available as a bathing spot for the local population when the river level is low. Trudging through the sand in the rain, we arrived at the road and boarded excursion bus No 4, one of several chartered to carry those about to proceed on an 'Eco Walk through Santa Lucia Arboretum', as it was described in the booklet of Shore Excursions 2011 issued by Cruise & Maritime Voyages.

The local guide introduced himself and ascertained that passengers in the rear of the bus could hear his commentary – 'just about' when the bus was stationery, but inaudible once the engine started and we moved off. He did, however, introduce the driver, describing him as being a very good driver. From past unfortunate experience, beware such statements. This once again became apparent as the driver gained speed on the winding and undulating two-way road with an 80kph speed limit, which he ignored, and proceeded to overtake the buses which had departed before us. Brazil has produced some world famous racing drivers, but not to be emulated by the driver of a public service vehicle carrying passengers.

We alighted from the bus in a narrow, rutted and muddy slip-road soon to become congested with the arrival of the other buses. We were divided into two groups of sixteen and, with a Polish priest as guide to our group, we proceeded into the forest in single file along a narrow path with the need to monitor every footfall. The description 'forest' being the operative word, as it was not by any stretch of the imagination an arboretum – defined as a collection of trees and plants established for scientific and educational purposes. This was merely a long-established area of rainforest.

Communication, and hence any educational advantage which may have been salvaged, was almost non-existent. It was available only to the first two or three at the head of the single file. Several indigenous trees were pointed out before we returned to our starting point after an hour or more. There was no visit to a museum of wood, nor did we enjoy any fruit and refreshing juices as promised in the publication.

The worst was yet to come. There was necessarily much manoeuvring by the assembled buses in the narrow slip-road, resulting in bus No 4 having front and rear nearside wheels bogged down in the mud. Now, the driver may have had ambitions to be a Juan Fangio [Argentine 1950s world champion racing driver] but he was clueless with regard to the procedure necessary to extricate himself from this situation. He revved the engine and embedded the wheels further and further into the mud, almost up to the axles. Attempts were made by others to pack vegetation behind the wheels to allow a grip, at which point the driver attempted to drive forward, rather than backwards, tyres smoking from the friction.

Attempts were made to dig out some of the soft mud. A wheelbarrow-load of gravel was called for, but the wheel of the barrow hit a rut and the contents spilled on the road. Here we had a situation where one of the guides with a machete could have cut some brushwood, packed the same to the front and rear of the wheels – for the sake of an incompetent driver – and the bus could have driven out. This was obviously too simple a solution and the assembled passengers continued to wait, in all for 45 minutes, until finally the bus was towed from its embedded situation. Bus No 4 was not the only vehicle to experience problems, another had to be towed away as a result of a mechanical fault, and another had to be refuelled from canisters.

Back in poll position, bus No 4 moved off, tyre-treads packed solid with yellow mud, onto the wet road, and proceeded to make up time. Meanwhile, the passengers gripped whatever holds were available in the hope of an arrival back to the ship without accident. Once again the speed was excessive and requests via the guide from several passengers to have the driver slow down were ignored. On one occasion, the bus was driven across a corner kerb.

The local guide agreed to report the unacceptable driving to 'his boss' but we have no evidence that this measure was undertaken. The ship's excursions assistant travelled in the same bus but kept a low profile and said nothing of which we were aware.

On return to the ship, we proceeded to complain to the shore excursions manager, an obvious reject from the charm school. On being asked if he knew the definition of an arboretum, his answer was, 'Well it's trees.'

We then pointed out other misrepresentations in the excursion brochure. At this point our tickets for other pre-booked excursions were taken, the charges removed from our shipboard accounts, and we were told that we would not be accepted on any further *Marco Polo* excursions.

by Clive Leatherdale (Cabin 725)
There is an unspoken assumption about this cruise; it is eco-friendly almost to comical limits. The ship now carries tens of thousands of stray beetles, lizards, cicadas, moths and heaven knows what. Each specimen is examined and photographed with due reverence, passengers queuing or manoeuvring to get the best shot. Not for a moment would a cockroach be happily stamped underfoot as might happen if the same beast was discovered back home. Not once did I expect to see any Amazonian visitor deprived of life and liberty. So it was with mild surprise at breakfast that I espied deck attendants with brooms and buckets sweeping up everything that does not belong. There you go mate, into the bucket, and that's the end of you. I half expected the eco-generals among us to rise up and demand that these poor beetles, surely on the verge of extinction, should be released into the wild forthwith. Though how these creatures are expected to survive onboard, before being conveyed to the chillier conditions of northern Europe, was not obvious.

It is common-sense capitalism that when a cruise ship arrives, bearing 800 wealthy Europeans with money to burn – likely to be in town for a few hours at best, and wanting to snap up everything from bottled water to trinket souvenirs to posh jewellery – they should be feted at every turn. You want to pay in sterling, madam? No problem. You prefer Moroccan dinars? That's even better. Please come this way!

Is it like that in Brazil? Like heck it is. Despite ship assurances that US$ are acceptable, the overriding experience is that only Brazilian reals will do. Otherwise, get lost. This is exasperating to the passenger and economic madness for the Brazilian. There must be some explanation behind this, and it will probably repay further investigation.

Alter do Chao provided the biggest tourist invasion we have inflicted so far, for no more then 2,000 people live there. We are here mainly on account of sandbanks and beaches, a novelty here in the Amazon. Some on board have forked out £55 for an eco-walk, which will probably have been a waste of time and money. My guidebook speaks of locals who will take you to 'virgin forest' for much less.

Of the four tenders lowered into the water, one was directed straight to a sandbank to act as a dry bus-shelter, another never moved, meaning only two tenders carried passengers. This delayed those going ashore. It was gone 11 by the time I got off, but at least I witnessed a commotion to warm the cockles. In the attempt to fill tenders to bursting (sinking?) point, they crammed in as many late-comers at possible. This proved too much for some fainthearts. I heard a Scottish voice yell, 'It's too full.' One couple refused to stay on. They forced their way off, thereby clogging the stairway as they struggled up past others coming down.

In the interests of impartiality, I can reveal that our lifeboat had a clearly stated capacity of 60 passengers, and that at no stage were there more than 56 on board. The squeeze was presumably due to ample bottoms, of which there were a good number. Some of us made a mental note to avoid the Scot in the event of an emergency, because being forced to get off and wait for the next lifeboat might not be a good idea.

This place is idyllic for those affected by golden beaches, and the sandbank stretching across is undeniably winsome. Unfortunately, it was a bad day to admire it. It was raining when we left the *Marco Polo*, raining when we disembarked from the tender, and within half an hour we were battered by the mother of all cloudbursts. The wind was strong, the sky black, and there was no sign that this might be a quick shower. This left opportunity only to inspect the tourist shacks, with their wooden piranha fish, Indian facemasks, and blowpipes. There was a 'native' on hand to fire 'poisonous' darts at a piece of wood. The blowpipe played a happy jingle when you turned it upside down.

Poor Richard Sykes has been receiving complaints from passengers who got soaked. He came on the intercom at 6pm to remind everyone that this was a rainforest and we can expect to get wet.

Even in the rain, you could see the appeal of Alter do Chao (Clive Leatherdale)

DAY 19. SANTAREM

*'As we will be staying overnight in Santarem, it's impor-
tant to note that ship security does not extend beyond
the ship's perimeter. If the Port Authorities advise that
the surrounding area is safe, then please take care when
going ashore. We recommend you travel in groups.'*

by Caroline Clifford (Hutch 468)

James had decided to go solo, preferring a leisurely tour of Santarem to
a 'jungle trek' through the Tapajos National Forest. All kitted up, I disembarked (far too early), only to be met by the frenzied departure of passengers from the Ana Beatrix III, who had travelled like sardines for three
days from Manaus. Its economy deck took 300 passengers sleeping on
the floor and in hammocks, with just two toilets between them. First class
had wardrobe-sized cabins with bunk beds. I mentally promised not to
complain about our 'hutch' again. Another local boat was filled with
motor bikes destined to terrorise pedestrians on the already crowded and
pot-holed roads.

Our cruise staff, 'pretty in pink,' greeted me and, instead of berating
me, assured me that my early arrival would guarantee me a good seat. The
charming local bus had just been 'slopped out' by the driver, every plastic seat still filled with a puddle of water. The prized front seat was raised
on a platform over the wheel, offering an excellent view. I felt a little selfish, but not for long. And who should squash in next to me but 'woody
woodpecker'. I must straight away apologise to her for my previous diary
entry concerning her laugh. She was a most interesting lady from the
Congo, and between the compulsory spiel from two guides, we swapped
notes on our various travels.

First stop – home of the forest guide who climbed aboard, but not
before two coachloads of passengers availed themselves of his toilet. The
queue was horrendous and eventually the men were told to find alternative facilities – a tree in the garden. For the ladies, the facility was first
class, clean, modern and with paper.

'Woody,' or Michelle, as I should now call her, got very excited about
a few passengers who appeared not to appreciate our tight schedule, but
eventually we drove into the National Forest. We were put off the bus,

divided into groups, and set off into what, at first sight, appeared to be impenetrable jungle. A few yards in, one of the group complained of feeling dizzy and was promptly sick. Not a good start, but it was put down as a bad reaction to malaria tablets. The rest of the trek was only remarkable as a result of the extreme amount of rain that fell. Although there was a spat at the front of the 'jungle line', those at the back just heard raised voices – 'selfish' and 'pushing'. I have an idea who was involved (actually I know who was involved). As usual – a man with a very long lens and possibly a woman with a long back to lean it on.

The walking pace was slow, and we were mainly instructed in the use of plants and trees for medicines. This included a cancer cure taken by the guide's father, who had passed away. We 'heard', allegedly, a tapir and a toucan, and we saw two spiders – one poisonous.

We were all soaked through and, to top it off, the guide told us it was the coldest day of the year. Past caring, two women squatted beside the track, no cares, no modesty. We just wanted to get back to the comfort of the *Marco Polo*. I must admit to feeling a little guilty, or maybe smug, when we passed the Ana Beatrix III, whose conditions our guide had described as 'intolerable'.

by Lizzie Mayes (Cabin 494)
We got a taxi with another couple from the ship to have a look around Santarem. The driver took us to the market, cathedral and town museum. The couple we went with had lived for many years in the Philippines – I think he was a professor. She was anxious to see the meeting of the waters, which we saw from a viewpoint, but it was a 'been there, done that' thing, and they weren't particularly interested in us or our company – we were just someone to halve the cost of a taxi.

She forcefully talked me out of buying some of the wonderful copaiba oil in the market, which she assured me was far too expensive. I know I will regret not buying bottles of it – they looked lovely and, I realised later, cost next to nothing.

In the afternoon we set off for yet another trek in the rainforest. This time, we were in a national park and we were assured it would be a totally different experience to yesterday. Yes, the paths weren't so well worn, but the brazil nut trees, rubber trees, etc, were just the same. And it rained just as hard. I have never been so wet in all my life (except for yesterday!). I sat in soaking wet clothes in the bus where all the windows leaked – one lady solved the problem by putting up her umbrella *inside* the bus – for the one and a half hour journey back to the ship. I don't ever want to see another Brazil nut tree again. It was a much better trip than yesterday, but an awfully long drive from the ship. Back on board for the deck party and supper. Richard provided a great end to the day with some retro rock.

'Educational Patter' by Mark Edwards (Cabin 423)
Interesting that on every organised excursion in all the countries that we have visited, each of our local guides has had the same patter. They have been, without exception, at pains to explain how much the education system had developed in the last few years. How the primary school education was now working well, and feeding up into the secondary schools, and then into higher education, and finally into university education. Even the Amsterdam trip did this, though it was at pains to explain how it was now working for a deprived area that we drove through. Is there a universal international tourist guide standard developed by the USA that they all have to stick to? It would not have been noticeable had it not been for the fact that it was every country and every guide.

by Dinah Read (Cabin 422)
The best things here are the birds. I photographed four kinds, which I will identify later. There were black vultures, turkey vultures, and the 'see here' birds (from their call). I think they are a species of tern, and snowy egrets and some handsome little fellows with yellow undersides – as tame as robins. Best of all I liked a black and white bird with a long forked tail that perched on the rail very close to me. He was very dapper.

We watched with interest while the crew went through a practice drill for 'Abandon Ship'. Sensible and necessary, of course. They wore their yellow lifejackets and marched along busily and in unison. By then it was approaching 11am and getting hot again. Jack went below and after a while I followed. He lies on his bed wearing only his underpants, totally at ease. I do love him. We rested together, a lovely interlude. We went on deck again and watched a whole family of river dolphins, including females with calves. That was a real treat.

by Clive Leatherdale (Cabin 725)
Rule number one for a happy cruise. Don't get injured and don't get ill. This imperative is all too easy to ignore, but the consequences for those who fall foul can be painful – and not just in the physical sense. Cruise ships are inherently dangerous. Their motion is unsteady, their surfaces are hard and unforgiving, and the *Marco Polo* is decorated throughout with yellow and black 'danger' zigzags to mark raised steps or low doorways. Every day passengers come a cropper somewhere or other by falling, tripping or colliding. And the growing number of sling-casts seen onboard

testifies to the misery inflicted, for if your arm is in a sling you can't eat and can't dress properly. Never mind it messing up your holiday.

I had steered clear of physical injury, and with it an unwelcome visit to the ship's hospital. It had never even occurred to me to include the medical wing in the scope of this book. All that was about to change.

I woke early. Something was wrong. I went back to sleep. Then woke again. Something was definitely wrong. A pain in the lower left side of my back. Retching. I swallowed painkillers, but the relief was minimal. I knew I faced a dreaded trip to the ship's hospital.

But when should I go? We were tied up in Santarem and not due to leave until 7pm. Suppose I went now and the doctor ordered me off to whatever hospital Santarem possessed? No, I wanted to remain on the ship at all costs. I looked up the medical centre's opening times, 9-11am and 5-7pm. I would present myself just before 7pm. Early enough to be seen, late enough not to be put off the ship.

I had the whole day to kill. I might never see Santarem again, so set off to walk to the centre two miles away. I did so, listlessly looked around, then returned to the *Marco Polo* to count down the clock.

The medical centre is strategically sited in the bowels, Deck 5, amidships, at the point where any motion sickness is minimised. No windows, artificial light. Bright, cheerful, efficient, with a potted bamboo plant on a table and stacks of thank-you cards and emails pinned to the wall. The waiting room consists of a sofa which seats no more than three patients at a time.

Anonymity is impossible. This is partly because of the confined space and partly because on a small ship most passengers are familiar by sight, if not by name. Nurse Daisy shoves a thermometer into my ear. I give samples of urine and blood.

It isn't long before a voice calls, 'Mr Clive'. I enter the surgery of Dr Antonis Papadakis. He is a familiar sight around the ship, in his all-green tunic and trousers, but we had never before spoken.

'Sit down, Mr Clive,' he says. 'I do not have good news.'

I feared the worst and heard it. Fever, blood in my urine, kidneys failing. Whether it was his words or his face I cannot recall, but I sensed I might be in trouble. I was wired up for drip-feed antibiotics and told that on arrival at Manaus, two days away, I would be sent to a private hospital for ultrasound tests. The results would dictate if I could stay on the ship. With luck the antibiotics would by then have killed the infection. Had I delayed seeing the doctor until tomorrow, he would have had no choice but to disembark me in Manaus, for the antibiotics would not have had time and there was no other 'good' hospital within six days.

DAY 20. PARINTINS

'Between November and January the village becomes an island due to the low river level. There are no roads to Parintins — you need to sail there or to fly! In fact, the principle types of transportation are donkeys and carts and motorcycles.'

by Lizzie Mayes (Cabin 494)

We decided to go to the Boi-Bumbá Festival as we were assured it would be one of the highlights of our Amazon adventure. Admittedly with some trepidation, we booked our tickets. We were greeted at the stadium by young girls dressed in feathers, brief tops and thongs, their young brown bodies smooth as silk. I have never seen so many old men's eyes pop out of their heads. They all rushed to be photographed with one girl on each arm. We were plied with drinks — caipirinha — a local rum and lime drink with lots of ice, and the show began.

I am sure at carnival it is a wonderful sight but I was bored in spite of the huge carnival-type floats of parrots, fish and other animals which were wheeled on, while the almost bare-bottomed dancers gyrated to the rhythm of the most monotonous music ever. In fact 'Girlbumbá' would be a more appropriate name! It would have been fine as part of a street carnival, like Notting Hill, but as a show, it was awful. However, I was in the minority and most people seemed to love it — albeit that they saw most of it through a camera lens. They then descended on the inevitable tourist stalls to buy dyed feather headdresses (some even wearing them as they returned to the *Marco Polo*), which I would lay money were made in China, and yes, DVDs. I am sure when the actual festival takes place each June with 50,000 spectators, the atmosphere is amazing. I bet the doctor's surgery will be full of dirty old men with high blood pressure tonight.

by Jeremy Tait (Cabin 715)

The main attraction in Parintins was the flamboyant, imitation Boi-Bumbá festival performed by some one hundred local inhabitants in a covered arena. Although the drum music was strictly rhythm and the dance steps were unimaginative, the costumes and props were fabulous.

In fact it was almost impossible to tell which of the dancers were male and which were female, because of the profusion of feathers that they wore, although a closer inspection soon revealed that, as all the dancers wore little else than feathers, this made their sex very much easier to determine! Interestingly the costumes, the dance steps and the use of animal effigies were reminiscent of the Zulus.

by Catharine Fox (Cabin 705)

We took the tender to the quayside, where many pedicabs waited. These are tricycles with a box on the front and a bench across it to sit on. It feels as if you are sitting in the ice cream container of a 'stop me and buy one'! We clambered in and greeted our driver, who was rather older than most of the others – a thin, wiry figure with nut-brown skin, curly black hair and twinkly eyes. We all set off in our pedicabs together, but it was soon apparent that our rider was really a boy racer at heart and had no intention of being at the back of the bunch, taking every opportunity to overtake the younger ones. He was very skilled at avoiding potholes, of which there were many, and although we neither spoke nor understood Portuguese, we recognised an expletive or a discontented grunt when someone raced past or stopped in front of him. We encouraged him, of course.

by Dinah Read (Cabin 422)

Everyone was trying to take pictures and it was hard to get a clear shot, but I did get some. It went on for an hour or so and I was thrilled by the whole thing. Once again my only sadness was that Jack was missing it and not there to share it with me. Such a loss for both of us.

Clive had a sudden kidney infection yesterday, which explained his absence at dinner. The salient factor in all this is that he is plainly and avowedly alone on the ship and had no one to take the burden of anxiety off his shoulders.

by Clive Leatherdale (Cabin 725)

I slept well. At 9, I braved the medical centre, found other passengers in the waiting room, and did not know whether or not to say hello. Another antibiotic session and I was given the all-clear to go ashore. I felt fine.

Out of the frying pan, into the Amazon. Or nearly. The current was so strong and the waters so choppy that our tender could not manoeuvre away and crashed heavily bow-first into the side of the *Marco Polo*. A senior officer had to jump on board, push the coxswain aside, and steer it away himself.

Parintins is a freak. A small town with nothing to commend it except its annual folklore festival. This takes place each June in a vast outdoor stadium and draws 50,000 visitors to a town that has only a couple of hotels. But this was January, cruise ships need to see a show of some sort, so tourists are herded somewhere or other – I couldn't work out where – to see a feathered and plumed pantomime.

For those fascinated by the architecture of sports stadia, the genuine Bumbódromo is a treat. It stands a mile from the pier, empty, apart from a security guard watching his own private television. Rather than shoo me away, he beckoned me and even stirred himself from his rocking chair to open the gate. The horseshoe arena ('bull's head' to the locals) can squeeze in an improbable 35,000 spectators – more than double that of Wimbledon's centre court. The seats of one side were painted red, the other blue. The actual 'playing area' was surprisingly laid out in the form of a handball court, with goals and nets at either end. I had never seen anyone playing handball in Brazil, and I never did.

'Murder on the Marco Polo' now risks being still-born. Suppose I am whisked off the ship tomorrow in Manaus? I tour the decks, trying to find fellow scribblers in order to update them and collect as many email addresses as I can. Valerie and Alan Waite tell me it's easy to remember their names; just think of the 'V&A Museum'. But my mind keeps coming up with Vivian and Arthur, which confuses everyone. The easiest way to remember them is to recall how they met, half a century ago. Keen badminton players, she bent down to retrieve the shuttlecock and Arthur, sorry Alan, was smitten. He still is.

I try remembering 'D&M', as that refers to David and Mary Skippen, although they mock themselves as Hinge & Bracket (H&B). Mary takes no nonsense from anyone, though she seems to have a soft spot for me (or did have, until she reads this). She winks to invite me over to join them for the afternoon quiz, which I feign to ignore, but she knows I'll come if she winks hard enough. She suggests I publish her cookery specialities, and demands to know why the Indian head chef insists on dunking every dish in rosemary.

There's an M&J on board. I haven't met them yet, though 'M' raised eyebrows at dinner by dismissing the east European waiters as 'from the Gorbachev charm school'.

I note Lizzie Mayes' necklaces, heart-shaped 'NedX' and 'OllieX', each one engraved with a tiny indented finger-print of her grandsons. All these initials and abbreviations are making my head spin. I type all this up outside, facing what I call the Dutch Ghetto, where the Dutch smokers congregate on Deck 9. Later, this was recast as The Hook of Holland.

'Germans' by Richard Sykes (Cruise Director)
A question for all those who drive – 'How good are you at driving?'.
Above Average? Average? or Below Average? Without awaiting a reply,
it's fair to assume that most, if not all drivers would call themselves either
average or above. But that's impossible. By definition, at least one in three
readers, and arguably one in two, should be below average.

Next question ... 'How polite are you?' Have you ever met anyone
who considers themselves to be rude, ill-mannered, boorish or a nuisance? Certainly not. Often a denial of these traits is followed by two simple words: 'I'm British!' QED.

And yet, without fail, the single most-heard complaint from the logs
of *Marco Polo* is pointed towards 'other people'. More particularly, 'other
people moaning.' On the whole, Brits get along. Yes, we 'tut' and seethe,
but there is a tolerance for each other that makes the whole thing trip
along beautifully.

But our tolerance for other cultures is something that has caused the
most squabbles. In particular, the Germans.

Marco Polo was chartered from 2008 to 2009 by Transocean Tours, a
German company. The ship was then sub-chartered for part of each year
by Cruise & Maritime Voyages. Transocean ran the German season and
CMV managed the British season. The cruises were separate. The hosts
were different. The passengers were ostensibly single-nationality. Then
came the winter cruises. It was decided to give an equal allocation of cabins to the Germans and the British, and run each cruise as a dual-nation-
ality adventure.

I've cruised with a few different nationalities and noted the way in
which many countries seem keen to live up to, rather than quash, their
hard-earned stereotypes. But the German politeness, sense of restraint,
and humour, have always struck me as being incredibly 'British'. I've
worked alongside German staff members and officers, and always got
along superbly.

So how did a Caribbean cruise with equal numbers of German and
British guests reach the point where our German shore excursion manager was prodded with a walking stick and asked, 'When are you going to
realise who won the bloody war?'

It's always the little things. For instance, announcements. These were
read by myself and our German-speaking cruise director, Romana
Calvetti. The first announcement was in English, with the translation following for German guests. However, British guests, having heard their
announcement, chose to discuss it immediately, which meant the translation couldn't be heard. There were German complaints. In the next

announcement, an addition was made to ask the British guests to remain quiet so that the German guests could hear their announcement.

This seemed to make things worse, as some of the Brits chose to discuss not having made any noise previously to drown out the German translation. There were complaints. So Romana and I changed tactics. The German announcement would now precede the English translation. Perfect, what could go wrong? Sadly, some of the Germans chose to make a point of how inconvenient it was to have your translation talked over by pointedly talking over the English translation. We hadn't even set sail! There were complaints.

The solution we found was to do the announcements in German first on one day and in English first on the next. This confused the passengers so much that they fell silent for the whole announcement.

It doesn't take a massive leap of the imagination to guess how this played out. Point scoring and petty squabbles became part and parcel of each day. German tours being called first, German translations on the reverse side of the menus, too much German cuisine, too much British cuisine … then there were sunbeds. Oh, dear Lord, there were sunbeds.

Constant patrols were set up. Rules were enforced. But one sunseeker managed to bypass every sanction. It was 2am, and Reception was alerted to a grating noise coming from above a cabin. Security checked the situation, but the noise had stopped. The next morning the same sound at the same time. Security were dispatched and again were left scratching their heads. The noise also happened at 8am. It was a couple of days before the scraping and scratching was traced, and a heavy, wooden steamer deckchair was discovered in a passenger cabin, having been dragged onto and off the deck each and every day. The passenger doing the dragging was frail, female, and British.

Then came tomato-gate. The Caribbean had just borne the brunt of a huge series of storms. Crops had been devastated and islanders were reluctant to part with food, so *Marco Polo*'s fresh provisions were very low. Lettuce was scarce, fresh fruit became rare, and tomatoes were off the menu. Or so it was assumed. No one knows how, but after a week without seeing stamen nor seed of a tomato, a huge bowl of flawless cherry tomatoes appeared … at the German deck party. That's when the wheels came off the wagon, and a very British man marched in a very British way to our very German shore excursion manager, prodded her with his very stick-y walking stick and said, 'When are you going to realise who won the bloody war?' War it most certainly was.

The problem, I maintain, wasn't the mix of British and German sensibilities. It was the fact that there was exactly the same number of

Germans as Brits. 50-50. Straight down the middle. Consequently, there was no excuse for any bias. No one could legitimately claim that they were a victimised minority or a crushing majority. The equality of the endeavour was its undoing.

I asked a lot of passengers at the end of the cruise how many British passengers were on board. They all felt that there were about 100 more Germans than Brits. I never got around to asking them if they were good at driving.

IF YOU'RE GOING TO HATE ME, HATE ME FOR ME. NOT FOR WHAT YOU'VE HEARD, WHO MY FRIENDS ARE, OR FOR THE PERSON YOU THINK I AM.

These unusual words were seen on a wall in Tobago (Clive Leatherdale)

Part of the extraordinary stadium in Parintins on the Amazon, which comes alive for the annual festival each June (Clive Leatherdale)

DAY 21. MANAUS

'Amazonia's Capital, Manaus, the greatest city and port in the Amazon, lies 994 miles from the Atlantic. The city was founded in 1669 on the site of a fort built by the Portuguese against invaders, on the shores of the Rio Negro, four miles from where it meets the Solimoes.'

by Mave Eaton (Cabin 616)

Manaus, and we arrive early. This is the end of the line and the most important port for most passengers. We are to meet our son, Mark, here. He lives in Toronto but has acquired a gold mine in Brazil! He has flown in via Miami and will meet us with car and driver. We are early, of course. The car and driver are not the sophisticated limousine I had expected. Mark explains that it was arranged by his office and was probably someone's cousin.

Mark is hungry, but the driver goes round in circles for an hour looking for a café, although we pass many. The driver keeps asking the way until we point to one and insist on stopping. It is simple and out of doors, but the beer is cold and the plate of fish, rice, salad, bean soup and hot sauce excellent.

The rains come, so we retreat to Mark's hotel and the local drink of rum, crushed ice and limes. It is odd to have a son here, but delightful, as we meet infrequently. I endure lectures from him and husband about my refusal to remove my gold chain from around my neck. I have concealed it with an artistically draped scarf: no one snatches at my neck.

by Caroline Clifford (Hutch 468)

I'm standing, staring and sweating outside the Teatro Amazonas. The guard came up to me: 'Are you on the tour?' I don't know why I said yes, because I wasn't. But the anticipation of seeing the interior of this magnificent opera house had made me a liar. I gratefully squeezed through the wooden door to join the privileged few. The decor was a little twee and the stage rather smaller than I had imagined, but the carvings, marble, chandeliers and mirrors were remarkable, all brought from Europe towards the end of the nineteenth century when Manaus had become a boom town.

Now feeling lucky in my new career as a 'hustler', I took advantage of the free taxi ride out to Tropical Hotel offered by 'Amsterdam Sauer', fine jewellers to the rich and famous. I knew that James would only buy me something 'sparkling and expensive' in my wildest dreams, but a free trip through the suburbs was right up his street. What a great idea it turned out to be – a free beer in an air-conditioned building on the dock before a car arrived to collect us. Joining us was Alexis, butcher from the ship, who was looking for a diamond for his fiancée (the only ring James ever gave me was one he found in the snow outside Tesco). Alexis offered us cover for the time-wasting scam that we were involved in; particularly since he found a gem at €6,000, 'Much cheaper than in the Ukraine,' he said. Obviously *Marco Polo* are paying their staff way too much. James said he could remember buying two houses for that. No comment.

Duty Free it might be, but we found nothing cheap in the crazy 'bustle and toil' that is Manaus. And the rep from the jewellers reported that a couple from the ship had been robbed during their 'free trip', which for them had included a detour to the opera house.

by Marion Cox (Cabin 619)

At school I was spellbound listening to our geography teacher talk about Brazil. There were undiscovered tribes, explorers, the Amazon, and an opera house in the middle of the jungle. Famous people had travelled thousands of miles to perform there – bet it wasn't for the tribesmen.

And here I am, 60 years later, in the auditorium. It's everything I expected, and more – more ornate, more elaborate, incongruous, crazy. A monument to the long past rubber industry. A fellow passenger laughed at my achieved ambition. 'I never knew it was there,' she said. 'I thought they all lived in wooden huts.'

by Lizzie Mayes (Cabin 494)

We arrived at this, the largest city on the Amazon, Manaus, and our journey up this vast waterway ends here. We had nothing fixed for today so decided to take a walk round the city. Sunday is obviously Funday here – everyone is out on the streets – market stalls everywhere, selling stuff that it's difficult to imagine anyone would want to buy. A sea of white plastic chairs and tables, full of people chatting, eating and drinking. Stall upon stall of hideous tourist crap, and others with the usual t-shirts and baseball hats. Most fascinating were the kiosks selling mountains of underwear the colour of grannies' old stockings – maybe better described as flesh-coloured. Who wears it? Certainly not the naked lady who ran across the road in front of us!

I wanted to buy a cool top or dress. The first shop I saw was C&A. Are all cities the same the world over, now? I was surprised to see the prices. It was impossible to buy even the cheapest t-shirt for under £12-£15, and they were pretty grotty at that.

We wandered up to the beautiful opera house. We managed to talk our way in without paying for a tour and we weren't disappointed. The ceiling, where you look up through a gilded Eiffel Tower with pictures depicting the four seasons, the polished floor where we had to put on felt overshoes, and memorabilia like Fonteyn's ballet shoes were all reminders of the city's lavish past. Dick and I sang a one-note aria just to check the acoustics were okay.

Tickets for this evening's performance cost just one real (40p) so we decided to come back, in spite of being told by the ship's excursion team that it was a show for children and not suitable for *Marco Polo* cruisers. That seemed to us to be a very good reason to go. All evidence of the day's market activity was now removed and the street reverted to an ordinary city road. The performance was due to start at 7pm and after numerous bells it finally got started at 7.15 to an eager audience of families with children as young as six months, a few intrepid Marco Polians, and Olga.

The orchestra of strings, woodwind and two enormous drums took their place in the pit before the curtain went up, and three huge white-feathered birds walked across the stage to a cacophony of sound. This was a ballet depicting a folk tale about the decimation of the rainforest – very dramatic and very loud, but the children sat mesmerised. There were parts where everyone laughed – otherwise they sat entranced. We understood not a word, but the message at the end was clear – a film of a flooded ex-rainforest followed by a film of the atomic bomb. Two different catastrophic events with similarly catastrophic outcomes.

by Jeremy Tait (Cabin 715)
Manaus lies one thousand miles upstream from the Atlantic and four miles from the point where the acid black Rio Negro and the nutrient-rich, yellow Rio Solimoes meet to form the Amazon River. Because of the different densities, speeds and temperatures of these two rivers, the black and yellow waters flow alongside for several miles without merging, and to see this unusual phenomenon, we were transported by a local river boat. At Lake January, now an ecological park, we boarded motorised canoes to navigate a jungle stream known as a garapé to view the flocks of heron, basking caiman and the occasional turtle and ariranha, which is a Brazilian otter. We then reached a remote spot where we were able to penetrate the rainforest by walking along an elevated wooden boardwalk

with numerous toucans, macaws, parrots and monkeys in the dense tree canopies, and the entire area was devoid of sunlight. This was one of the highlights of our cruise, and it was the deepest that we penetrated into the rainforest, and also the furthest point up the Amazon that we were to go. At the end of the boardwalk, we found ourselves on a platform overlooking giant Victoria Regia water-lilies floating on the top of a flooded pond known as an igapó.

by Dinah Read (Cabin 422)
After breakfast we went on deck to see our arrival at the pier at Manaus – at least I watched it. Jack (to my annoyance I must admit) sat on the sun loungers and saw nothing, though everyone else was lining the rail and we had a whole troupe of native dancers and musicians on the quayside to entertain us. Theirs were not as grand a display as the Boi-Bumbá yesterday, of course, but it was, nevertheless, colourful and lively. Jack, in spite of my entreaties, would not get up and walk literally five steps to see them so I am glad that I didn't spend £45 on a ticket for him yesterday, as I would so willingly have done. The singing and dancing are still going on.

by Clive Leatherdale (Cabin 725)
My experience of Manaus was different from others'. It was 11.15 before the port agent led me to a waiting taxi, through whose windows I was introduced to Manaus. No one could imagine driving far, for the city is isolated by water and forest. A virtual island. And a messy island, too. Garbage lined the streets, no house bore any resemblance to its neighbour, and of sensible urban planning there was no sign. The sky showed its disapproval, too, with a thunderous black scowl.

We pulled into the carpark of the Unimed private hospital. I was ushered to the emergency waiting room, where rows of anxious patients sat watching television – juvenile party games and cartoons. A dispensing machine served 7-Ups and bags of crisps. Patients were called by name by a bored woman who took their blood pressure.

After an hour, a kidney doctor arrived. He was tall, jeans, pin-striped shirt half tucked-in, half hanging out. He led me to the ultrasound room and found it locked and unresponsive. It was Sunday. The port agent swore. The doctor jumped in his car and drove to another hospital, with us following behind. Its ultrasound clinic was also closed. The port agent swore again, loudly. I became edgy. We drove back to the first hospital, with the exasperated agent bellowing Jesus Christ this, Jesus Christ that – until he saw a huge red and black banner and roared 'Flamengo', the name of his favourite football team in Rio.

This time the ultrasound door opened. I lay on my side as the gel was applied by a smiling middle-aged lady with a brace across her teeth. The doctor stared at the screen. The agent stood by me and translated. The doctor kept shaking his head, ominously, but he was shaking his head to indicate 'no problems'. 'You're fine,' said the agent. I stood up, dressed, and took a photo of this strange trio. 'You are an English gentleman,' said the doctor.

I handed over the medical forms given me by Dr Papadakis. The doctor disappeared to complete them. When they came back the box marked 'Is the Pax fit for travel?' was ticked.

Top: Waiting room in Manaus private hospital, complete with snack dispenser and TV.
Bottom: Huge 'puppets' in Manaus, into which you can climb and dance
(Clive Leatherdale)

Lisbon, 14th January. The iconic Belem Tower, seen from the *Marco Polo* on her way into the estuary. Built in 1515, the tower displays beautiful Manueline architecture (All photos in this section by Malcolm Whatcott)

Lisbon, 14th January. The famous bridge over the Tagus estuary.
Fog appears to have snapped the bridge in two

Tenerife, 16th January. Sailing into the harbour on a beautiful sunny day. The capital, Santa Cruz, surprised us by its size, rearing up into the distance from the harbour

Tenerife, 16th January. Mt Teide, an active volcano, overlooking Garcia's Rocks, which were named after a local shepherd

Cape Verde, 19th January. The *Marco Polo*, moored in Mindelo harbour, seems so small from the hills above the port, but it still dwarfs other vessels

Cape Verde, 19th January. Catfish Bay, which puts you in mind of David Attenborough. You half expect him to appear crouching over a pile of turtles' eggs

Cape Verde, 19th January. Mindelo Market, bustling with activity.
Fresh fruit and vegetables, all at incredibly low prices

Cape Verde, 19th January. The Artisans' Museum.
Many crafts were on display, such as these wire sculptures

Cape Verde, 19th January. The statue of Diego Afonso, the famous
Portuguese navigator, overlooking Mindelo's impressive natural harbour

At sea, mid-Atlantic. Deck crew painting the lifeboats' davits.
Maintenance like this was ongoing in suitable weather throughout the voyage

At sea, mid-Atlantic. The open decks were rarely empty once the *Marco Polo* reached warmer climes. This image shows the statue of Nureyev and an ice carving

On the Amazon, 24th January. Animal transporter moving livestock by river – the only feasible way of moving animals from town to town

Icoaraci, 24th January. Returning to the *Marco Polo* in the tender(s).
Fun, fun, fun – and for some – wet, wet, wet!

Almeirim, 26th January. This friendly boy wanted his photo taken.
The *Marco Polo* moored offshore sets the scene

Almeirim, 26th January. A shop for sale, a bored shopkeeper and no customers

Almeirim, 26th January. These friendly local children kept shouting and waving until I took their photo

Almeirim, 26th January. All the young dudes, sitting in the shelters watching the world go by. Moto-taxis like these were common throughout the Amazon towns

Almeirim, 26th January. Returning to the *Marco Polo* in the tender; a calmer experience than Icoaraci! Passengers transfer from ship to tender via the stairway shown

Alter do Chao, 27th January. The first boat to be unshipped was always the inflatable 'zodiac', which was normally used to carry out reconnaissance

Alter do Chao, 27th January. Sometimes one tender docked against another which had been secured to the pier, and which served as a dry waiting room in wet weather

Alter do Chao, 27th January. The one that didn't get away! Happy fishermen returning to port with their catch. Note the typical rudder with a propeller at the far end

Alter do Chao, 27th January. This homely houseboat with attached tender was moored in a scenic bay. For many visitors this seemed an ideal place to live

Santarem Fish Market, 28th January. Fish of all sizes –
mainly catfish, more catfish and, for variety, still more catfish

Santarem, 28th January. A tug pushing a heavy barge comes to an undignified stop close
to the dock and cannot proceed. The scene is watched by passengers from *Marco Polo*

Santarem, 28th January. Fishing, not for sport, but food.
Gathering clouds and thunder foretold the downpour on its way

Santarem, 28th January. A slow day at the office for this fisherman; only two small fish
caught by lunchtime. Note the typical Amazon ferry in the background

Santarem, 28th January. While the adults fish on the pier above,
boys hone their skills on the pilings below

Parintins, 29th January. Heading ashore in the tender, the *Marco Polo*
(and a deckhand) is framed in the rear windows

Parintins, 29th January. The town comes alive every June for its festival.
For the rest of the year bicycle rickshaws eagerly await the arrival of cruise ships

Manaus, 30th January. Sunday
street market. As in many
markets around the world,
'living statues' add that extra
'something'

Manaus, 30th January. Another 'living statue', white daubed, complete with animated 'baby' – very popular with children

Manaus, 30th January. The *Marco Polo* dwarfing the local ferries, berthed near the walkway into the passenger terminal

Amazon, upstream from Manaus, 31st January. A novelty on the Thames, perhaps, but floating fuel stations like this are common in major Amazonian ports

Amazon Ecopark, 31st January. Grass in the river is a problem, fouling propellers. The blockage can be difficult to remove and causes the boat to lean alarmingly

Amazon Ecopark, 31st January. Passengers were supposedly on their way to a
Meeting House, but actually just cruised the creeks

Boca da Valeria, 1st February. Traditional house (with satellite TV) on stilts to cope with
varying river levels. To the left is the village 'bar', which served beer at cruise-ship prices

Boca da Valeria, 1st February. Costume displays like this are arranged to greet passengers off the many cruise ships which stop here

Boca da Valeria, 1st February. A disturbing image of a dying catfish. Throughout the village the cry was 'Photo one dollar!' Hence the raised index fingers

Boca da Valeria, 1st February. Passengers were welcomed into most houses, for an entry 'ticket' of $1, escorted by local children who willingly held passengers' hands

Offshore, Boca da Valeria, 1st February. From the time of the *Marco Polo*'s arrival until its departure, local motor boats (wrongly described as 'canoes') stayed close to the ship

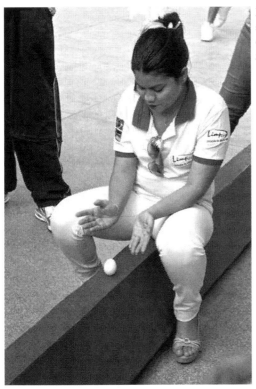

Macapá, 3rd February. Eggs can, apparently, only balance on their ends on the Equator (where there is no coriolis force)

Fort São Jose de Macapá, 3rd February. Some of the cannons were in remarkably good condition, as was the rest of the fort

Île Royale, 5th February. Landing site for the penal colony with a rusty old crane.
The *Marco Polo* is moored in the background. The other vessel is a tourist catamaran

Îles du Salut, 5th February. An external view of the old hospital block
for the penal colony on Île Royale, spartan to the extreme!

Îles du Salut, 5th February. Inside the hospital block on Île Royale where Papillon and others were 'treated'. Strange to think it was only closed in 1952

Îles du Salut, 5th February. The cells' entrance. Dark, foreboding, claustrophobic; they were cramped – no place you'd want to be!

Îles du Salut, 5th February. A corridor of cells – bleak and forbidding. There were nine cells either side of this central corridor

Tobago, 7th February. Argyle Falls, about an hour's gentle walk from the Visitors' Centre. A few swam, most didn't

St Lucia, 8th February. The *Marco Polo* berthed in Castries harbour.
This image was taken from Morne Fortune overlooking Castries

St Lucia, 8th February. Small fishing village with sailboats in the background.
Totally chilled

St Lucia, 8th February.
Returning from the Pitons,
our excursion boat towed a
catamaran back for repair

St Lucia, 8th February. Sailing back to Castries.
This massive black plume of smoke revealed a yacht on fire

Barbados, 9th February. Mushroom Rock – a popular tourist destination
on the north side of the island

Barbados, 9th February. Passengers found plenty of evidence of the previous season's
hurricane damage, here and on most islands

Barbados, 9th February. *Marco Polo* moored where freighters normally berth,
but only a few minutes' walk from the Passenger Terminal

The Bridge of the *Marco Polo*. Modern technology, alongside traces of the ship's past
(e.g. Russian religious icon)

A Very English Deck Party, 15th February, orchestrated by Richard Sykes (left).
Scots, Welsh, Irish and Dutch either tolerated it or they didn't

Richard Sykes, indefatigable cruise director, revealing even more of
his vast repertoire during the Very English Deck Party

Maintenance went on, and on, and on. The starboard side and some of the lifeboats being spruced up in Barbados

Remember the rubbish! At least one heavily laden truck relieved the *Marco Polo* of its waste in each port. The pipeline takes water onboard

Nearly home and Nureyev's lost his patina (after several hard days' polishing). I'm ready for my close-up, Mr de Mille

The *Marco Polo*'s Waldorf restaurant on a 'formal' night. Christian and Hristov are the waiters here. If the lady on the right is not careful she will get a jug of water in her lap

Ponta Delgada, Azores, 16th February.
The old area of the port with its distinctive Portuguese architecture

Ponta Delgada, Azores, 16th February. The marina to the west of the main harbour.
More, and larger, yachts fill the moorings as the summer approaches

DAY 22. MANAUS

'Since 1967 Manaus has been classed as a duty free zone, and thus goods, particularly electronics, are cheaper here than anywhere else in Brazil. Multinational companies were enticed by the prospect of tax and tariff benefits to set up their manufacturing plants here.'

by Lizzie Mayes (Cabin 494)

Today we had booked to go on a full-day cruise to the meeting of the waters. I woke up to a mercifully dry morning but within half an hour the deck was awash. I decided to take a change of clothes with me today.

We made our way to the riverboat, which was draped from prow to stern with blue plastic. I didn't know or recognise any of our fellow passengers. We set off, unable to see anything through slanting rain. The rain eased off slightly as we made our way up the river, passing countless floating petrol stations. We reached our first stop and were shown into the inevitable barn full of 'local' crap, I mean craft, where everything seemed to be priced at $10. I sound really mean, but I just don't know what I would do with a blowpipe clearly mass-produced for the tourist market.

The rain got even heavier as we boarded our motorised canoes, seating about twelve people, and set off in convoy for a wildlife-spotting tour through the creeks. Within five minutes we were soaked to the skin. We saw not a sign of any wildlife, probably due to the noise of the boats and the rain. A canoe appeared out of the grasses from a poor-looking house on the banks with a small girl holding a sloth, which Dick immediately wanted to hold. It was duly handed over, and Dick handed over the obligatory dollar. I am increasingly uncomfortable about the ethics of all this, but who can blame them for trying to supplement their meagre livings.

As we motored downriver we were given an impassioned talk by our guide about the ecological meltdown facing Brazil, in spite of efforts to slow things down. It is ever more depressing, going down this great river, the dilemma facing people because of the insatiable greed of modern western culture.

We came to the meeting of the waters and saw lots of dolphins, including the elusive pink one. On the return journey we pulled into the river's edge, where we were to be taken to a village to see more rubber trees.

I was going to give it a miss and stay on the boat to watch the dolphins but we were cajoled to walk into the 'village'. We went up the boardwalk to Terra Nova, a village of about twelve wooden stilt houses and the inevitable church. There is always a church. There was a staged demonstration of rubber making (clearly no rubber was being harvested here, other than when a tourist group arrived), of manioc [cassava] grinding and roasting and, of course, the ever-present tourist shop. As we left, a couple with a baby came up the boardwalk. The baby was wearing nothing but pampers.

I came away feeling I was in the wrong place at the wrong time. The guide said that many river people chose to live this way, as they don't have to pay taxes, but I think they are maybe making the right decision, if the alternative is a city slum. I was surprised to see 42in TVs in many of the homes, though it is true they have no running water and very little in the way of other possessions. Some houses have water tanks on stilts. I returned to the ship feeling confused emotions about the morality of this kind of tourism.

Back on board, we heard more and more complaints about the food, service, cleanliness, lack of chairs, chipped china, cabin service, etc. What kind of life do these odious people have at home; do they have clean towels every day, two five-course meals, afternoon tea, huge cooked breakfast, and free entertainment from morn till late at night? Do they *see* anything when they go ashore?

There is much discussion about this being only a 3-star cruise. What do they expect for the amount of money they are paying? If it weren't for the cheap labour on board – yet another form of exploitation – we would be paying double. We are waited on hand and foot, and have witnessed people living the simplest of lives, and yet some passengers whinge incessantly. I suppose Dick and I are used to the *Lonely Planet* guide type of holiday.

I enjoyed my dinner, served by the always cheerful Antonio and Dawson. We went to listen to violinist Olga, and finished the day with another wonderful 'Elvis' cabaret by the indomitable Richard Sykes. Went to bed wondering how everyone is back home.

by Jill Crocker (Cabin 514)
Various stops up the Amazon, all of them exciting. We took a riverboat trip but ducked out of the rainforest walk. Steve [Ragnall] was wise not to push himself too far [he contracted polio of the spine as a child]. We

made contact with some of the locals. One teenage boy made (I'm sure) some rather intimate gestures to me. I recognise the demeanour from my seventeen years teaching children excluded from school. I just smile.

Steve escorts one group of passengers on a 'sights of Manaus trip'. He got a bit flustered at times, and even tried to enlist a stranger in a red t-shirt onto the bus. Steve was certain he was with us when we left the ship. We and the guides spent some time trying to find him before the tour bus left the opera house, but there was no sign of him. I think he's probably a local, as the numbers on the bus are right.

We decide to take a river trip to the 'meeting of the waters' with a local boatman. He was a lovely man, he priced fairly, and we tried to persuade one or two passengers to join us, but no luck. Still, it was cheaper than the organised tour, and our money went straight into local pockets.

Drama. Our boat breaks down mid-river. We check the time, and it's all aboard in two hours. There is a blockage in the water coolant pipe. The captain fixes it, but it breaks down again. We limp across to the water lilies where the pipe is properly cleared. Phew. On the return our captain races a local boat (proving the blockage is thoroughly cleared?). We win. I'm so glad about that.

by Jean McGinley (Cabin 229)

Way back in March 2010 when we booked, it had seemed such a good idea – six weeks cruising to the Amazon, no flying. There was just one problem – it was our first cruise. After two weeks we got used to the routine of daily activities on offer, but I suddenly realised how long we had to go before returning home. I missed the grandchildren, my cat, feeding the birds.

One bizarre occupation afforded some amusement, spotting the 'lookalikes' or doppelgangers amongst our fellow passengers and cruise staff. There is Jilly Cooper, Terry Thomas, Judi Dench, a young Daniel Craig, Kristin Scott Thomas, Diane Keaton, Ruth Madoc, Alun Armstrong, Noel Coward, Joan Rivers, and the chap who plays the lead in *Garrow's Law*, whose name escapes me.

Our amusement increased as we neared Brazil and encountered Ronnie Biggs. To these people, who know who they are, my apologies and thanks.

Talking of Brazil, my low point was having my gold (plated, fortunately) chain pinched by a street boy in Manaus. Philosophically, I accepted the loss. I had been warned, after all, and at least I was not hurt. I also found it very hard to listen to other passengers' moans about this and that.

by Clive Leatherdale (Cabin 725)
When I emerged on deck I was greeted by a scene from Noah's Ark. The decks were under water, and the rain was coming down in a vertical avalanche. It continued to do so for the rest of the morning. Britain never sees anything like this. Our words 'deluge' or 'cloudburst' are so inadequate. Rain like this back home would create a national emergency.

I took the Amsterdam Sauer jeweller's shuttle bus to their store in the Tropical Hotel Manaus in the Ponta Negra district. I only went for the free ride, and it confirmed my experiences from yesterday. No town planning, no parks, no fields, just endless sprawl and filth. Not a single agreeable sight arrested my eye there or back.

The hotel was grotesque, so opulent that it is bound to be 'leased' to one of the football nations allocated to Manaus for the 2014 Brazilian World Cup finals. Having taken their free ride, I felt obliged to spend ten seconds in the jewellery boutique, but felt affronted that the assistant who shadowed me really thought I might pay €20,000 for a bit of stone.

As today marks the midway point in our six-week cruise, my convivial dining-table companions, Dinah and Jack, Bernadine and Angela, shared a toast with me. Other tables have long since splintered or fragmented, yet ours is, how boring to confess, all harmony.

A taste of what readers can expect in the coming pages on Boca da Valeria. Some passengers considered very young girls dressing like this was innocent 'natural Amazonian costume'. Others did not (Clive Leatherdale)

DAY 23. BOCA DA VALERIA

'The tiny fishing village of Boca da Valeria sits at the confluence of the Rio da Valeria and the Amazon. This remote and primitive Indian village of 75 inhabitants is typical of the thousands of small isolated communities within the Amazon basin.'

by Clive Leatherdale (Cabin 725)

I smell a rat. The loose insert (more of which shortly) in the day sheet about Boca da Valeria is part romanticised, part wrong, and part downright mischievous. But I shall hold my tongue and let other passengers have their say first. Many passengers wanted their say (this is only a selection) and they did not mince their words.

by Dinah Read (Cabin 422)

And now we have turned in the general direction of home. We are heading toward the open sea again. During the night when I got up to go to the bathroom I put my watch forward an hour (I could have sworn that I had heard an announcement that it was to be done). This proved to be an error. Perhaps I dreamed it.

Anyway, I had Jack up at 5.30 and we were both ready for breakfast and down there by 6.30am – an hour before it was available. We came back up and checked and spent the next hour waiting around. I was teased unmercifully by Jack, who knows just how to get about it. The end result was that we came back to our cabin where we 'forgave' each other happily.

At lunchtime neither of us was particularly hungry. We had intended to go ashore this afternoon but it was raining heavily and Jack called it off. Jack is asleep now and it is just gone 3.30pm. It has stopped raining and I think I could and should go now. So I did.

by Aileen Singh (Cabin 708)

When we saw in the daily programme that the next day there was a trip to an Amazonian village, there was an air of excitement and anticipation amongst us. We went to the boutique and got some sweets and other useful items like shampoo. These were not ideal, for had we known before leaving Manaus, we could have procured pencils, exercise books and story books more relevant to Brazilian education.

Neville and I were on the first tender to arrive after the preparation crew. Many children were there on the jetty to greet us. They immediately slipped their hands in ours in an effort to lay claim to us. Even after we gave them 'gifts', they still wanted to stay with us and escort us through the village. Some villagers had taken the trouble to dress in traditional costumes of feathers and headdresses. Others had pets, which to us are wild animals (although they had tamed them) on show.

Although we shared very little oral language, we seemed able to communicate through gestures and facial expressions. The villagers had laid a 'road' of loam which helped to alleviate the effects of heavy, persistent rain and mud. Our small group led us to the end of the village, where the family in the last house welcomed us into their home. It was very sparsely furnished, but pride of place was a television set showing Sky TV.

In the schoolroom some children were playing a computerised piano and some indigenous instruments. There was a provision for donations to the school and we were only too pleased to help. At times, the children seemed bewildered, but who could blame them with some 500 people descending on their little corner of the world.

Our small donations to their economy won't go anywhere to help with their future needs, but the goodwill and intentions from both sides is a beginning.

by Neville Singh (Cabin 708)
Another touching memory was our visit to Boca de Valeria to meet the villagers who gathered at the landing. The children took our hands and escorted us along their houses and would not let go. It was as if they wanted to prolong this fleeting contact with these exotic strangers from another world.

To these children and their elders, the river was a street theatre and the passing boats living props, with players plying their trade, baiting their hooks and occasionally bagging some bargain. Against this scene, the arrival of our *Marco Polo* must have seemed an extravagant costume drama with so many extras.

The villagers went to much trouble to 'show off' for their visitors, and for the next two hours we were shown their houses (some with electric power and television), their school (with old computers) and their church. The houses were built on stilts, with chickens and pets ranging freely in the yard. One man showed a huge catfish which was still alive and panting. Photos were invited, to do justice to their show.

Only one boy spoke English, and spoke it so well that I wondered how he came by it; perhaps through TV. It was obvious that some children were gifted and would grow into leaders. Their culture has been impacted. Nudity was once a natural lifestyle born of the heat and humidity. But now they had found style and moved on.

The village lacked some amenities but not savvy; one man ran a busy bar with ship prices! Canoes were out and outboard engines in. The girls were very pretty, some curious but not awed. The place buzzed with dancing eyes and smiling faces, gracing us with a warm welcome even in the wet. The rain had joined our party.

Some 50 years ago, while surveying the rainforests for roads in British Guiana's interior, I met indigenous people and learnt their bushcraft, which was vital for survival. These are resilient folk. Their tools are new but their skills endure. They have also embraced change.

I can only hope that some of these children can also free their village and know the world. Who would deny them that dream?

'Magical Boca da Valeria' by Vivian Walsh (Cabin 609)
As I looked from the ship, I said to myself: 'What a beautiful place Boca da Valeria is.' It has a winding inlet to the right, just big enough for a small tender to moor. My eye was caught by a very pretty girl, dressed in a yellow leopard-skin patterned t-shirt and shorts. She had a charismatic way about her as she beckoned us to come to her village. As soon as our tender arrived I was surprised by a wave of small children holding on to me. I seemed to float up the beach on a sea of children. I was overwhelmed by their wonderful welcome. And, uplifted by their warmth, I continued floating until I was washed up into a bar! By this time I was so filled with euphoria that I bought all the children soft drinks, willingly parting with what little money I had, until it was was gone. Then, just like a wave dissipating, so had many of the children, except for two little girls who still hung on to me. We made our way along the beach. I could see local people, who had made an effort to dress up for us. I now had no money, but they didn't seem to mind, and were happily smiling as they held up their pets for me.

The two little girls, still holding on to me, led me to their family. This consisted of mum, with a small baby, an aunt, and a brother, who treated me like a long-lost friend. How trusting these people were, allowing a complete stranger to hold the hands of their children and walk up the beach.

I said to myself: 'This could not happen in England, we trust no one.' Later, I met a group of teenagers, one of them was called Mia, and she was the big sister of the two girls I had been holding hands with. Mia was bright and wanted to know more about me, so with a few words only, and hand signs, I feel I communicated way beyond words ever could. As I was leaving, Mia and her friends remembered my name and called me back to give me their email addresses. Mia's mother asked me for my umbrella for her baby. I wished I had given it to her now, as her need was so much greater than mine.

by Jeremy Tait (Cabin 715)
After leaving Manaus we anchored close to the tiny and unspoiled fishing village of Boca da Valeria, literally Mouth of the Valeria River, which was in striking contrast to the modern cities of Belem and Manaus. This remote and primitive Indian village, which is without roads or vehicles and is surrounded by dense rainforest, has a population of only 75 Cabocio, who are the descendants of early Portuguese settlers who intermarried with the local Indians and maintain their livelihood by hunting and fishing.

These people live in stilted huts constructed from grass and reeds, with openings for windows and doors. When the river is in flood, their livestock are kept on their balconies.

Scores of children, many of them with painted bodies and dressed in brightly coloured feathers, greeted us with their pets, such as tapirs, monkeys, sloths, lizards and tropical birds, and they held our hands in a natural and spontaneous gesture of trust and friendship, so unlike the slum children of many of the Brazilian cities who beg for money.

We gave them small coins and sweets as gifts, and the thrill and excitement of meeting such an obscure people was tempered with a feeling of sadness that such primitive conditions still exist in the 21st century – yet the Cabocios appeared to be happy and content and eager to meet passengers from a modern cruise ship.

However, the reaction of some passengers who went ashore can only be described as remarkable and – dare I say it – indicative of a total ignorance of the marvels of evolution and an inability to differentiate between, on the one hand, primitive emotions and instinctive behaviour (both of which are pure and unadulterated) and, on the other, western decadence (which is contrived and calculated).

Discussion after the visit showed that many passengers were shocked, and in many cases disgusted, by the sight of half-naked children holding out jungle animals for inspection, posing for photographs, showing people their beds, and their belongings, and accepting sweets and other small gifts from the visitors.

What we witnessed in Boca da Valeria was a spontaneous and pure outpouring of natural behaviour from an isolated tribe which had virtually no contact with the outside world. These children and teenagers were naturally excited by the spectacle of a modern cruise ship and white-skinned strangers wearing baggy trousers, printed dresses, floppy sunhats and brandishing umbrellas and cameras. To show their friendship and to welcome the visitors, what could be more natural for the children than to show the strangers their favourite pets (for they had no toys or dolls) and the huts where they lived? Many children simply held hands with passengers as they walked through the village. This marvel was a spontaneous gesture of friendship and affection, never to be found in modern cities.

One male passenger later told us that a teenage girl painted in bright colours and dressed in little else but feathers said she would be happy to sleep with him for US$10, which made her a prostitute. I suspect that the man himself had made the suggestion and that sadly he had not realised that her agreement to sleep with him was an offer of friendship and the sharing of pleasure, which is not unusual in tribal communities.

When little children in the jungle hold the hands of tourists and pose for photographs out of pure innocence and for the thrill of a new experience, how can any normal person object to this little bit of primitive behaviour? It will not last for ever, so let us understand it and enjoy it while we can.

by Margaret Atkinson (Cabin 504)
Overcast skies with malevolent looks loomed overhead. We sailed into what appeared to be an area of islands, wooded, but with an underlying rock of red sandstone. Further ahead was an area of cleared forest, where the new growth of light green contrasted with the black threatening sky. As the ship anchored, heavy rain descended. Tenders were lowered down on the port side of the ship, ready to take passengers up the inlet to the village.

As our shoes had not dried after yesterday's deluge, we decided to remain on board. Despite the heavy rain, a flotilla of local wooden narrow boats came out and gathered around the ship. Some contained just two people, others three, five and even eight. They were mostly children. All looking up at us. Waiting. Expecting. Some boats contained various fruits; others, local creatures, sloth, terrapin and green lizard could be easily seen from our deck. But what other creatures were there lurking in their boats out of sight?

Having been told that these were very poor people, we remembered we had a bag of sweets and a bag of chocolate eggs. We decided these children should have them. We threw the bag from the deck to the boats. Although the boats were cheek by jowl, our bags missed their target and fell into the Amazon. They fell between two boats in what seemed to be a very small gap about six inches wide. Yes, we had messed up, and we felt rather sad.

Later on, we heard from some returning passengers that they were none too happy about their visit. The 'poor village folk' were not as they had expected. They had visited some basic homes. All had the latest TVs, fridges and other electrical luxuries not normally associated with destitute people. A comment was heard that a stall set up with 'for sale' items were in fact Western, or, perhaps, Made in China, and were not local as expected. They might even have come from passengers from previous cruises.

If so, chuckle, chuckle. One can only be impressed by the villagers' entrepreneurial spirit. Waste not, want not. What a brilliant way of bringing in the lolly for more luxury goods. Good luck to them. What great initiative.

Although the rain continued, these stoical people remained alongside us, regularly using bowls to bail out their boats. Whatever is said about their lifestyle, these people never gave up. What a spirit! An indomitable spirit that is lacking in Western living these days.

by Daphne Carden (Cabin 618)
How generous of the people of Boca da Valeria to open their village to us. I felt humbled as we walked around. The children, so excited, as most children are the world over when rare goodies are offered. The stalls set up with handmade items on offer – as we do at our craft fairs; the shyly smiling, proud father and his three children, colourfully dressed ready for our cameras for a small fee. I learned they were collecting for their simple church and school, or family needs – as we do. Native people from an adjoining village were also attending the 'fair', specially arranged with great anticipation, judging by the welcome given to *Marco Polo* passengers.

As I slipped and slid around on the mud, I noticed one of our passengers (a disabled lady) sitting on a box surrounded by native children. She had a box of trinkets on her lap and was placing strings of sequins around the necks of the delighted children. An elderly native man stood amongst them, quietly and firmly making sure the children behaved themselves and retreated once they had received a gift.

My legs began to ache, so a 'sit down' was necessary. I made my way up the steps to the 'refreshment shack'. A young boy of about eleven was sitting near me with a baby on his lap, which he was lovingly caring for, planting a kiss on its head and giving it a drink from a plastic bottle.

Noticing my gaze, the boy signalled as to whether I would like to hold the baby, which I was pleased to do. James (a singer from the *Marco Polo*) was passing and noticed me cuddling the baby. He stopped to take a photo, which I have in my cruise collection. Later, as I headed down to the quayside, a smiling native woman approached me with what appeared to be the same baby. She placed it in my arms and indicated they were twins. More children came alongside us and she proudly touched the heads of four other children. They were hers, too! An elderly couple were sitting nearby under the shade of a tree. The young native woman gave me to understand, as we all joined them, that they were her parents and grandparents (note: no '$' signs in their eyes or manner). I felt a warm bond of unity as we stood there together. We all share this small planet in our brief span of life, which is a struggle for us all in a great variety of ways.

by Caroline Clifford (Cubicle 468)
Dear Diary, I'm sorry I didn't talk to you yesterday but the sheer misery of paying £42 for a tour [in Manaus] to sit, staring at a blue tarpaulin and listening to rain so loud that it drowned out the guide, made me feel miserable. James was on a downer, and then joy – he lost his cool and refused to get in the [tour] canoe. He had the last laugh – some boating arsehole forced us out of the narrow channel into thick weed. The floating weed wrapped round the propeller, the outboard failed, and we had to beg a tow from a passing 'canoe'. James, meanwhile, enjoyed a cocktail with the riverboat captain, or 'commander', as his cabin read. So, back on board *Marco Polo*, we cancelled all our remaining tours.

I didn't care what the weather threw at us today, as we didn't have to keep to a strict schedule. I just hoped that the rain would hold off till after lunch, and then all those wishing to rush ashore would piss off early.

The first view of Boca da Valeria was enchanting – like 'Narnia'. Then a cloud of black smoke, and I realised the first tender had gone on a recce. You rarely visit such tiny, out of the way, places on a cruise ship the size of *Marco Polo*.

The village, its neighbours and all their animals, had come together to create a 'tourist fest', a little like a 'pound shop', but with everything costing one dollar. You could even buy sweets to give to the children, for one dollar. Funny, since the Bank of Brazil wouldn't even touch the yankee stuff.

It was, however, the best opportunity for many to see lizards, sloths, capybara, monkeys, parrots, even fish, but could we really condone the sad little faces of these creatures and the way they were paraded for the rich and fortunate? The sloths looked mildly amused, and I saw one grab at an umbrella at some considerable speed. And then there was the monkey happily playing with dollar notes.

The girls, however, were dressed more like hookers than carnival queens. James commented that they were fitter than the pro's in Manaus and would certainly make a few old men happy!

I did wander a little way out of the village, up a slippery dirt track and was happy to see that some of the locals were ignoring the money-making festivities and carrying out their daily duties. The visit was certainly 'different', but what could you expect when 750 people invade a settlement inhabited by just 75?

by Tim Major (Cabin 469)

At Santarem and Manaus we had tied up alongside, so our tender crews had no opportunity to practice their new skills until we arrived at Boca da Valeria. Here the weather was again rainy, so there were relatively few customers for the tender. I certainly saw no benefit in being one. I suspected, and subsequent reports confirmed, that the only hostelry at which one could both find both shelter and refreshment was likely to be oversubscribed.

I was also suffering from what the doctor the following day diagnosed as acute bronchitis. It seemed, indeed, that our tender crews acquitted themselves well enough. When reports filtered back that a passenger had unintentionally ended up in the river, I was prepared to assume it would be the 'usual suspects', but in this I did them an injustice.

It turned out to be a passenger who had clearly decided to set new standards in nautical ineptitude and elected to take a canoe ride on the Valeria River.

Not content with this piece of bravado, unwise, with Health & Safety Brazilian Style ensuring that the canoe carried no life-jackets, he also demanded to demonstrate his proficiency with a paddle. The enthusiasm with which he wielded the paddle was only exceeded by his incompetence. Within minutes, with a particularly vigorous stroke he succeeded in pulling himself out of the canoe and into the water.

It was at this point that his wife pointed out that he could not swim. Fortunately, she didn't dive in to rescue him, as it turned out she couldn't swim either!

Whether their Amerindian hosts were accustomed to fishing suicide-inclined tourists out of their river, or they merely adapted their skills gained from dragging dead caiman into their canoes, our fellow passenger was successfully retrieved, with wet clothes and a rather tattered reputation as his only injuries.

'Survival in Boca da Valeria' by Kay Rainsley (Cabin 543)
The rain sloughed down as we were funnelled between groups of hopefuls holding cards, 'Boat trip – $5 per person – one hour.' It was muddy and the air smelled of disillusionment.

Ahead lay a cornucopia of fairground attractions minus the fun. Small, gum-chewing boys and girls paraded capybaras, spider monkeys, baby sloths and splendidly hued birds in a hideous menagerie of tied, bound and clipped creatures. The children extended their palms towards us. Pretty young girls wearing pseudo-Amerindian outfits of gaudily coloured feathers posed for photographs. Rough painted stripes were juxtaposed with their decorated smiles. One teenage girl showed off her skimpy outfit, fringes, feathers and lean legs. Cameras clicked. Thinking about my granddaughters, I moved towards the school building.

A dark man ran his fingers over an old keyboard. The rhythm unsettled me as I studied the ancient globe, wooden boards and Dickensian seats. A 'how to write letters of the alphabet' poster jostled with a list of countries. A display of children's work covered one small area of wall. On one side of the room lay a few books, games and teaching materials. I wanted to ask questions but had neither the language skills nor the appetite.

Outside there was a relentless press of small hands against larger ones, brown faces and bodies drenched with rain against plastic-covered white ones; youth and old age coming together in a bizarre ritual of giving and taking.

A large catfish gulped and stared, its eyes bulging as I hurried past. A man stroked its soft, expiring, body – did I want to touch it? I did not. A pole of six multi-coloured birds, wings fiercely clipped, perched end to end, tweeted in vain.

I fumbled to open a bag of sweets. Suddenly they felt dirty – like a bribe. I snapped three young girls with their mother, framed by luscious, red, tropical flowers and gave them the whole packet.

Peacock-man stood, resplendent in his 'dollar a photo' outfit, preening himself in the largest house. 'Guns n' Roses' boomed incongruously. He postured, shaking his grotesque headdress as the cameras flashed, clocking up the cash. 'Welcome,' said the sign. I surveyed the bare floor, meagre bed covers, hammocks and frugal clothes. The spacious kitchen contained a gas cooker, table and a selection of cooking pans. Rickety shelves held an eclectic mix of utensils. Feeling like a foreign voyeur, I left for the church.

'Feliz Natal,' happy Christmas. Cheap paper chains looped from the ceiling. White-wash. Rows of austere seats faced the tiny altar.

Unrelenting rain was spreading mud and misery. I photographed two smiling girls in their feathered headdresses and quickly looked at their mother, who was holding a younger sibling. Her expression had changed from the previous fixed smile to something else, distaste perhaps? And in that split second our minds met.

I retreated, past the still gulping catfish with its bulging eyes and its useless teeth, and wondered how long it could survive.

'Then and Now' by Jack White (Cabin 341)
(Jack White was making his second visit to Boca da Valeria. Seven years earlier he had also stopped there on Fred Olsen's *Braemar*. Jack found the differences between 'then and now' striking.)

THEN (18 DECEMBER 2003): As the *Braemar* sailed down the Amazon towards the village of Boca da Valeria, we were told that this was a very small native village whose residents would be dressed in traditional costume to greet us. The going rate was US$1 per photograph and was generally accepted. If they took the trouble to put on a display, they deserved something for their efforts.

We tendered ashore in fine weather, and a pathway through the village was lined at intervals with displays – a child with parents standing by, an adult or a family group. Moving forwards and pointing a camera prompted a pose. The $1 was graciously accepted. Some passengers took shots from the side to avoid payment. One lady, not in costume, posed with a toucan. Displays varied in quality and one had to be selective; otherwise it would have cost a fortune. A 'warrior' outside his house looked rather flamboyant.

Halfway through the village stood three communal buildings – one for local archaeology, a church and a school. I do not recall much in the way of archaeology, but a huge structure of a bird stood by the building. The church was well-maintained and obviously in use, while the school had less reverential treatment.

A house at the end of the village offered better value – multiple shots for the dollar. A few children roamed independently and they were happy to walk holding hands with passengers.

NOW (1 FEBRUARY 2011): We had come prepared for photographs with a supply of $1 bills, so we were surprised when we were told that the villagers would be interested in clothing, pens, pencils, sweets – anything really.

In dismal weather we tendered to a new jetty at the other end of the village. To the right were youths advertising boat trips upriver at $5 per person. This was new. To the left was a crowd of children 'begging' for anything you were carrying. My wife's umbrella was not on offer. This was different, many more people, and more aggressive. Not a good start. Fortunately, we were not carrying any bags, so we were not 'targets'. We were able to proceed unmolested.

Where had the archaeology building and the bird structure gone? Passengers who did not have a supply of $1 bills to 'scatter' made contributions to the church and school, but these were now run-down. We heard that another school upriver had computers.

A disturbing feature of the modern displays was the number of animals used – birds, monkeys and sloths. Sloths, looking like a bundle of rags, were particularly distressed. Most disturbing of all was a huge catfish. If passengers are prepared to pose beside a gasping catfish in its last throes of life, then God knows what photo opportunities will be provided in the future.

An 'age of innocence' has yielded to aggressive commercialism. With a sad feeling that a genuine native village had disappeared, we returned to the ship.

by Margit Latter (Cabin 335)
This place took me back ten years to when I stayed with a family in the Peruvian jungle. Ten years ago those children wanted to hold my hand and walk with me. Mothers invited me into their homes, but nobody held their hands out for dollars, like here in Boca da Valeria, or wanted their photos taken with animals held tightly on ropes. Nor were little girls of ten or eleven dressed up to look like little madams.

The day ended with a boat ride to another village upriver, where the woman who 'captained' the small boat for four took us to her home. She and I chatted all the way about her life – her Spanish was good. She told me about her private life.

Her husband worked with wood and cooked the meals for her and their two boys. He never beat her and only drank on Saturdays. They owned 35 cows, chickens and ducks, and grew vegetables in a disused boat filled with earth.

'What we don't eat, we freeze,' she said proudly, pointing to her freezer in her stilt home. It was huge, almost the size of a commercial freezer. She opened it and offered us an ice lolly, and I saw it was filled to the brim. I asked her where she got her other foodstuff, things which would not grow.

'Every three weeks my husband and I take the boat into town, go to the market and supermarket, and it makes a wonderful day out for me. I am in heaven here.'

by Sarah Broadbent (Cabin 305)
Local boats were heading up the enchanting creek beyond Boca da Valeria. We branched off the main stream and after about five minutes reached a lake. Our boat-owner's house was at the head of the lake. It was built on stilts in a position to die for, and had mains electricity. Chickens, ducks and dogs ran around outside. There was also a church and a school, both seeking donations.

We landed at a beach and were taken into the house, where we found his wife and mother. There were four rooms, two with hammocks, one with a pile of clothes and a Singer sewing machine. The living area contained a wonderful wooden table with benches each side and a colour TV. A cardboard box in the corner housed a cat with tiny kittens.

There was a kitchen at the back which had open sides, and we were shown a bowl of rather strong-smelling fish which was their dinner. Sadly, on our leaving, the mother asked us for money. On the way back to the river a couple of very smart speedboats overtook us.

by Lizzie Mayes (Cabin 494)
This looks as if it will be the highlight of our Amazon experience. The daily information sheet informed us: 'Boca da Valeria ... forms a startling contrast to life in Brazil's modern Amazon cities of Santarem, Belem and Manaus ... a gasoline generator runs in a hut supplying the electrical needs of the village,' and so on.

The day sheet continued: 'The villagers – their numbers swelled by people from other nearby villages flocking to witness the spectacle of a cruise ship – will greet you warmly, in particular the children, who will be more than eager to introduce their pets to you – in the form of tapirs monkeys, sloths, lizards, parrots, spiders ... some villagers may even proudly don typical Amazonian costumes. Note: you may wish to take some small gifts ashore with you, such as sweets, soft drinks, pencils and trinkets – as an offering in exchange for tours of the inhabitants' houses or other courtesies.'

The morning rain eased off, and by 2pm the sun was beginning to appear, so we decided to go ashore. Alarm bells started ringing the moment we got into the tender and a canoe appeared with unsmiling children, sloths round their necks, iguanas and turtles tied to the boat with string, and a hard-faced mother looking on. As we got off the tender, a line of children was waiting to greet us. They took us by each hand to lead us through the village. There were trinket stalls, children with an assortment of tatty-looking parrots, agoutis, monkeys and sloths lined up for photo calls, and young girls dressed in bright green feathers were draped on tree stumps – next step prostitution in a red light district somewhere?

Children appeared from all directions with open hands, asking for dollars. We walked to the end of the sad little display and disengaged ourselves from the children, handing them a small gift of a pencil and some soap, and some small coins we had in our pockets, and walked along the beach on our own. We then walked up into the forest behind the village, where we were invited into a house by a toothless old man. It was in many ways extraordinary – a small wooden bed, a cooker, rows and rows of aluminium pots and pans, a string of fairy lights, which he delightedly switched on for us. The house comprised two rooms, quite spacious, and a veranda. It was clean and tidy and the old man was very smiley and clearly proud of his house, but I did feel I was intruding and can't think of any reason I would take a complete stranger into my house and show them everything. He had bags of crisps hanging up. As we found we had a $5 note, we bought about ten packets. Dick gave him a mouth organ, which he found very amusing.

We made our way back to the boat – with conflicting feelings about the visit. Dick was a lot easier about it than I was. I really hated the scent of corruption. At dinner tonight, I was surprised to learn that John and Sue had decided not even to go ashore when they saw the people begging in canoes around the boat.

Postscript: I'm still thinking about Boca da Valeria and how it could have been better. I feel that perhaps we should have had a contribution box on board so that the only money given could have gone directly to the school, and that perhaps even the small gifts could have been put in a box to be shared out amongst everyone after we had gone. I feel anger about the destructive effect of this kind of tourism on small communities living a simple life in tune with nature. Hundreds of sanitised, smugly affluent professional cruisers barging their way into people's lives and homes, feeling very good about it because they have handed over the odd dollar, coloured pencil or chocolate bar.

'A Penny for the Guy in Boca da Valeria' by Dick Mayes (Cabin 494)
In the wilds of west Somerset in the village of Wobbliscombe a meeting had been called to discuss the forthcoming annual church fete. Present was the vicar, the chairman of the parish council, the local bobby, the headmaster, various committee members and some guests from a nearby village. The following is an extract from the minutes:

'So, we are all agreed that the money raised will be divided between the church infrastructure fund and the school. We have decided on 30

June, as it coincides with the SAGA group holiday weekend in the Castle Inn and also with the Twinning week with our friends from Oberammergau, so we can maximise on numbers and hence takings. We now need to discuss the various activities and attractions.

Mrs Pimpernel said she is happy to run the children's fancy dress competition again. Are we all happy with this, particularly as last year a number of the entrants were rather scantily clad. What do you say, vicar?

"Well personally I have no problem with this and I do think we tend to overreact to newspaper reports of what are mainly isolated incidents. If some people had their way, children would spend their lives indoors in front of the TV or computer games perverting their own little minds. No, I think it should go ahead as last year."

Also, last year we had some of the children walking around with their pets collecting donations. There was young Nessie Jackass with her donkey who collected £4.50, Kevin Cavie with his guinea pig, who collected £1.53, and his brother Rupert with his pet earthworm which managed to find its way down the front of Lady Squeamish's dress. She is refusing to open the fete this year. Collecting by children is probably illegal but it certainly added to our takings. What's your view on this PC Faircop?

"I'm not quite sure of the law. I could check with my superiors but I think that in a village setting nobody's going to complain. We can all remember collecting a penny for the guy when we were young. Unless we created a nuisance to passers by, the police would turn a blind eye to it."

Mr Reed, I hope we can count on you to give your demonstration of thatching again this year? It's certainly been very popular with our visitors from abroad in the past.

Mr Turner, your wife has put your name forward to fit up your foot-operated lathe to demonstrate your skills at making wooden bowls. Headmaster, do you think you could persuade your art mistress, Miss Picasso, to do the face painting again?

I intend to hold the same side-stall attractions, such as the coconut shy, the archery contest – Mr Tuck, I hope we can ask you to dress up in your Merry Men of Sherwood outfit again and, of course, the Wobbliscombe Morris Men.

The Women's Institute have agreed to sell homemade cakes and home-grown plants. Headmaster and Rev Aspiring-Bishop, there would be great disappointment all round if you don't agree to go in the stocks for wet sponge treatment. Farmer Hereford, despite the unfortunate accident with the Women's Institute stand, your welly boot-throwing contest has always been very popular and it would be a shame to leave it out this year.

So, before we move on ...'

Meanwhile, 4,000 miles away in the wooden school building of the small village of Boca da Valeria, the village elders and those of a nearby village have assembled to discuss the visit of the passenger cruiser *Marco Polo*.

Então vamos concordar que o dinheiro arrecadado será dividido entre a renovação da escola e a igreja ... (So do we agree that money raised will be divided between the school refurbishment and the church ...)

by Bernadine Ryan (Cabin 527)
TO THE PASSENGER COMPLAINTS DEPARTMENT
AN OPEN LETTER TO CRUISE & MARITIME VOYAGES LTD

'All hail to the mighty white man who cometh forth handing out gifts.'

This seemed to be the message tranmitted to the local community on our arrival at Boca da Valeria. It brought home to me the need to inform the passengers on board the *Marco Polo* of their responsibilities towards supporting and not destroying the way of life of the indigenous community. This responsibility to foster understanding, appreciation of and mutual respect for the culture and way of life of everyone who shares Planet Earth ultimately lies with Cruise & Maritime Voyages.

On principle I did not got ashore. Having read the information provided in the ship's day sheet, and subsequent personal observations from the deck of local villagers in their canoes begging and displaying in return for money the indigenous animals, including a sloth, I knew this was not the place for me. I was particularly disturbed by the bulletin's suggestion that handing out such items as sweets and soft drinks would be appropriate. 'The great white man hands out trinkets to the lowly natives.'

This ultimately fosters a generation of beggars. What ignorance would encourage previously unknown tooth decay when the nearest dentist is inaccessible hundreds of miles away? Why corrupt their natural healthy diet with the junk food that is the scourge of the Western world?

I cannot comment from first-hand observation what went on in the village itself, but I did spend time on the tender deck listening to passengers as they returned.

The vast majority 'enjoyed' the experience, handing out dollar bills like confetti. Their photos of
young girls in pseudo-ethnic costumes, looking more
like under-age hookers, disturbed me. In most
instances their generosity was simply sadly misguid-
ed, not malicious. If they'd been suitably informed
beforehand with relevant information from the ship,
how much more positive the experience would have
been, both for the passengers and the tribespeople.

European explorers of the past decimated the
indigenous tribes of the Amazon basin. Are European
tourists in the 21st century continuing this trend by
upsetting the balance of nature?

I would have expected that common sense would have
decreed a minimum dress code for passengers going
ashore. What impression of 'civilised Europeans' is
given to the indigenous populace on seeing a European
male dressed in skimpy swimming trunks under his rain
jacket (to all intents and purposes looking as if he
had forgotten to put on his trousers) accompanied by
a bikini-clad European female wearing a transparent
rain cape? Inappropriate and totally unacceptable. Is
this what they wear in their own neighbourhood on a
rainy day in England? I think not.

If *Marco Polo* continues to anchor off Boca da
Valeria, it could be the perfect opportunity to foster mutual respect between our world and theirs. It
could benefit this and neighbouring communities in a
positive manner by funding essential amenities such
as clean drinking water, efficient sanitation, medical facilities, adequate power generators, supplies
for the school, or paying a living wage for the
teacher. This could be achieved by collecting a vol-
untary donation of US$1 per passenger to be matched
dollar-for-dollar by Cruise & Maritime Voyages – what
a difference this would make to the community and its
neighbours! They could reciprocate by proudly showing
visitors around their village and their homes, without the need or being encouraged to beg. Everyone
would benefit.

The crew seemed to be better informed than the passengers about the needs of the community. Advance
information disseminated to all passengers prior to
embarkation could result in financial donations as
well as material gifts in the form of school supplies,
clothes and medicines (not junk food!) to benefit the

whole community, not just the aggressive few. Education of the passengers is as necessary as education of the indigenous peoples. *Marco Polo* could be in the forefront of change for good.

Yours etc
Bernadine Ryan

by Mark Edwards (Cabin 423)
TO THE PASSENGER COMPLAINTS DEPARTMENT
AN OPEN LETTER TO CRUISE & MARITIME VOYAGES LTD

Sir, I write to complain about the *Marco Polo* visit to Boca da Valeria on 1st February 2011. The visit was a serious lapse of ethical judgement on behalf of Cruise & Maritime Voyages, as it was tourism of a style that was reminiscent of the 1970s or 1980s.

I am not anti-tourism *per se*. Tourism is a form of trade, and all trade has its set of ethics. This moral code becomes refined over time. The visit to Boca da Valeria appeared to have little of the ethics that currently prevail. Many of your passengers will not have considered the moral principles involved in tourism, and Cruise & Maritime Voyages have a duty of care, as the tour operator, to advise what is acceptable behaviour in a village situation, where there is no guide. It significantly failed to do this.

In following sensible guidelines, I would expect the village men to take tourists off in their canoes at a price per head, for they are using their skills to give enjoyment to tourists.

I can accept, with reluctance, the use of wild animals and birds for photographs where it can be argued that the animals can and have been tamed. This would apply to the sloths and capybaras at Boca da Valeria. However, I also saw the restraint of an iguana by a string tied around the abdomen, which is not acceptable.

I can also accept, again with reluctance, the presence of a bar selling beer and soft drinks in such a small village, because it could be argued that in the dry season this could be a necessity for visitors spending some time observing the flora and fauna of the area.

We were informed that this was a very poor village. By whose standards are we judging this? If we judge by our 'first world' standards, yes it is poor.

Yet by the Brazilian standards that we have been shown previously by our Brazilian guides, it is not poor. It has a large church and a school, both built out of bricks. It has piped running water, it has electricity, the house I went into cooked by gas, and had a radio.

Having said this, I have no doubt that the village requires very much more funding for its school and local education, but how does giving individual children sweets help the village and its education? Surely the tourism norm of a donation to the teacher, or a village elder, is the effective and acceptable method of supporting the village.

As a retired dentist, I have seen little evidence of the use of sweets outside the big cities, and certainly no evidence of decay in the children's teeth. For me, the giving of sweets and crisps to these rural children, so that we may introduce them to the western problem of dental decay, is unforgivable.

I turn to the use of children in the village. It was very noticeable that it was the children that were touting the animals to be photographed. No doubt this is because the image of children and animals together is difficult to resist. The faces of these particular children will be with me for many years.

They were not the faces of the savvy tourist street traders, who know that they will 'win some, loose some', and still have a cheeky smile. These children had the faces of hard avaricious adults who were out to get every dollar they could out of the punters. How can it be morally acceptable that these children have lost their smile before their tenth birthday?

We, the tourists, have turned them this way, but it is outside our acceptable ethical boundaries. Last year I was in Assam, cruising along the Bramaputra river. The boat was an Assamese boat that used the principle that they would never stop at the same river village twice, and that they would donate to the village school or community via the head man. Why is your company not following a similar protocol?

Finally, I must speak of the tribal costumes. The Cruise & Maritime Voyages handout said that it was possible that the villagers would 'proudly don typical Amazonian costumes'. What it did not say was that it would be the children that would be wearing the costumes, and that they had been taught to be the perfect paedophilic dream. I saw only one adult, a man, wearing costume.

In fact, the costumes were worn by children from about age four to twelve, mainly girls. The older girls had been taught to stand as if they were prostitutes, hands on hips, at a height that made their sexual presence felt. No smiles, this was business. It was nasty exploitation of the worst kind. Tourists have taught them this, and Cruise & Maritime Voyages, by stopping there, are continuing to support it.

The sad thing is that the village has so much to offer without this unpleasant behaviour. The birds, insects, butterflies and plants were different to those we have seen previously on the Amazonas, as it has a slightly different micro-climate with its rocky outcrop. Why are we not supporting them to utilise all this?

It is said that Brazil is a country of contrasts. This disgraceful, degrading, demeaning visit is the antithesis of all the other visits of this cruise, where the tourism has been conducted in a structured, non-invasive style by qualified guides.

I would ask that you remove immediately the stop at Boca da Valeria from any future Amazonas Cruises that you operate.

Yours etc
R M Edwards

'For a Fistful of Dollars' by Clive Leatherdale (Cabin 725)

As the *Marco Polo* headed east after leaving Manaus, beginning its homeward run, the mood on board was one of contemplation. The best was over. But how wrong we were. For many, the stop at Boca da Valeria the next day would be the highlight of the whole cruise; for others it marked a wretched low. Many of those who missed it – whether deterred by the rain or who dismissed the village as 'not worth the bother after the opera house in Manaus' – would rue their decision. Others refused even to go ashore, for moral reasons. Few came away from this place untouched.

Prior to departure from England, I had struggled to unearth anything about Boca da Valeria. It was as if it didn't exist, and as for the river Valeria, that too was impossible to pinpoint. What kind of place was this?

The cribsheet prepared by Cruise & Maritime and distributed to passengers put me immediately on guard. It had the tone of *Billy Bunter in Brazil* (1949), picturesque descriptions of plucky natives clamouring for a pencil or a liquorice allsort. A box at the foot of the page declared it to be a 'small, typical Amazonian village'. Nothing could be further from the truth, for the simple fact that no other Amazonian village welcomes fleets of cruise ships. Boca da Valeria is remarkable only as a stop on their Amazonian itinerary. But for that, it would indeed be as anonymous as thousands of other villages up and down the river.

For a start, I wanted to know why the *Marco Polo* was stopping here. I could not imagine negotiations between an international cruise line and the head man of a village via satellite phone, telex or whatever. It turns out that the link-up was made via Amazonian port agents many years ago. They spotted a wheeze. We know from Jack White [page 174] that cruise ships have been coming here for at least seven years, and Boca da Valeria is now a fixture on the circuit. Nor are visits few and far between: *Braemar* arrived here just a few weeks after *Marco Polo*.

The cribsheet said the *Marco Polo* would be met by 'canoes'. I thought canoes were propelled by paddles, not outboard motors, in which case I didn't see many canoes. The first shock came when climbing into a tender to take us ashore. A 'canoe' manoeuvred alongside and a boy of about ten peered up into a sea of faces. He was holding up an animal. I cannot tell you what it was because my eyes were struck by the boy. He was a child in years only, for his face was hard, hard as nails. He might have been a street urchin from Rio. A passenger sitting near me made the mistake of taking a 'cute' photo of boy and beast. Quick as a flash, the boy thrust up his index finger. It was a 'demand', not a 'request'. He wanted one dollar and he wanted it now. We had not even gone ashore, yet already the exhortation to bring 'small items such as sweets, soft drinks, pencils and trinkets' seemed to belong to a bygone age. Bugger that, these kids wanted money and knew how to get it.

It got worse. As we slithered ashore, up a path churned into a syrup of mud, it was to discover that the supposed 75 inhabitants had swollen several-fold in anticipation of rich pickings. The nearest building to the jetty was not a school or a church. It was a bar, bigger than many of the houses, an open-air circular bar under a thatch roof with a sign in English offering 'cool beer, soft drink here'. It was already packed with people off the ship. Nearby were two portaloos, male and female, and a satellite television disc! Someone with a straight face was peddling the line that this was a typical Amazonian village.

Pubescent and pre-pubescent girls stood by the path clad in as little as possible. We were expected to believe that this was traditional native costume, all feathers and war-paint, though their skimpy outfits clearly owed more to Hollywood than to anything their mothers and grandmothers once wore.

Looking through my photographs of that day, I am struck by how well nourished these children looked and how well dressed in their fancy new t-shirts, shorts and dresses. It emerged that many of these clothes were provided by *Marco Polo*, which raises more questions than answers. Of poverty, as I understand it, I saw little evidence. The fact that a house stands on stilts does not make it poor. Passengers hoodwinked into thinking they were buying native crafts to boost the local economy returned to the ship to discover poorly made or mass-produced kitsch.

It got yet worse. I stood back to observe passengers strolling through the mud with a child, sometimes two, sometimes three, clinging to each arm. From my detached vantage point, I watched tiny fingers sliding into bags and withdrawing what they found. This pilfering was sometimes apprehended, but the would-be thief was seldom reproached. I later spoke to one of the victims. A child had opened her purse. 'It's alright,' she said. 'They were only looking for sweets!' This 'typical Amazonian village' had become adept in the black arts of pick-pocketing and aggressive begging, 'skills' unknown to traditional villages.

I watched astonished as dollar bills were handed out, here, there and everywhere, without thought to the consequence. It was the brashest and pushiest kids who got most of it, while the quieter ones at the back got nothing. They will learn.

I did some sums. Suppose 500 passengers went ashore today, and each handed out an average of US$10. This meant that after *Marco Polo* left, $5,000, mostly in one-dollar bills, was swilling around the village. That sum could easily refurbish a church or school, but Jack White noted that those buildings were more run down today than they were seven years earlier. Among *Marco Polo*'s passengers were international aid experts. They, too, were dismayed by what they observed.

So where did that $5,000 go? There is no bank to put it in and there are no shops to spend it in. One passenger insisted she saw money pass from child to adult, from adult to the bar, and from the bar to a tin box at the back. Even if true, then what? And why insist on American dollars? Passengers knew from hard experience that dollars are almost an illegal currency in Brazil.

No wonder villagers from miles around swarm into Boca da Valeria on cruise day. And not just villagers. Every hoodlum and ne'er-do-well in northern Brazil must know what's going on. Keep the church and school poor to tug at the heartstrings, then spend the proceeds on speedboats, industrial-sized freezers and satellite TV. That's clever. Several passengers asked, 'Who's exploiting whom?' Any curious journalist who fancies a bit of Amazonian delving would be advised: 'follow the money.'

DAY 24. AMAZON

'Many of you will know that Clive Leatherdale of Desert Island Books is compiling an account of this cruise to be published later this year. Could all existing contributors and anyone else interested please come and join the meeting today at 11.00 in Scott's Bar.'

by Judy Chapman (Cabin 419)

Where has the time gone? Soon we will be on our way to the Atlantic, and the Amazon will be just a memory. Each port of call was special in its own unique way, from the bustling market in Belem, to the poverty of Parintins, to the faded glamour of Manaus. Who could ever forget standing on deck in the port of that city, observing from above the comings and goings of a people whose lives are shaped by the mighty Amazon?

We've jumped on countless tenders – good practice for the crew if they ever have to 'man the lifeboats' for real; we've travelled in rickety old local buses; walked through eco-forests; canoed down creeks and explored numerous street-markets. We have negotiated cracked, uneven pavements, holes in the road, maniac motor-cyclists and open sewers. All of which would give British 'elf and safety' experts nightmares.

But there comes a time when you've seen enough of these sights. All the market stalls sell the same 'Made in China' tat; one eco-forest or zoo begins to look like another, and while one drenching in a tropical rainstorm might be fun, several are simply frustrating. For me, this is what cruising is all about – relaxing, spending quality time with Mike, and forgetting all my worries back home. Periodic text messages have let us know that all is as well as can be expected with mum [aged 94]. For the time being, home is here on the *Marco Polo*. This is real life. England is that cold grey place thousands of miles away.

An unexpected but pleasant advantage of a long cruise is that the crew/staff (I never know which is which) become familiar faces with names and personalities. Fellow passengers become, if not friends, friendly acquaintances, each with a story to tell. There is the serene elderly lady who lost a child in tragic circumstances; the lively, sparky grandmother who is recovering from breast cancer, and the perfectly matched couple who met through a lonely hearts ad. There are the men who have travelled worldwide during their working lives, and a surprising number of couples who have forsaken the UK and retired in Spain. Many couples, Mike and I included, are on their second marriages, and many others are not married at all, but live in unwedded bliss. Co-habiting is not just for the young.

When convenient, Mike and I like to lunch in the Waldorf restaurant. The luxury of being waited on beats the scramble for food in Marco's Bistro any time. The open seating at lunch is also a great way to sit with and get to know fellow passengers. We have long since abandoned our allocated dinner table in the evenings to join Lee ('No, no one has ever said I look like Bill Gates') and Margit, and four others at a happy, lively table in the corner.

'Halfway Thoughts' by Lizzie Mayes (Cabin 494)
So many people on board see nothing beyond their own personal comforts and desires – their interest more about saying where they've been and not what they've seen, and more concerned about the price of drink on board, the food, the room service, etc. I dislike their well-travelled naivety, strutting about in t-shirts and baseball hats boasting former travels. Fortunately we have been on board long enough now to avoid most of these people and have found interesting and compatible cruise-mates.

I understand why I have no need to be constantly travelling – the baseball cap and 42in TV has found its way into every far-flung village, people are moving in huge numbers into city squalour to improve their living standards and live in ghettos to scavenge rubbish tips; everything you buy is stamped, 'Made in China.' Thank goodness no cruise ship will ever come up the Bristol Channel and disgorge 700 people on the Quantock Hills to trample the purple heather, gorse and golden grasses and terrify the wild ponies and their foals, the larks, sheep and the red deer.

On the other hand, it has been a good experience seeing this amazing waterway and its communities, only connected to each other by the water. I loved the bustle of Manaus on Sunday; the markets piled with wonderful fruits and vegetables, and all manner of extraordinary fishes, the boats docking alongside us, laden with people coming ashore from places all along the river – some with suitcases, some with a small box of fruit or vegetables to sell, some adventurous travellers with a rucksack on the back, the lines of coloured hammocks for people to sleep in as they make a journey of several days to the town.

I loved the experience of feeling the torrential warm rain as we waded through the forest and the sound of frogs singing their hearts out. I loved being part of the community in the performance at the opera house surrounded by wide-eyed children, and wish I'd had some basic Portuguese. We went to the *Marco Polo* show this evening – a repeat of 'From Russia with Love'. We have noticed the same people are in the front row every time, and have named them 'the bolters', as they must eat their supper very fast to get into the lounge so quickly. The 'basters' are still pursuing the mahogany tan before arriving in the Caribbean to show it off, and the smokers are still packed tight on the 'puffin deck', whilst those in the 'parrot house' are steadily encroaching into the non-smoking area.

I am beginning to hear rumours of a bug on board – that several people have been ill following the floating restaurant lunch in Manaus. It seems we were lucky not to be afflicted. These poor folk, and anyone else with tummy upsets, are confined to their cabins with their partners (who may not be ill at all) for a minimum of 48 hours. I suppose it's necessary, otherwise it could spread like wildfire. I am being particularly diligent about sanitising my hands, which are beginning to look like new potatoes with layers of skin peeling off.

'My Funniest Moment' by Alan Waite (Cabin 223)

It was a warm, balmy evening and the *Marco Polo* was anchored in the mighty Amazon river. I was on Deck 9, looking down on the party taking place on the deck below. My attention was attracted by a 'lady' who was dancing by herself, gyrating her hips and twanging on an imaginary guitar whilst listening to an Elvis Presley track.

But as I watched, spellbound, it suddenly got even better. An insect, attracted by the lights on deck, alighted on the dancer's hair and then proceeded to go down the front of her dress. This had the effect of making her gyrate even more wildly. Her husband now got involved, trying to help the poor insect out, or failing that, to try to squash it inside her clothing. No easy task, considering the jumping up and down of the victim. A performance worthy of winning any Elvis lookalike contest.

'A Missed Chance' by Piet Pieterse (Cabin 127)

A cruise to the Amazon. What a chance. The word 'Amazon' means something mysterious in itself. Everybody has heard of it: the huge river. And many have heard about the awful woodcutting and burning of great parts of the rainforest. Almost all reactions are superficial. And what about the reactions of the *Marco Polo*'s passengers? I have heard some surprising remarks:

'What a big river.'

'I didn't know that a cruiser could sail up the river for 1,000 miles.'

'I only see green banks on both sides.'

'How boring it is.'

'Where are the woodcutters?'

'Each day there are downpours for hours at a stretch.'

'There are even ATM machines in Manaus.'

On board ship we were informed about the Amazon by one of the lecturers, who admitted he was not an Amazon expert, and by brief info-papers from the excursion desk. But that was all. I should call this 'A Missed Chance'. We were told nothing about the natives, how they live, their education, religion, about the cooperation between the eight Amazon countries, their products, like fruit and wood. About medicines relating to the forest plants. About cosmetics, jewellery, ceramics, ornaments, and about Fairtrade products.

What could have been organised on board? DVDs and discussion groups during the five days crossing the Atlantic. This was enough time to inform the tourists and make British and Dutch passengers more conscious of the influence of the rainforest on our lives. When we globe-trotters get back home we can convince relatives and friends how important Fairtrade products are. These cruises have a big opportunity to help change our behaviour, but the *Marco Polo* missed that chance.

by Clive Leatherdale (Cabin 725)

The number of 'book club' contributors turning up continues to rise. We even had our first Dutchman this morning. The reverberations from yesterday's visit to Boca da Valeria show no sign of abating. One man described *Marco Polo* passengers as 'human piranhas'. A woman was reduced to tears when describing the shame of what she had witnessed.

I dread this book project going cold. Passengers might be fired up while they are on board, but they could lose interest when they get back home and are overtaken by daily drudgery. I try to give encouragement, acknowledging that showing one's written thoughts to a stranger can appear daunting, rather like stripping off to show our private parts to a doctor.

Quick as a flash, Richard Sykes winds up the meeting, inviting those present to 'Go and show your private parts to Clive'.

DAY 25. FAZENDINHA, MACAPÁ

'Capital of the Amapá region, which stretches from the Amazon delta to the borders of French Guyana and Suriname, Macapá is the only major city in the Amazon to actually be situated on the banks of the river, lying right on the Equator.'

by Mave Eaton (Cabin 616)
We arrive off Fazendinha for Macapá at the mouth of the Amazon. There is irritation amongst the passengers, as we are not using the dock but have to tender again. Is it an economy measure so that dock charges are not paid? The passengers pay £5 each for the return bus journey into Macapá, which takes 25 minutes. It is very hot and humid. Shops are small and sell mainly cheap clothes and shoes. I wish to find a supermarket to buy alcohol. We are directed to Top International – a long hot walk accompanied by mutterings about walking city streets. We see Top International. It is the largest and newest building and is surrounded by a steel fence. A sign flashes on and off – Duty Free. But it is a mirage. This very smart air-conditioned shop sells everything but drinks. I meekly agree to visit the fort, where every stone was brought from Portugal.

We rush back for a return bus, and are almost the last to find a seat. An ageing Englishman sits alone and looks very ill. There are requests that we return to the ship immediately for his sake, but the cruise representative is brusque and says we must wait to fill the four remaining places. Sick passengers must take a taxi to the hospital. After ten more hot minutes we are allowed to leave. The ill man vomits into a green plastic bag. A compassionate lady finds tissues and water and cools and cleans him. The sick passenger's wife slowly comes from the back of the bus to give succour. We are glad to reach the tender and to leave him. Rumour has it that one passenger has already died on the ship. [Not true, no passengers died on the trip. Editor]

by Tim Major (Cabin 469)
This should have been our last port on the Amazon, but rumours of a jail-break at Macapá by 40 violent criminals gave our intrepid tender crews another chance to shine. With some 25 escapees apparently still at

large, the local authorities determined that *Marco Polo*'s planned berth at Santana would be unsafe, so we were directed instead to anchor off the pilot station at Fazendinha.

The tender crews, in the event, gave quite a good account of themselves. My main concern centred on the ability of the pilot's flimsy pier to handle the impetuous docking, and the heavier pedestrian traffic than that to which it was accustomed. I still retained my cautious policy of trying to sit in the covered bow, and this was fortunate, as it meant I avoided the rain water which had collected in the rolled-up awning and was intermittently poured down passengers' necks by the rolling and pitching of the tender. Worse was to come, as we sailed through a heavy rain shower, and the crew only began to lower the side-awning after exposed passengers had been well wetted.

And on the return, our coxswain decided to let rip, with the result that passengers on the windward side and aft were given their last sound dousing with Amazon water as the short chop spilled into the tender.

'Buying Coca-Cola in Macapá' by Catharine Fox (Cabin 705)
While visiting the fort in Macapá, we spotted a market where we attempted to buy a large bottle of Coca-Cola to take back with us. Most of the stalls were small cafés but by mime and gesture a young girl sold us a glass bottle of coke with a metal cap. It was quite expensive and, as we'd paid, she took the cap off. We said, 'No, no,' waving our hands. 'We want to take it with us.' She endeavoured to fix the cap on again, and we walked away. Just then the owner of the stall returned, a tired-looking lady with two young children and pregnant with the third. She sent the girl after us, so we came back, and she seemed to be pleading with us. As this was all in Portuguese we had no idea what was going on, so we shrugged and moved off again. The young girl chased us and caught hold of my arm. By this time all the stall holders were standing, watching in silence – not threatening but we felt uncomfortable. In desperation I asked, 'Does anyone speak or understand English?' Silence! Eventually we were allowed to go. Back at the ship, as we transferred the drink to a safer plastic container, we noticed on the bottle that it said 'returnable deposit'. Was this what it was all about?

'My Last Five Minutes' by Pat Pickering (Cabin 440)
I was last off the coach, dropping down onto the gritty surface of the forest track. We were back in the small clearing among tall spindly trees, just a stone's throw inland from the river and from where we'd departed earlier in the day en route to Macapá. I watched idly as the driver made a

precarious three-point turn, bumping over the sun-hardened furrows and easing over the tangled green verges before lurching off down the road towards the village of Fazendinha and to the city beyond. In the opposite direction, already some distance away, trudged my weary fellow passengers, no doubt looking forward to afternoon tea or a long cool beer back on board.

Suddenly I remembered: this was my last day on the Amazon, and now we were down to the last five minutes. With that thought came an unexpected heightening of the senses, a realisation perhaps that memories of a place and time have to be supported by infinite detail. I resolved not to miss a single thing!

Beneath my feet the gravel pathway took on a new importance, its reddish-ochre reminding me of the old-fashioned municipal tennis courts of my childhood. Maybe I was searching for reference points from the past to strengthen my memories for the future.

As I lingered, a long file of centimetre-sized polished mahogany ants zig-zagged their way from left to right across my path, several of them breaking ranks to investigate my shoes, before rejecting them as a source of food and rejoining their platoon, which was fast disappearing into the shorter, scrubby grass at the edge of the verge.

Turning my back on the river and looking inland, I saw for the second time today the dilapidated stilt house visible earlier from the coach. Now, from a lower vantage point, half-hidden by undergrowth in the middle distance, I realised that it was empty and abandoned, its upper storey and roof sun-bleached and leopard-spotted by the light filtering down through the camouflage-webbing of the treetops above. The wooden plank walls of the single-roomed structure had weathered a soft greyish-brown, and the door hung outwards supported by only the lowest of its three rusty hinges.

Its dark interior was barely visible through the frameless window, and some young leaves and shoots of an exotic variegated creeping plant had begun a sly incursion. Alongside, lay a small patch of roughly cultivated land, where a straw-hatted head and shoulders and the upper part of some long-handled farming implement could be seen moving forward and backward above the level of the bushes. Had the house once been his home or that of his parents or grandparents? Was it abandoned to the forest for all time or would they some day reclaim it, and where did the last occupants live now?

I was distracted from these musings by a vivid flickering coming from over my left shoulder and passing within arm's reach. Brilliant crimson and muted amber alternated into my line of vision as a small ornate unknown species of butterfly came to rest in amber mode on the foliage directly in front of me. Dissatisfied obviously with this particular spot, it took off again and fluttered upwards to re-alight, this time in crimson mode, on the edge of a cluster of trumpet-shaped tree blossoms, their pale lemon-yellow acting as a perfect foil for the dazzling red.

'Flora and fauna together – almost too good to be true,' I thought, as I reached gingerly for the camera: but at the first tensing of my muscles, the delicate creature took off in alarm and resumed its aerial meanderings upwards and out of sight.

Up till now, I'd been aware only of form and texture and colour, but soon the scents and sounds of the clearing came into focus, too. From the opposite side of the track, in the shade between the verge and the river, and in a spot where the trees stood further apart, came the smell of woodsmoke, sawdust and petrol and the murmur of male voices. There, surrounded by an untidy confusion of upturned small boats, discarded outboard motors, assorted timber, oil cans, car tyres and ropes of various thicknesses, stood the sizeable hull of a typical Amazonian ferry propped upright and under repair by a trio of workmen.

On the ground stood, possibly the foreman, sporting a black baseball cap and a faded 'Ronaldinho' football top, looking upwards to the rim of the vessel, while his two compatriots, perched high up above him on the deck were gesticulating downwards towards a rusty hole in the bow, about the size of a dinner plate and roughly the shape of Australia.

A little way off towards the river, an older woman clad in a navy spotted dress was crouched down, fanning with a tin lid the flames of a small campfire. The fire was enclosed in a ring of unevenly shaped stones and covered with a wire mesh grid on which was balanced a battered, blackened cooking pan.

As she worked, she glanced from time to time behind her to a purple, blue and white checked cotton hammock, recycled no doubt, from some item of household linen which was suspended between the door handle of a mustard coloured Renault saloon and the lower branches of a convenient tree. Inside, an infant slept.

I wandered on now in the direction my fellow travellers had taken, and followed a raucous screeching sound coming from the far end of the clearing. Here, the track petered out onto grass, then undergrowth, then denser forest. The disturbance was coming from my left. Was this some indignant primate, perhaps a bushy or a spider monkey who had taken exception to our passage through its territory or disturbed by the discordant clanging of hammers on different gauges of metal now emitting from the direction of the shipwrights? A few more steps, and peering upwards through the branches, all I could see was a lone oriole blackbird, perched on a bough with his head tilted downwards but with his beak firmly closed.

Lowering my gaze, I made out behind the thin tree trunks, the structure of another homestead, this one clearly inhabited and being vigorously defended by a pair of dove-grey mottled guinea fowl with their several tennis-ball sized, tawny coloured, powder-puff-shaped chicks teetering at their feet. Then, as if to assert its presence too, the oriole blackbird joined in the avian chorus with its own short, higher pitched and sweeter call.

The clock was ticking. It was almost time to leave and I was reluctant to set foot on the wooden boardwalk of the jetty that led from here out over the river and away. Was there anything more that I could possibly see? I took a few tentative steps onto the pier and glanced backwards to my right.

How could I have missed it? Lying half on its side, partly in the water and partly on the muddy embankment, like a huge animal shot for sport, was the enormous bulk of the strangest craft imaginable. Rising from a dark green hull, its three storeys of decks were covered in cracked, peeling paint in fading colours of sky-blue, daffodil yellow and white, while its convex sloping decks were totally enclosed round the entire superstructure with closely spaced slats.

In the foreground, several small boys were sitting on the muddy 'beach', intent on their game of making tiny canals by drawing their fingers through the soil at the water's edge and watching the river flow for a few seconds inland.

I decided to take the risk! 'Bom dia – desculpe,' I called down in greeting and to excuse myself for disturbing their vital work. 'O que e aquilo?' What is that? With shy smiles the replies came back in a babble as they all tried to speak at once, and with an accent and vocabulary that went far beyond my very basic Portuguese.

Seeing my lack of comprehension, the oldest of the mudlarks moved into the water and resorted to the delightfully basic form of communication that is mime. Making an undulating gesture with the palm of his hand across the surface of the water, he uttered one simple syllable that was soon taken up by the others as, amid gales of laughter, they chorused 'Moo, moo, moo, moo, moo'. Ah – it was a cattle transporter!

'Obrigado.' I was still chuckling as I strode purposefully down the jetty towards the small wooden huts of the pilot station at the far end, and still smiling as I stepped into the tender for the short trip back to the *Marco Polo*. It had been a glorious last five minutes in the Amazon.

by Sue Edwards (Cabin 423)

It started with diarrhoea, not a good sign. I went a few times in the night. And I'm still not right. Mark goes off on a tour of Macapá while I go to the doc's. I am now confined to my cabin with dodgy air-con and no means of escape.

The phone rings (to check I have come back) as soon as I get here, and then a steward arrived with a bottle of water, then lunch which is horrid, and also for the person who is not ill – Mark. When he returns from his trip he will be confined also for 48 hours from my last symptoms, that is from 8am yesterday.

I have an injection in my bum and am given two lots of tablets to be taken three times a day, and some Imodium to be taken every time I have a loose movement.

Mark returns and goes ballistic. The doc then arrives to see us and explains the problems of cabin-mates passing on infections. There are quite a few cases on board, and he only needs another two cabins to be sick in order to have to report the epidemic to the port authorities, who could impound the ship. So behave, or else!

Mark was not impressed with his cardboard dinner, which was very poor in quality and content. He rang twice to say I did not want any, but it came anyway. Twice he sent it away, but he regretted it after he had eaten his paltry offering.

We are knackered with doing nothing. Mark is champing at the bit at his lack of exercise and seizing up through lack of movement.

We played a few games of rummy.

'Don't Get Food Poisoning on a Cruise Ship' by Mark Edwards (Cabin 423)

Being a well person, to be quarantined for 60 hours gives time to ponder. How is *Marco Polo* actually controlling the spread of gastro-enteritis, over and above the normal level of cleaning and hand sanitisation?

I was ashore when my wife Sue was quarantined. On returning to the ship, a crewman leapt out and squirted my hands as I was about to hand my card to security. That meant the only place to put my card was between my teeth whilst I rubbed my hands. That card then contaminated the security man and several following passengers.

After my first in-cabin meal, no one came to collect the tray, so I rang Reception, who told me to put it outside the door. I replied, 'No, my cabin is quarantined'. I had told them the cabin number, so obviously they don't know which cabins are quarantined, and this was confirmed by later room-service visits. When the steward eventually collected the tray, he held the big red bag open and I tipped the whole lot in, tray and all.

That's good practice, but he had no protection of apron, mask or gloves. That's bad practice.

What would have happened if I had followed Reception's advice? Had our cabin steward spotted it, she would have instructed me to take it back in. She had already told us, 'Nothing outside the door.' But what if she wasn't there?

As it was a 48-hour quarantine, we expected that our bathroom would be disinfected. In an attack of gastro-enteritis, it is the toilet and wash-basin that are overused and carry the largest infective load of bugs. Nothing at all happened in the first critical 48 hours. We kept everything washed down with soap and water, using 'progressive dilution technique', a well-documented way of getting the infective agent under the 'minimum infective dose'. Not that there was any advice from staff.

When room service do appear, aproned at last, I keep being asked to sign the chitties with their pen. So that's another four crew members carrying our potential contamination. One stewardess, straight from the Captain's Club, actually walked completely into the cabin and placed my beer on the table.

After 48 hours we had run out of towels, tissues and loo rolls. I stuck my head out and called to our cabin steward (there isn't any other way of summoning her). She appeared, properly protected with apron, mask and gloves, with her red bags for everything coming out. Carefully not entering the cabin, she passed towels and loo roll in to me. She will come back later to clean at 1.15pm, so that we are the last cabin of her shift. She scoots straight into the bathroom and starts to clean. Everything is well washed down using the shower hose.

Sue asks if she can have a cloth and disinfectant to do the major surfaces, light switches, drawer fronts in the cabin itself, and is told no. Too late, as Sue has reached in and grabbed the necessary cloth and disinfectant. 'Don't let anyone see you,' was the worried instruction from our steward.

Why not, as sensible practice is to have her inside our cabin for as little as possible? The only thing that our cabin steward missed was to wash and then disinfect the door handles. Without it, that will just help the nurse carry our contamination around the ship.

At the end of our quarantine period we were expecting our cabin to be 'deep cleaned', but it wasn't. We were just released with verbal instructions that we must not eat in Marco's Bistro and told that the instructions were written in our release letter. This advised that we avoid Marco's and suggested we might like to avail ourselves of complimentary room service for breakfast. Sensibly, they wanted to keep us away from any buffet

service for 48 hours, but somehow couldn't bring themselves to positively say so.

I took my library book back as soon as I could, asking about quarantined books.

'They never come back,' says the librarian.

'This one has.'

'It will be quarantined for a further 72 hours.'

'But only if you are told about it!'

So why are there no sensible written instructions for quarantined passengers during and after their confinement? Why do Reception and, by
extension, room service, not know which cabins are quarantined?

The level of general cleaning within the ship did step up, but there
does not seem to be crew-wide understanding of how gastro-enteritis will
spread by touching contaminated objects. The ship must have luck on its
side, as the carriage of infection from quarantined cabins is all done by
crew and not the passengers.

by Clive Leatherdale (Cabin 725)

Deck music has turned to Enya. I wonder if they will play her *Orinoco Flow*
to remind us of South America's second great river.

I heard this morning about the 'trifle woman'. The cook in Marco's
Bistro had prepared a tray of trifle, decorated with four cherries in each
corner. This woman picked up a serving spoon and plucked out the four
corners, plus the cherries, leaving the rest.

Macapá was busy, prosperous, civilised and livable. Wide streets, clear
road signs, neat white kerbs. I saw two Mormons, the first I had encountered in Brazil. One was Brazilian, who could not speak English, the
other American, who could not speak Portuguese. He told me there were
fourteen of them in Macapá alone, and he had been there six months
already, which was a long posting.

Macapá has a pier, like Southend, with a wee train, like Southend,
though it is not clear if Macapá's train ever moves.

Wandering the side streets in search of anything unusual, I came upon
a place that exceeded expectations. At first sight it appeared to be a grassy
garden selling kiddies' old clothes, toys, dolls. A few women sorted items
for display. A glance at the wall behind showed I had discovered, loosely
translated, a Refuge for Victims of Domestic Violence.

I hesitated, for by definition men were the cause of whatever distress
lay beyond those walls. But I did not hesitate for long, because I was
warmly beckoned within. The door gave onto a waiting room, inside
which was a female security guard and a receptionist busily taking down

a young woman's details in a hand-written ledger. The walls were plastered with graphic posters which hardly needed translating, such as: 'Violência contra a mulher – Denuncie' (Violence against women – Denounce).

I wondered what facilities were on offer, for this was a spacious building with plenty of rooms. Doors were opened to show interview rooms, medical rooms, and at the far end what served as an auditorium. I was shown in to find about twenty women, young and old, seated around the walls, facing inwards. Most had a notepad in their hand. One end of the room housed a projector screen. The lights dimmed and I was invited to sit through a presentation on the whys and wherefores of domestic violence in Macapá.

The reason for such an establishment is not hard to explain. The police turn a blind eye. They side with the men. The brochures that were pressed upon me emphasised various types of therapy for various types of abuse. These ranged from the obvious, physical assault, to the far from obvious. Under the category 'moral violence' could be found what is best translated as character assassination, spreading lies about a woman by others.

The list of women's issues catered for was long and extensive. Women have the right to choose how many children they have, not to be forced into having sex, or be denied their sexual orientation. Breast examinations are best performed one week after a period. Counselling and legal assistance are available to all, and do not delay, victims will be seen immediately, today!

The Centre for Female Victims of Domestic Violence in Macapá (Clive Leatherdale)

DAY 26. AT SEA

'A relaxing day at sea, navigating our way out of the Amazon and into the Atlantic Ocean. Did you know? Since leaving Tilbury we have consumed 4,325kgs of potatoes, 37,276 eggs, 2,170kgs of poultry, 3,677kgs of meat.'

'Banned from Brazil' by Dianne Hall (Cabin 474)
With some uncertainty my husband, Rod, and I had boarded the tender which was to allow us to set foot in Brazil. Our fellow passengers shared no similar uncertainty, but they weren't Australians who had flown halfway round the world to join this cruise, and they didn't need visas to visit Brazil.

We had originally booked on the *Marco Polo*'s sister ship, the *Ocean Countess*, which was leaving for an identical cruise to the Amazon three weeks after the *Marco Polo*. Before Christmas we were notified that the *Ocean Countess* voyage had been cancelled. We were offered a full refund or a transfer to the earlier *Marco Polo*. We chose the transfer, but then realised that we no longer had the ten working days required by the Brazilian Embassy in Australia to issue visas. We were left with an unenviable choice; stay at home and lose thousands of dollars, or soldier on and risk being denied entry to Brazil. We took the plunge.

The officials on *Marco Polo* seemed confident there wouldn't be a problem, and no Brazilian immigration officers boarded the ship before our first port of Icoaraci. Once on shore, our trepidation evaporated. We enjoyed the life and colour of this outlying suburb of Belem, congratulating ourselves that our fears seemed groundless and that we would be free to visit other Brazilian ports. Ironically, as it turned out, we seemed to be the only passengers who succeeded in extracting Brazilian reals from a local ATM.

When immigration officers finally boarded to check passengers' documents, uncertainty again crept in. The ship's officials again reassured us that all would be well, so we took the plunge and booked a series of shore excursions.

That evening at dinner, our cabin number was called, inviting us to Reception. Our hearts fluttered when told we had been summoned by immigration officers. What followed left us shaken and emotionally drained, and with a greater understanding of the angst suffered by asylum seekers.

We were led to a side-room in which three Brazilian officials had passengers' passports racked in front of them. A deal of conversation took place in Portuguese, and then one officer announced in English that we would not be allowed ashore. We stood there like errant schoolchildren in the headmaster's office, attempting to put our case, but to no avail. We were bustled out unceremoniously and abandoned to our fate.

Stretching before us were ten days as prisoners on board *Marco Polo*. From that point on, our plight was ignored by the ship's officials, who seemed to avert their eyes whenever we loomed into view.

Our fellow passengers were wonderfully sympathetic, but we grew weary of explaining our situation and answering the ubiquitous question, 'Going ashore today?'

Tendering days were the hardest, as we floated in the middle of the Amazon with small towns tantalisingly close across the water. In port it seemed easier to bear, as we were close enough to catch the flavour of the port and see the locals coming and going about their business. The weather also helped, as seeing others setting off on excursions in torrential rain failed to arouse our envy. Nevertheless, we often felt lonely and isolated, unable to share conversations about shore experiences or compare notes on the horrors of particular excursions.

It took all our internal resources to remain cheerful and positive in the face of our incarceration, but there have been some positives. Our cabin has not become a Chinese laundry draped with drenched clothes; we have experienced the Amazon without the souring experiences of beggars, muggings and filthy streets. We have had ample time to observe dolphins at play, birds soaring and diving, and the amazingly varied river traffic. Even the changing cloud patterns and the ominous darkening of the sky heralding an approaching storm served to fill our days.

Our feelings on our last night in Brazilian waters were mixed; sadness at leaving the mighty Amazon behind and exhilaration that we were now free to be like all the other passengers. The open sea and the Îles du Salut beckoned and we were more than eager to set foot on terra firma again, even though it seemed like rough justice that our first port of call should be a former French penal colony.

by Mave Eaton (Cabin 616)
We are en route to the Îles du Salut, so this very wet and windy day is at sea. Disgruntled passengers search for empty chairs in the lounge.

Interim bills had been delivered to cabins in the night: perhaps more bottles of expensive cheap wine have been ordered than they realised. A queue forms at Reception as passengers argue over perceived errors. Two cabins down from us, we see staff with masks, rubber gloves and hospital gowns pulling all the bedding outside. Food is delivered on trays and handed across the threshold. We fear the norovirus or some other bug has struck. This ship is fanatical in its use of alcoholic gel: the cleaning never stops but this is a virulent germ. I rush in and scrub my hands.

by Caroline Clifford (Cell 468)
On a day at sea, the highlight (apart from the anticipation of reading the dinner menu and salivating over the dishes presented 'Japanese style') is the daily programme. Once my day is planned around the lectures (which fortunately clash with the exercise sessions), I can schedule visits to the Waldorf restaurant.

I haven't missed a lecture to date, but singing sea shanties doesn't hit the spot. Besides, I remind myself that I can't sing a note. Tom Lehrer and Allan Sherman at 4pm – now you're talking – with lecturer Stephen Smith, alias Harold Bishop. That does hit the spot.

But that's hardly enough to fill the spare time between meals. So I read the programme again, and again, and yet again.

I remembered Richard Sykes mentioning the ever-increasing 'kind reminders' for inconsiderate passengers to desist from doing something or other. But do they apply to me? I haven't yet occupied a table at Marco's Bistro, so 'vacating my table swiftly' doesn't apply. And I've heard the Dutch passengers describing how long it takes the Brits to dunk a teabag, so I won't be using the tea and coffee station. I have not, and probably won't, use the jacuzzi, so also not applicable. As for reserving sunbeds, a chance would be a fine thing, but I am planning to take Richard's advice and store one overnight in our cabin.

But, yes, I put my hand up to 'power walking' (if you can call it that) but only once did I do it before 8am, the earliest time allowed. I did feel guilty as I ducked down a flight of stairs when I saw an irate passenger, in his pyjamas, remonstrating with a sturdy and determined lady walker. I pretended to look for dolphins. I saw the same man later, now dressed, attacking the poor receptionist, describing his disturbed sleep and demanding that an announcement be made over the public address system. I ducked out again.

I have already identified today's deliberate mistakes in the programme, but there's nothing crucial, since we won't be tendering today. Some might, however, argue that the sea is far from the 'calm' stated.

And then there's news about Valentine's Day. I'm not anticipating 'Wooden Roses' but James is writing me a poem. I had a quick sneak at his masterpiece when he was in the bathroom – if he does enter this into the ship's competition, he will be paying for a long, long time.

by Lizzie Mayes (Cabin 494)
So the Amazon adventure is over and we set off on the next phase of the cruise. I am past caring now. We are definitely in the minority, being virgin cruisers. People's faces still glaze over when we respond to the question of how many cruises have we done. I suppose it cramps their style if they can't compare previous experiences.

Some statistics in our daily hymn sheet for today – since leaving Tilbury we have consumed 4,325kgs of potatoes, 37,276 eggs, 2,170kgs of poultry and 3,677kgs of meat. They didn't mention fish, but as it is on the menu twice a day we must have eaten several thousand kilos of that, too. I think that 20 per cent of the people eat 80 per cent of the food. It's astonishing to see what some people manage to get on a plate – I saw one man with three fried eggs, two sausages, bacon, beans, hash browns, mushrooms and several slices of toast at breakfast one day.

We saw the captain for the first time for days today. I said to him that I thought he had jumped ship as we hadn't seen him around, and he explained he hadn't been off the bridge for seven days coming back down the Amazon. Even with the pilot on board, it is a treacherous journey, with shallow waters and sandbanks.

by Sue Edwards (Cabin 423)
No gut problems during the night. At 7.30am Mark rings for two cups of tea – 45 minutes later they arrive. No breakfast yet. What more quarantine delights do we have in store? I only had a banana last night.

Mark does some basic exercises on the floor between the beds. He risks injuring himself on the furniture or walls. Methinks the gym is looking more enticing than ever to us.

This incarceration reminds me of when I was in hospital after having Gemma by caesarean section 33 years ago and I was kept in for ten days. It was a great summer and eventually I checked myself out. But I don't think this prison allows that, as there is nowhere to check out to. I hope the nurse comes soon and declares me fit and safe to mingle with the rest of the ship. I could always wear a note saying 'unclean'. I am surprised there is not a red cross on the door.

I will soon be driven bonkers by the irritation of Mark doing step-ups on the sill to the bathroom. Can't one just die in peace? If I were really ill, I would be seriously peed off instead of moderately cross. He is like a novelty ticking clock, step up, onto the metal sill, step down, onto the carpet, tick-tock, tick-tock, every second. Oh, silence. 'That's five minutes,' he says. It really seemed like fifteen to me. Mark goes for a shower.

Would you believe it, breakfast arrives at 8.45. I am a 'sick' person, so I get oatmeal, two bananas, two slices of horrid dry toast, and tea – no milk provided. It's a good job we have some from the canteen. Mark gets no choice either – sausage, scrambled egg and beans, and dry toast – no nanas, butter or jam.

Along with breakfast, we also have our interim ship's bill to peruse. It's a good job we are confined, as the last one took hours to check.

Mark says it is like being back at school, but his school sanitarium was better, as you could walk around. Our only highlight to look forward to is *Chicago* or *Chocolat* on our cabin TV.

At 12.30 comes lunch – ugh – consomme and fish. Mark has a piece of meat and veg and jelly, and gives me his jelly.

The seas are still heaving and, if I start to vomit, it will be with seasickness. I continue with 'my notes from a small room'. Mark gets a choice for his dinner, but having a choice means a long delay, 30 more minutes. Mark is pacing like a caged lion. He can't be hungry but he says he is just bored.

For dinner I get the compulsory invalid's broth. It is served in a party paper pudding dish wrapped in tin foil. It never stays solely in the dish, so when it arrives some has escaped into the tray. It is easier to drink this than slurp it from the plastic spoon. Pudding is, as usual, a banana, of which several are now piled up on the bedside desk.

I hope this is my last experience of sickness (not that I feel hungry) but it is making me feel worse.

by Clive Leatherdale (Cabin 725)

I ask Ben and Miep (a Dutch couple) why no one can name six famous Belgians, when almost every Dutchman you can think of is either a brilliant painter or a fantastic footballer. After all, Belgium and Holland, are neighbours and similar in size and in population. The spread of talent should be equal. Ben replies with this solemn story:

A Dutchman, Frenchmen and Belgian are discussing their daughter's education. The Dutchman peers inside his daughter's satchel while looking for a pen and finds three packets of fags. 'I didn't even know she smoked,' he remarked. The Frenchman looks inside his daughter's desk looking for a ruler and finds three bottles of whiskey. 'I didn't even know she drank,' he said. The Belgian opens up his daughter's pencil case while looking for a pencil sharpener and finds three condoms. He exploded: 'I didn't even know she had a dick!'

I have discovered an intriguing couple, he a retired Dagenham car worker, she a mental health social worker. They met through a dating website long before the days of the internet. She had studied theology, considered herself an agnostic, but had discovered so many 'guardian angels' on this ship – by which she meant supportive friends – that she yearned for a leap of faith.

There are some serious personal dislikes festering onboard, on this our first full day at sea after leaving Brazil.

Looking across from Île Royale to Devil's Island. The torments experienced here, and related so graphically in *Papillon*, are so recent that traipsing around the prison cells and infirmary left many feeling deeply uncomfortable (Clive Leatherdale)

Day 27. Îles du Salut

'Until the 1940s the muggy, oppressive climate and malaria-ridden forests of French Guiana were considered the perfect way to punish criminals and undesirables from Mother France. From 1848 the region was used as a penal colony until its abolition in 1948.'

by Caroline Clifford (Cell 468)

Great excitement on deck when some 'twitchers' spotted a female frigate bird flying over the ship. All too much for me before breakfast.

Fortified and satisfied after my salmon course, I collected tender ticket 'C' from the ever-smiling Susan [McKinlay, ship librarian]. In a very efficient manner we were en route to Île Royale a mere ten minutes later. Armed with a map, I set off to circuit the island, walking as far and as fast as possible, and hopefully to spot some wildlife. On landing, however, the heavens opened and my tired umbrella closed, inside out.

The earth track passed through coconut palms and mango trees. Climbing up the hill, I was distracted by the sign, 'Beware of the Caiman.' I hovered around the pond and a sizeable iguana posed for a picture. True to form, my camera revealed 'low batteries'. Past the cemetery, by now the proverbial 'drowned rat', I watched an agouti scurry across the track in a business-like manner – things to do, places to go, before the mass of human passengers arrived.

By the time I had rounded the island I was a strong contender for the wet t-shirt competition. James, I found waiting at the pump house. He was itching to point out a brand new Danfloss pump ready for installation, and the generator house next door – all in excellent condition. 'No expense spared,' he explained – 'all thanks to the EU'. His excuse for sheltering, not walking, was that 'like Everest, it would be showing off to climb up twice'. He had been chatting with a French-speaking visitor who mistook him for a workman.

The 'very efficient' tender service dissolved into chaos when two posh catamarans took our place at the pontoon, discharging French Guianese weekenders with a plethora of humungous cool-boxes. Tender rage was rife, horns were sounded, and our poor passengers, waiting to disembark, got soaked – in sweat, not rain. But they still took time to snigger at my drowned rat impersonation. I was more than happy to see the rain return with a vengeance.

James continued my compulsory education by pointing out that a new set of injectors for the Volvo Penta engine would cure the tender's black smoke problem, and that tender No 06JZ7 should be consigned to the scrap yard. He wasn't too happy about the gangway stairs to the ship either, which he said had seen about 50 years of intensive wear.

There was a grin on the face of the tender crewman who pulled down a tarpaulin, giving James and the last remaining dry passenger an unscheduled shower.

'Text between Papillon fans' by Marion Cox (Cabin 619)
Text: 'Here in Paradise on Devil's Island. 80 degrees. Not seen Dustin Hoffman feeding the pigs yet.'
Reply: 'Here in Canada its minus 35. Hell! Are you getting back by making a raft and jumping in after the seventh wave?'
Reply: 'Six days at sea coming up. Force 4. May need more coconuts on the raft.'

by Lizzie Mayes (Cabin 494)
We awoke to find ourselves moored in the midst of three lush green islands with white surf beating their shores. We were tendered off the ship as the tropical rain came down relentlessly.

It felt strange and eerie that these islands were the scene of so much tragedy but are now tranquil and a wildlife haven for monkeys, agoutis, humming birds, macaws and lizards and iguanas. We also saw turtles swimming off the island.

It was hard to imagine what it must have been like as a mosquito-infested prison. Some of the buildings were classically beautiful. It felt strangely sterile, as there are no children living on the islands (just a baby and a couple of toddlers). Children were such a large part of the Amazon experience. I suppose this is because there wouldn't be enough of them to sustain a school.

The names of prisoners are listed in the church and there is a moving cemetery where many children of prison workers are buried. A party of French tourists were on the island. I thought, as probably most passengers did, that I must reread *Papillon*.

Late in the evening, while we were talking about our visit on deck, a rank odour engulfed us, and we took off like 100-metre sprinters. The ship was clearly discharging something into the ocean and I promptly discharged my dinner onto the deck.

by Jill Crocker (Cabin 514)

Steve [Ragnall] keeps going on about this sea-shanty lecture he wants to do. I am sick of hearing about it, actually. I can't see how it will work. Anyway, I'll leave him to it.

The Îles du Salut are lovely. We took no coats, since we thought we'd seen the last of the rain when we tendered ashore (strange word that, nothing 'tender' about the process at all). Wrong. We got soaked through to the underwear – mention of which highlights my relief when Steve volunteered to launder his own underpants, our combined efforts in this activity reducing the company's profit margins even further.

by Dinah Read (Cabin 422)

I went ashore at about 9am for two or three hours. It was showery, to say the least, but after all, that is normal in these latitudes. Île Royale was a curious antithesis of a place, quite beautiful – the ideal of a tropical island, coconut palms and mangos and papayas and hibiscus, and all kinds of luxurious foliage and flowers from bougainvillea to shrubs with sprays of bright pink flowers and their attendant humming birds. I have seen them in Canada, too, and it is scarcely credible that they make that epic migration on such tiny wings. But then so do monarch butterflies! There were parrots, too, and surprisingly charming cane rats the size of cats.

And yet, and yet, this place was a harsh nightmare of a penal colony. How could such a paradise double as a place of dread, where men, innocent or guilty of some terrible crime, many of them insane or sinking into insanity over the long years, were confined in cramped, iron-barred cells in unbearable heat and humidity? Many of them awaited death by execution. Others simply died, half-starved as they were, and were often fed to the patrolling sharks. Even the guards had much to fear, malaria and yellow fever were endemic. There are three cemeteries here and one of them was for children. At its functional best (!) there was a church, a hospital, a school and a lighthouse, still standing. What a paradox.

by Tim Major (Cabin 469)

At our final tender operation, at the Îles du Salut, our crew tried to capitalise on their last chance to cause accidents by standing resolutely and unsupported in front of the best handholds and insisting on taking passengers by the hand to help them in and out of the tender. Knowing that there was no way that a man half my size, standing on an unstable platform, and not holding on, would be of any help in stopping me from falling should I lose my balance, I was equally insistent on waiting for them to get out of the way of the firm handhold they were obstructing so that I could ensure my own safety. They did yield politely once they worked out why I was waiting.

The clear sea water was so pleasant that there was no fun in dousing us, so the coxswain had to satisfy himself by gunning the tender away from the pier and enveloping a nearby French catamaran in a thick black cloud of diesel smoke. Its crew luckily took this in good part, exhibiting a tolerance worthy of the entente cordiale, possibly because they watched as our coxswain proceeded to race after the black cloud so that we, too, could enjoy it.

For me, I was glad to be back on board safely after my last tender experience, and would have helped myself to a celebratory cordial had the antibiotics I was on not precluded such self-indulgence.

'Where the Devil are we?' by Kay Rainsley (Cabin 543)
Isles of Salvation or Isles of the Devil? Rarely can a group of islands have excited two such diametrically opposed labels.

Barely a league in size, these three verdant outposts of neighbouring French Guiana appear like mini-Edens, replete with a pleasing array of flora and fauna. Agoutis scurry beneath the trees, running and foraging in family groups. Drooping, dripping, fronds of coconut palms line the walkways; there is no motorised traffic save for the quad bike used by the resident police. We circumnavigate the largest island in twenty minutes at a leisurely pace in the pouring rain.

A reservoir, once providing drinking water for thousands of inhabitants, is choked with water hyacinths and tropical plants. A caiman relaxes in the warm water, its snout fixed open. Along the surrounding dry stone walls, soaking up the sun between downpours, is a pair of good-sized iguanas.

Macaws scream as they wheel across the sky, flashes of red, blue and green coming in to land. Cicadas chitter and monkeys chatter, thrilling the visitors by coming within camera range. Humming birds sip nectar from the yellow-petalled blooms and a red butterfly displays its wings in a kapok tree. Wings of freedom. I think of that other Papillon and his stay in the former French penal colony. Leg irons, chains, harsh stone walls with rigid rules and heavy doors. Forced labour in the hostile jungle, ferocious fevers and inadequate diet led to a survival rate of just 10 per cent at one point.

Incarceration, insanity and guillotine prevailed. We gaze across from Île Royale at the two smaller islands, Île St Joseph and Île de Diable, two benign-looking patches of land anchored in a clear but treacherous ocean. We see the remains of the tower which was used to jerk provisions across to one of the islands by means of a cable. We swim in the sea, descending the steps hewn out of the rock and scattering hundreds of sea bugs in the process. The sea heaves and I remember Steve McQueen in his final bid for escape astride a sack of coconuts. Then I see him in *The Great Escape* and I think of how he sought to assuage his misery at being confined. The crumbling remains of the butchery can be clearly seen close to the water's edge.

The walls of the solitary confinement cells and the hospital stand firm, although some roofs have collapsed. We gaze at the remnants of harsh metal bars and cold stone barriers which were home to the unfortunate inmates. Tiny rectangles pierced high walls, too high to afford a view and too small to afford much refreshment from the relentless sun. Heavy doors with peepholes hung crazily on tired, rusting hinges. The spaces were stifling, claustrophobic, fetid, dark and gloomy. I was glad to get out after just a few minutes.

Amazingly the church was well appointed and adorned with the usual paraphernalia. Inside, a selection of postcards designed by inmates gave their interpretation of island life as a captive. It stands as a symbol of hope or despair.

In a bizarre twist of fate, nuns moved to the island from mainland French Guiana to escape yellow fever, giving it its former name, whilst French prisoners sought to escape from the island.

by Sue Edwards (Cabin 423)
Breakfast included porridge for me and a banana – not too bad – and a cup of tea. Mark gets croissants and dried apricots. We say we do not want bread as we are hoping the nurse will sign us off quarantine when she arrives this morning.

No such luck. She says she might tonight around 7pm. I have now been confined for two full days, and it seems like longer. By 7pm tonight it will be nearly 60 hours of quarantine with *no* symptoms.

So we cannot go to see Îles du Salut, as the ship leaves there at 3pm. Mark types his complaint letters. We can't even go upstairs and send emails.

Mark orders a beer – fortunately our invalid lunch does not arrive and we eat half a tin of dried apricots and half a banana.

The nurse comes at 7.30 this evening and does not release us in time to eat at Marco's Bistro, at which Mark goes ballistic. We eventually go to the Waldorf instead and get fed immediately. It is so good to eat tasty food. Why couldn't they serve smoked ham salad in our cabin? It was our first proper food for five days.

by Clive Leatherdale (Cabin 725)

I had always admired the writing of *Papillon*, so it was a treat to visit the scene of the action. Of the three islands constituting Îles du Salut, only one, Île Royale, the largest, is inhabited, part living museum, part up-market resort. I found the old cells, nine to each side, separated by a narrow corridor. Papillon, who was short, measured the length of his cell at five paces. For me, very tall, it was just three and a half.

In the middle of Île Royale was a hotel-cum-restaurant-cum-bar-cum-tourist shop, which meant you could buy drinks and enjoy them on a terrace overlooking Devil's Island, which was a vouyeristically disagreeable sensation.

I did not wish to leave, and caught the penultimate tender back. There must have been a swell, for our tender crashed about and smashed into the ship. When it reached the stairway it was not securely tied and passengers could easily have fallen into the gap when getting off.

In the evening I presented myself at the medical centre, with luck to be signed off after my kidney infection. Dr Papadakis reassured me that everything was now normal. As I got up to leave, I asked him if he knew about my book. He did. There are few secrets on this ship. I badly wanted to arrange an interview with him, and to my surprise he said he badly wanted to tell his story, as nobody really appreciates the conditions under which he works.

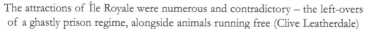

The attractions of Île Royale were numerous and contradictory – the left-overs of a ghastly prison regime, alongside animals running free (Clive Leatherdale)

DAY 28. AT SEA

'Susan, the librarian, would like to hear from anyone interested in speaking at a Royal Navy and Nautical Get-Together on the 10th of February. Please see Susan during the library's opening hours.'

by Caroline Clifford (Cabin 468)

I'm always the last to know about 'ship's gossip', but this morning there was a distinct air of mystery.

Next door are not dead. Last night there was coughing aft, as well as forward. James, bless him – just when the snoring abates, a loud piercing cough fills the cabin. I went out for fresh air.

On the aft staircase there was a man who appeared to be dressed in a giant condom. He wielded a pressure wash and mumbled something from behind his mask. Sanitation was the order of the day, and despite the clocks changing yet again, breakfast was eerily quiet.

When Patrik came to sort out the cabin he was still wearing apron and mask, and still refused to say how many passengers had contracted the dreaded lurgi. Several people are spreading the rumour that the ship will not be allowed to berth in Tobago because of 'sickness' on board. Hopefully this bears no more resemblance to the truth than the rumour I tried to start that we would all get refunds for the miserable tour in Manaus.

There are certainly a few more damaged limbs on show, presumably victims of the North East Trade swell that has hit us again.

And then there was the mystery of the disappearing steak tartare. I was over the moon to see it on the dinner menu, but by dinner time it was not there. James said I was hallucinating, but later 'Stalin' confirmed that I was not – 'it had been a mistake'. Raw steak is probably not the ideal diet for sick people. Other cruise lines allow you to sign a book if you request raw or 'blue' meat, but sadly that's not an option here.

Fact, not gossip. Tony Rice [lecturer] was 'incarcerated' (his word, not mine) in his cabin with his poorly wife. He was told he would be arrested if he tried to go ashore in Île Royale. One must assume that the other 'disappearing' passengers are confined to quarters.

by Lizzie Mayes (Cabin 494)

I'm beginning to totally relax now. Somehow it is a relief that the Amazon part of the trip, with all the expectation, the highs and lows, is over, and we can just get down to the business of enjoying whatever is thrown at us. I love being at sea and not having the pressure to decide what we will do on these oh-so-short times ashore. There will be no more organised shore excursions for us after the glass-bottomed boat in Tobago – no more herding. I wonder if the tour excursions are a branch of Cruise & Maritime, which would explain why there is so little help and information for those who prefer to go it alone. Again, perhaps this is our lack of cruise experience and that most cruisers are happy to be herded and have the security blanket of the organised excursion.

There is more talk about the number of people who have gone down with this bug. Also there are more slings and bandages every day. I don't envy the ship's doctor, what with so many old and clearly – judging by the numbers of pills taken at breakfast – not very fit people on board. I guess he can't take any chances.

I am intrigued by the Probus Meeting in the Palm Lounge – am I just plain ignorant or are they really an organisation lobbying for people to travel by bus? I will have to google them when I get home. I see they are getting a Royal Navy & Nautical meeting set up – I bet Dick will avoid that one. Sitting in the Palm Lounge, I was amazed by how many people were ordering their official photos – like £100 a time. I have to admit I have been avoiding them like the devil, as I don't want them to waste their film on us. We will never be tempted to buy even one! We went to the 'Caribbean Show' to get in the mood and afterwards went 'out through those doors' or was it 'those doors' to get some much needed fresh air on deck.

by Margaret Atkinson (Cabin 504)

A day at sea. The weather appears to be more settled today, but with a huge swell. The ship was rocking a bit and it was hard work walking to the front of the bridge deck. We looked at the wide, wide sea; just sea and sky, blue sky. Planes there were none, ships there were none, but flying fish aplenty. The sunlight glistened on their bodies as they flew through the air. As we continued to watch we noticed a brown patch. Immediately, we thought it was some algae. We looked again. No, it wasn't algae. Surprise, surprise, it was a brown turtle. Where was it going, swimming alone in the opposite direction? What a moment to be without a camera.

Bernie the Bag drew one's attention today. 'Bernie the Bag' is our nickname for a passenger with a distinctive walk. He reminds me of a past tennis player. He has an almost constant companion, a companion in the form of a red and white plastic carrier bag. He is seen here and there, on deck, on tour, in the lounge. Where Bernie goes, the bag goes.

It has been said that strange things happen at sea. Happen they do. Happen even at the Sunday morning church 'field service'. The pianist was practising the tune, *Austria*, for the hymn *Glorious Things of Thee are Spoken* when she was approached by no less than Bernie the Bag. The conversation could not be heard.

Before the service began the reverend [Haines] made a comment that we may not always like some things in our lives. The hymn tune is also the same tune as used for the German National Anthem. As Christian people we must rise above the past conflicts of nations. The congregation stood up and the hymn was sung. Only Bernie the Bag remained seated.

We are now headed for Tobago. Pity that the head chef presented us with an Indonesian dinner. And that was today, that was.

by Sue Edwards (Cabin 423)

We can't find any loungers, so resort to chairs. These make my neck sore, so I lie down on the deck. Mark says I've been getting funny looks. One chap said, very concernedly, that he thought I'd fallen off the chair. I pointed out that I hadn't had a drink yet. Mark still paces round the deck like a frustrated, aged hamster.

I spoke to Tony Rice after he had given his lecture on 'Beneath the Waves'. He, too, had been locked up for 48 hours. His wife had had a bout of vomiting, and no one was telling him anything either. He thought it ironic that we could not escape *to* Îles du Salut, and had asked what would happen if they went ashore despite their quarantine. He was told they would be arrested. Irony, irony, irony.

We took our dinner wine up to the pool deck afterwards, but it was quite breezy. My wine glass sailed across the table on a film of rain drops, but I successfully caught it before it went over the edge.

'Who's Pinched my Palate?' by Mark Edwards (Cabin 423)

Why does all the food seem bland? Why have I lost all enjoyment of food, and am only eating because it is a sensible thing to do? We started the cruise thinking that the food was quite reasonable, given the size of the catering problem. Dinners in the Wardolf restaurant were about the right size, and the flavours and textures were pretty well balanced. We don't really do lunch, so that was something out of the Bistro, as and when, depending on the amount of exercise.

Obviously the ship restocked in Europe, and everything is pretty fresh. As we go through the cruise we start to lose the enjoyment of eating, but I can't really put a finger on it. Is it because it is the same formula all the time, but with more and more coming out of the freezer? Are they running short of some ingredients? I mean, why serve roast pork with rice? It doesn't work, and more and more daft things like that start appearing.

Is it the blandness of the food that we never noticed before, or has it actually lost its oomph? Was it the incarceration in our cabin, eating off the cheapest of cardboard plates, so that everything tasted of cardboard? One thing is for certain, the Dutch are going to be happy with the cheese, as it is their type. Where are the English cheeses? They live quite happily in our freezer at home, so why not in *Marco Polo*'s?

Four weeks in, and Sue and I both suddenly commented about the food. It was obvious that we were delaying eating at every occasion. It wasn't the sea, because we hadn't left the Caribbean. Have we been away too long, and are missing the normal delights of cooking at home, with all the smells and anticipation that goes with it? Or the ability, if neither of us is really hungry, to have something small but really tasty? Or something oh so simple – fresh raw carrots, peppers and hummous? Now there's a thing: all the ingredients of hummous are storable, why don't they make some, or is it too exotic? Have we got stuck in the bland tourist food, that sounds grand, but is organised to please the peasant masses, whose ageing palates don't taste anymore? After all, my mother's palate deteriorated very badly in the last five years of her life, and so did her cooking.

Another strange thing, normally a wee drink before a meal wakes up my appetite. Nothing doing at the moment. And there again, as an exercise freak, I normally need to eat after training, wolf it down, and although the volume of training is high, I'm not interested in eating.

Please can I get home now, and let that enjoyment of food return. Where are the Nigel Slater cookbooks?

by Kay Rainsley (Cabin 543)
I spoke to 'V' – her father had committed suicide at 58. When 'V' got to 58, she wondered whether she would want to. He had left no note, no explanation, nothing.

She is now 81 and thoroughly enjoying life – determined to live life to the full. Life's too short to moan. She worries about her grandson. He has two small children, two and six months, and he has bought a wolf! Apparently it's a third generation domestic wolf, and cost him £700. She doesn't trust it with the children. She says people value pets too much, higher than family. She can't understand people who won't leave their pets behind to go on holiday.

by Pat Pickering (Cabin 440)
If you were to take a colossal knife and slice the *Marco Polo* vertically down its entire length to create a cross-section, like some illustration from a child's picture book showing the workings of Cook's *Endeavour* or Nelson's *Victory*, you would see us all scurrying around like ants, moving from deck to deck, area to area, room to room, and perhaps hovering for a time in one location or another before scuttling off again, driven by our social needs and interests.

It's a Sunday at sea. At home you would probably have a late, leisurely breakfast, browse through the Sunday papers, flick through the colour supplements until lunchtime, go for a long walk or a drive or just potter in the garden. But on board it's far more challenging – you have to make difficult decisions. Anyone for the quick quiz in the Captain's Club or a session of bridge in the Nansen room? There's a craft session with Pam here later for those who like to get creative with cardboard, paper, scissors and glue.

Maybe you need some exercise after all those desserts you've indulged in, persuading yourself that the buoyancy at sea cancels out the calories. There's aerobics for oldies with Louise in Scott's Bar, or carpet bowling amidships on Baltic Deck, but that's not recommended if the ship begins to roll!

If you've come cruising for pure relaxation, perhaps the perfumed ambiance of the Beauty Parlour on Columbus Deck is more to your taste, or one of those enormous, comfortable leather armchairs in the library. Susan the librarian is quite used to seeing readers dropping off for 40 winks, and tolerates gentle snoring.

No? Have you tried Steve Ragnall's sea-shanty choir, warming up now in the Palm Garden on Pacific Deck? Tony Rice is lecturing on 'Creatures of The Ocean – Part Two', with his usual enthusiasm and amazing photographs, if you can get yourself to the Marco Polo Lounge by ten o'clock.

A word of caution, however. If you arrive too early you'll have to kill time in 'heathen's corner' while the reverend brings morning worship to a close. There really is something to suit all tastes, but if none of that appeals, you could always just saunter around looking for familiar faces or like-minded groups with whom to pass the time of day in idle gossip. Where to look for them?

You could head off up to the 'Hook of Holland', outdoors on Amundsen Deck, starboard side, where the Dutch smokers generally gather for a first cigarette of the day, or you could go higher still to the 'toast rack' on Navigator Deck by the jacuzzis, where the golden-bronzed ones spend their morning horizontally under the sun. If you prefer some shade, perhaps you'd be better off down on the pool deck, port side, where there's often a congregation of down-to-earth Yorkshiremen and women in 'The Dales' by the tea bar. Across the way, starboard side, beneath the overhang just outside the Bistro, you'll find the hardy souls from north of the border taking their coffee, and perhaps something stronger in 'Scotch Corner'.

I've tried to find out if our fellow travellers from 'the land of song' have some secluded valley of their own on board, and got quite excited when Richard announced that a 'leek' had been discovered in Scott's Bar, but it was a false alarm – wrong kind of leek!

I've yet to get round to establishing if the southerners amongst us are as warmly gregarious or as cosily territorial as the northerners appear to be. Perhaps there is some forgotten corner of the Captain's Club that is forever Berkshire, Sussex or Hertfordshire, some 'wold' or 'fen' or 'level' for those of that ilk, and maybe I really should have paid more attention to the monitor screen in the cabin, channel 8, for evidence of covert clusterings of West Country folk who may well have already staked their claim at the bow rail of Columbus Deck for their own little 'Cornish Riviera'.

by Clive Leatherdale (Cabin 725)
Lying on deck doing my notes, this tall, beanpole woman raced by on another lap of her morning power walk. Lizzie calls her the Belfast Sink for the way she barges laggards out of the way. By chance, the Belfast Sink came to sit by me when she had finished her daily assault on loiterers. When I asked her about Boca da Valeria, she said she had taken pots of free jam and biscuits from the ship. I bit my lip and said nothing about the plague of tooth decay she was inviting.

Yesterday, I went to Reception to tell the lovely Ukrainian lady that not all British were complaining bastards. Someone told me a campaign has been started to complain about the complainers.

Dinah Read remarked at dinner this evening that the carrot salad they served us was the kind of thing you gave to ponies as a treat. Angela Ryan confirmed that she had prayed for me during my kidney illness, and she had also prayed for an Indian lady recently seen in a wheelchair. And she had got up and walked!

'To Jack 2011' by Dinah Read (Cabin 422)
Look at me man,
  With your sapphire eyes
And I see the young man
  That you were, long ago.
An angular jaw,
  A body taut and muscular
And those eyes
  A hint of challenge then as now
Melting into the loving look
  I know so well
Under your self-sufficiency
  And your pride there dwells
A little boy in need of love
  And the years count for nothing.

Every town and village in Portuguese-speaking Azores and Cape Verde seemed to have a 'bandstand' at its heart. This one is in Mosteiros, Azores (Clive Leatherdale)

MEDICAL FACILITY CHARGES

Doctor's consultation within working hours:	
In medical facility	45.65£
Cabin visit	50.85£
Doctor's consultation outside of working hours:	
From 8:00 until 22:00:	
In medical facility	50.65£
Cabin visit-	55.50£
From 22:00 until 8:00:	60.05£
In medical facility	65.85£
Cabin visit-	
Seasickness injection within working hours:	
In medical facility	31.25£
Cabin visit-	35.70£
Seasickness injection from 8:00 until 22:00:	
In medical facility	35.25£
Cabin visit-	41.50£
Seasickness injection from 22:00 until 8:00:	
In medical facility	40.95£
Cabin visit-	45.50£
MANIPULATIONS:	
I/M injection	11.74£
I/V injection	27.92£
I/V treatment (infusion) start	33.43£
Minor operation under local anaesthesia starts from	120.67£
Half plaster cast	157.30£
Full plaster cast	212.62£
Cauterization (nose bleeding)	120.15£
CPR	507.45£
Intubations	300.05£
First aid on the spot (any emergency case)	211.03£
ICU treatment / per hour	105.20£
Oxygen therapy / per hour	70.10£
Cardio monitoring / per hour	43.55£
Urinary tract catheterisation	150.05£
Stomach catheterisation	50.85£
Vital signs checking	5.72£
Saturation of oxygen (SpO₂)	7.28£
Eye wash	15.87£

The *Marco Polo*, like all cruise ships, is reluctant to publicise its medical charges, but they are pinned to the wall in the ship's hospital. It's a long list, but here is the main page – with apologies for the poor quality photograph; my hands were shaking in case I got caught (Clive Leatherdale)

DAY 29. SCARBOROUGH, TOBAGO

'Tobago is the smaller of the two islands that make up the Republic of Trinidad and Tobago. It features lush rainforest and glorious beaches, and is surrounded by colourful coral reefs with more than 600 species of fish.'

by Caroline Clifford (Cabin 468)

Was I cutting off my nose to spite my face? We had cancelled our original excursion of Tobago in favour of taking local buses. It was 30 years since my last visit, so there was a fair chance that the bus timetable would have changed. And although I was confident of getting to our target destination, Charlotteville, in the north-east of the island, could I be so sure of getting back?

We didn't even get as far as the bus station. The advertised taxi fares were US$25 per hour, fair value, but Charlotteville was charged as a five-hour trip, whilst *Lonely Planet* reckons it takes a mere 1½ hours each way on the bus.

We met taxi driver Anail Corbin. Although I felt sure that we were stitched up at US$55 return, it seemed the safer option – that was until we saw his car, and I was convinced that James would go off on one. It was a twenty-plus years old, largely falling to pieces, Nissan 2.8. 'There's six boys jumping up in there,' Corbin proudly explained. No air conditioning, ripped upholstery, and an ancient automatic gearbox. At around 16 miles per gallon, our round trip would probably cost him US$10. 'I never touch the engine,' he said. 'I just put oil in. This car put me on my foot.' We asked what mileage the car had done – he couldn't tell us – the instrument panel was 'fucked'.

Corbin asked me my name. I replied Caroline. From then onwards he referred to James as 'Mr Caroline'. It had rather a nice sound to it. Corbin also appeared to be a good friend of the policeman outside the cruise terminal, so I was confident that he wasn't planning to mug us on some remote road. He filled us in on the wildlife when prompted – 'no monkeys' and 'no snakes' – not strictly true; and he asked us about our marital status! He enjoyed that discussion since all three of us were divorcees and all agreed it was a satisfactory status.

Corbin was a careful driver and he knew everyone on the island, shouting greetings out of the window – 'Hey man', or, 'Alright nice man?' or, 'One love, one love.' At one point he tossed his empty water bottle out of the window into a rubbish bin on the other side of the road. He beamed with pride when I called, 'Good shot,' from the back seat.

Religion plays a big part in Tobago life, and Corbin was no exception, his life based on the teachings of God, whose words, he said 'are dear wisdom'. He asked James if he was Catholic, and James, for once, was diplomatic and said he 'was brought up as a Catholic'. In fact, James went to a Jesuit college, which is probably why he is now a confirmed atheist.

The other road users were not so prudent, a number of them bordering on the insane. 'Dick head,' Corbin yelled out of the window when some lunatic overtook us inches in front of an oncoming car.

Lush vegetation, coconut palms, mango, papayas, bread fruit and brilliant red flame trees bordered the twisting road which passed through the small towns of Goodwood, Pembroke and Glamorgan. We passed the turn-off to Argyle waterfall, where we had originally planned to 'tour', through Roxburgh and Speyside, and then up a particularly steep stretch, across the north of the island, to Charlotteville. The dilapidated car really struggled at this point, and at the steeper bends Corbin held the gear lever firmly into 'first'. 'It's one mile up, one mile down,' he explained.

Tiny mini-markets built on stilts hung on the sheer drop beside the road. We passed another 'acquaintance', this time riding a donkey laden with fodder. A group of men approached us, and Corbin explained they were on a hunting trip. I stupidly asked for what. 'Wild meat – agoutis, iguana and tattoo.' I'm not sure what tattoo is, but I'm sure it tastes nice. 'Iguana see dog, iguana take off – he not getting away at all. If he getting away it's a miracle.' And yes, Charlotteville is a good place to see the giant leatherback turtle, and yes, Corbin does eat them.

We loved the island and I loved the banter between James and Corbin which developed into a 'when in Rome …'. I still have a mental picture of James with dreadlocks, drinking Mount Gay and smoking something stronger than SuperKings.

Back in Scarborough, James extracted himself from the front seat while I fumbled for my purse. 'Are you going to get married again?' Corbin asked me. I hope that wasn't a proposal.

by Lizzie Mayes (Cabin 494)
Woke up to grey sky and a choppy sea – not what I expected on my first visit to the West Indies – where were the blue seas, blue skies and palm-covered beaches?

Anyway, we went off on our last excursion, to the Buccoo Reef. We went by bus to Pigeon Point and packed into our glass-bottomed boat crewed by three hunky black men. The water was still a little bit choppy – not ideal for snorkelling, but we were soon seeing lots of fish on the edge of the coral as we motored out to the reef.

Then the boat stopped over the coral and we saw a kaleidoscope of colour – brilliant fluorescent fish, puffer fish, angel fish, and parrot fish darting in and out of their coral castles. I was mesmerised at my first ever visit to a coral reef, until the inevitable voice from beside me announced how much better the colours are in the Great Barrier Reef and how disappointing this was.

How to ruin a girl's day in a few words. We moved on after a while, in order to find a place to stop for snorkelling. There was quite a bit of swell but most of us decided to go in. I panicked with the mouthpiece – really gagged on it – so decided to give the snorkelling a miss and just enjoy a swim in the beautiful warm water, though it was a bit scary. Dick had quite a long snorkel, so he was happy. Back on board we were fortified by a very nice rum punch served by our delicious crew.

We then headed for the nylon pool which, we were reliably informed, if we swam here, would make us all look ten years younger. Who could turn down an offer like that, so we all plunged in with great hope. By now the water was calm and warm, and we could see right to the bottom. We got back on the boat and didn't recognise anyone as we all looked so youthful. But I have a feeling that might have been something to do with the rum punch.

by Kay Rainsley (Cabin 543)
Complaints escalate. 'J' says that Reception won't help with anything. 'J2' tells of one woman who has hated everything since day one!

The crew are working really hard, cleaning everything in sight. We see them in their white coveralls, wearing masks and plastic gloves and carrying buckets.

The Caribbean is bliss for us. We are back in our comfort zone – diving. Great. We go to Crown Point and get two dives in. First, to see the wreck of the *Maverick* – a former Tobago to Trinidad ferry. Second, to the Mount Irvine extension, a reef dive. We dived with Les (husband) and Dean (Aussie – travelling the world with his girlfriend), Julia (Scottish), Jan (Dutch guy from our ship with his wife Poppy, a non-diver), Katie (our dive leader from Penzance).

The ship is rolling today – the sick bags are out. Les is putting bags of ice on his knee – he can walk more easily but it's still swollen.

'A dive to the Maverick' by Jan and Poppy Greefkes (Cabin 240)
Midnight, 6-7 February, and the temperature and humidity in Cabin 240 are still abominable. Jan gives up all attempts to sleep and opens the cabin door in order to stay alive. He starts to write an article about a recent scuba dive on the battleship *Krohnprinz Wilhelm*, part of the Kaiser's fleet scuttled in Scapa Flow after the First World War. The intense heat and poor ventilation take his mind back to the extreme living conditions endured by those sailors. No food, no cabin heating, and little hope of returning home. In the morning Jan will dive the wreck of the *Maverick* located near the Crown Point area of Tobago. Aged 67, he needs his sleep in order to dive safely.

His partner, Poppy, a non-diver, organises a take-away breakfast to enable them to leave the ship early. On shore, Poppy and Jan, weighed down by his heavy diving equipment, find the local tourist office. They are in luck, the pretty lady behind the desk takes the details of two diving schools, contacts one and confirms that Jan wishes to dive to the wreck of a former cargo ship, the *Maverick*. It is an artificial wreck, sunk for divers, lying in 31 metres of water.

The taxi driver is a gentle Caribbean woman who's keen to show them points of interest along the way to Crown Point. Several times she stops to ask for directions. Once there, Poppy boards the dive boat with Jan to enjoy the ride. After waiting for ten minutes, there is an unexpected surprise. Kay and Les, very experienced scuba divers from the *Marco Polo*, also come on board.

Two beautiful wreck and reef dives follow. Kay and Poppy take some fantastic pictures and a new *Marco Polo* friendship is born.

by Clive Leatherdale (Cabin 725)
Our taxi driver was Wayne, who said he would take five of us round the island for three hours; US$15 each – $75 in total, which seemed fine. The trouble was that the middle row of seats kept collapsing backwards like sleeper beds and it took a while for them to be bodged.

The conversation turned to famous cricketers – I was dubbed 'Clive Lloyd', the driver 'Wayne Daniel'. The guidebook said that Bacolet Bay, just east of Scarborough, was the setting for Walt Disney's *Swiss Family Robinson*, starring John Mills, which was shown again on TV not that long ago.

We walked down the 118 steps to the beach (Suzette counted them). Small, concave, and steep, you could see why the beach was so ideal, but we were to discover that the whole of Tobago was studded with similarly isolated beaches.

Wayne's easy, laid-back drawl sounded like a foreign language, but he understood everything we said except the word 'urban'. 'Excuse me?' he enquired. He came up with some funnies. Wayne Rooney's mother-to-be had visited Tobago and chanced to see the taxi driver play football and score many, many goals. She went home, gave birth to baby Wayne, and named him after the taxi-driver. You didn't have copyright on the name, I pointed out, and Wayne reluctantly agreed.

Wayne also told a tale about himself and two other Waynes, who went out walking and stumbled upon an enormous deadly snake. The biggest Wayne had a huge beard and turned out to be the most cowardly of the three. He ran away. Our Wayne teased him about it whenever they met.

We asked him if there were many suicides here. No, said Wayne, it was a happy relaxed place, where everyone went to church on Sundays and that explained why Wayne loved Tobago. There were certainly all manner of churches here, including more than the island's share of Seventh Day Adventist Churches.

He took a mobile phone call from his wife. She had locked herself out of their house and wanted his key. But we were now in Charlotteville, on the other side of the island, so could not help, and she blamed him, in the way that only women can. He related this with good cheer, saying her moods changed so quickly and that men get 'beaten up' every so often, but with a shrug of his shoulders added, 'But what can you do?' The last call from her was to say that she had not locked herself out after all.

In the afternoon I set off to inspect Scarborough on foot. It did not take long, partly because it is so small, partly because there is little to see. It appears to lack the basic infrastructure of a regional capital. It was very hot and the hills steep. Tobagoans were less enthusiastic about being photographed than were Brazilians, who would pose at the slightest opportunity and give the thumbs up afterwards.

The Phantom Orinoco

'It is very much regretted that the visit to Puerto Ordaz and the Orinoco will not now take place, but the uncertain conditions in that region have left little alternative, and the safety and security of our passengers and crew cannot be compromised.'

by Clive Leatherdale (Cabin 725)

For a man well travelled on many continents, it was an oddity that this cruise should scour the atlas for unfamiliar places. Almost the whole itinerary was fresh to me, even Amsterdam and Lisbon. That was one of its temptations. The one destination I knew was the Orinoco. In 1988 my 39-year-old self had travelled the length and breadth of Venezuela by bus, by boat, by thumb. I knew the country for its dangers, its beauty and its extraordinary landscapes.

The *Marco Polo* had been scheduled to stop at Puerto Ordaz, which can be hard to locate on some maps, for it is the 'new part' of Ciudad Guayana. Puerto Ordaz lies west of the junction of the Orinoco and Caroni rivers and connects with the 'old part', San Félix, by bridge.

I yearned to return to the Orinoco, not just for its own sake, but to try to hunt down Luis, the local boatman from nearby Barrancas, who ferried me down the Orinoco delta in his tiny boat. I had hired Luis to find Padre Basilio, who had run a remote mission station in Araguaimujo for over half a century. It had seemed like a good place to visit.

Among the maps and guidebooks now spread around my cabin were photos I had taken in 1988 and my notebook. If I found him, I wanted to thank Luis for taking care of me, for there were times on the journey back when I feared his boat would be swamped by currents and we would disappear without trace, to the eternal anguish of those dear to me. Now, my photos would remain unshown. But here are some of my notes:

(Thursday, 7 April 1988) Barrancas is a strange, one-horse town. Everybody lives along the promenade, with a panoramic view of the Orinoco. Pirates, cut-throats and vagabonds everywhere, with a sinister air. Surprisingly, many people speak some English – the first time I found this in Venezuela. The bus stop is by the cinema. A hotel with a surly bastard was on the main street. 'What you want?' he asked.

I was hassled on the quayside 'Donde va?' [Where are you going?] I told him. B3,000 [bolivars] demanded the first chap. I don't know if that's single or return, or what. I feel ashamed of myself, and found another chap who spoke English. He showed me people from Georgetown [in neighbouring Guyana], doing great illegal trafficking in God Knows What. He negotiates with Luis, who said he'd take B1,300 to leave at 5am tomorrow, or B2,000 to go now and stay overnight. We agree on B1,600. I go and buy food – bread, luncheon meat and sandwich spread, and two 2-litre bottles of manzana [apple] and Pepsi. Luis doesn't reappear until 3.20pm. He has gold-capped teeth and dark glasses – slightly sinister. His was the smallest boat, neatly painted in blue, white, red and green. He travelled fast, 2½ hours to get there, and overtakes a bulk carrier *Berge Helene* Stavanger. He showed excellent seamanship. He drank straight from the Orinoco in an empty paint can. The boats range from small, to very small, to extremely small in Barrancas.

We passed up the tiny Araguaimujo tributary – extremely smooth water. All the boats wave to each other – there aren't so many settlements here as in Tucupita.

Araguaimujo is extraordinary. It looks like a deserted fort, falling to pieces. It had its own sheltered mooring and missionary boat. Looks like a ghost town. Then a tiny old man, white hair, rheumy eyes appears, Padre Basilio, with his trousers 'around his ankles'. Slightly gaga, 87, he's lived in the delta for 57 years and written several books in his 'study'.

Luis put on his crucifix and was very servile. He said Padre and Sister were happy for us to stay. A friar was not happy, as 300 girls lived here.

I gave Luis bread, luncheon meat and sandwich spread. He went to his room next door, much spitting and snorting. I was given a bed by a nun but preferred my hammock. Extremely hot and sweaty. I was asleep by 9. It took time to realise I could sleep on my side in a hammock.

(Friday, 8 April 1988) Slightly chilly as always at 3-5am. Luis came looking for breakfast, but he didn't want luncheon meat! He'd got up with his torch several times in the night. I hope he wasn't ill. I didn't eat anything last night. Indian girls in dresses are traipsing through the building, chanting and sweeping up. They went through their recitations, led by Padre Basilio, in rickety old church hall. Luis took me another mile to show me the northern end of the village. Extraordinary spectacle. I was surrounded by Indians wanting me to buy things, like yellow and black birds.

[Later that same day I travelled by bus to Ciudad Guayana] There's a ghastly feel to San Félix. Hotel Yoli was B180 + 10% because I don't live in Venezuela. The room had cockroaches. No coathangers, the window would not shut, and AC that blasted me all night.

A young chap by the door had a rifle under his arm – 'vigilante priva-do' – to protect clients' cars. He kept wandering round the restaurant with it. Totally unfriendly waiters. It looked a dreadful area.

(Saturday, 9 April 1988) Ciudad Guayana looks even more dreadful than you imagine. It goes on forever, like a New Town.

The tiny boat (above right) in which local boatman Luis (below right) took me for two days through the Orinoco delta in 1988. I travelled to visit Padre Basilio (below left), who had run a remote mission station in Araguaimujo for over half a century. Excerpts from my 1988 diary (left) were intended to help me find Luis and thank him for taking care of me. The waves on the return journey had made me fear for my life

(Clive Leatherdale)

Day 30. Castries, St Lucia

'St Lucia (pronounced Loo-sha) is a small lush tropical gem. Its dramatic twin peaks, the Pitons, soar 2,000 feet up from the sea, sheltering magnificent rainforests and orchards of bananas, coconut, mango and papaya trees. Enjoy the vibrant Creole atmosphere.'

by Caroline Clifford (Cabin 468)

James was up on deck around 7am, moving the chairs outside Scott's Bar back to their rightful places, namely around the tables with ashtrays. Not that he smokes, of course. What a day this will be!

But it was going to be fun. We were taking a local bus and we didn't care where it was going. A driver stopped us outside the cruise terminal: 'You want to share a taxi with these people?' he called out. 'No,' yelled the people already inside, which happily saved me the trouble.

There was a sign for the public bus to Soufrière. Why not? We waited in the stationary bus for nearly one hour in the sticky heat. Every seat had to be occupied before leaving. A few disgruntled locals got on, and then off again, until the rastafarian driver took our US dollars (changing them at some arbitrary rate). By now, walking away was no longer an option for us.

We drove out of Castries, south on a scruffy road, the air filled with the smell of gas. I was jammed between James and the window, the bare metal frame jabbing into my shoulder as the bus sped along. The paint was chipped away where thousands of passengers had leant against the window sill. I pitied the poor woman on the other side of James, with just one buttock on the sweaty seat. He's not a small guy!

James said the Toyota minibus had plenty of 'woof' in it, considering the load. Alton Towers had nothing on this, as the driver tore up and down the steep, winding roads in an apparent suicide bid, reminiscent of a white-knuckle ride. I tried not to look at the vehicle graveyard far down below and concentrated my attention on a lemon that had broken loose from its packaging and was rolling around the floor of the bus.

This bus had looked the smartest on the rank, but clearly 'fully air-conditioned' means 'all the windows are open'. Everybody had said 'good morning' on boarding but then no one spoke again. The driver refused to acknowledge passenger requests – it was a 'non-stop' deal, no toilets and no photo stop! The nearside suspension made a sudden 'clonk' sound, which James explained was caused by wear; or in my opinion by erratic driving. James went on to say that this was an easy job, which just involved fitting a new knuckle. Codswallop!

Several stretches of road were washed away and landslides were common. An ambulance rushed past, and we spotted several tourist buses parked on a bend, one driver apparently being interrogated by the police.

I was happy to arrive in Soufrière. Our driver was characterless, and I was bruised. We made our way to a friendly bar, the intention being that James could relieve himself with some dignity; or at least he would have done if he'd remembered to do his flies up.

When we got back to the church where the bus had stopped we had that terrible sinking feeling – the queue of returning buses had evaporated. Suddenly, from behind a shack, our miserable driver emerged. He introduced himself as Silvano, apologised for not talking to us, and to compensate for this, wanted to put some 'jumping music' on the music player.

We boarded the bus and waited, and waited, and waited some more, until once again the bus was full. The St Lucian women have massive bosoms and they do take up a lot of space. On top of that, the woman sitting next to me, who incidentally had a beard, was drinking foul-smelling soup out of a thermos and kept exclaiming, 'Praise be the Lord' and 'Thank you Lord' every few minutes.

Most people fell asleep on the return journey, which was quite a feat in view of the tortuous nature of the road. James elbowed a dozing worker back into his seat whilst calculating Silvano's annual income at around US$50,000 – based on fourteen passengers paying US$4 each way, and the bus making three or four journeys a day. Allowing for his expenses, probably only fuel, not a bad earner.

by Margit Latter (Cabin 335)
The 4x4 jeep on the safari tour in St Lucia shook every bone in my body each time the driver/guide shot over deep, muddy holes on the jungle path. This seemed to have pushed the 'giggle button', because my friend and I could not stop laughing. At one stage I thought, 'My head is coming off,' but it stayed on firmly. Then, onto the beach – white sand, palm trees, blue skies – and I was able to hang my hammock (I never travel without one, but am forbidden from hanging it anywhere on the *Marco Polo*). Happily swinging between palm trees, it needed only a *Bounty* bar to complete a kitsch advert, except that the guide warned me, 'Look at the

big coconuts above your head: if one lands on you it could be fatal.' Obediently, I got out of my hammock, cursing all coconuts.

I might as well have another swim. Lovely waves, warm sea – then I let out a very unladylike scream, followed by terrible Anglo-Saxon words. The pain was sharp. Something or someone had bitten me on the top of my leg. The poor man swimming next to me looked aghast.

I got out quickly, blood pouring out of my leg. The little bastard not only bit into my mole but was still attached to it. I brushed it away. A woman came quickly with a mediwipe, and the guide provided two plasters. He also gave me a form to fill in, for my name and cabin number.

Back at the ship, staff already knew about the 'fish bite', which showed that the jungle drums were working well on the *Marco Polo*. [to be continued on Day 32]

by Lizzie Mayes (Cabin 494)
Panic once again sets in as we near the port and we have precious few hours onshore. How to make the most of it, though today we are lucky to have a whole day.

First thing, as usual, was to find a bank and get local money. On the way there a jolly young man accosted us, offering a three or four hour trip for US$25. We explained we had no money, but he said that was no problem, as he Albert, the Man, would find us a bank on the tour. So we capitulated, somewhat relieved to have the responsibility taken away from us, and found we were sharing a minibus with five other Marco Polians from whom he had extricated $35. The other five didn't seem overjoyed to see us, and we didn't recognise them from the boat, so it was a bit of a risk. However, we sallied forth.

One of the women had a list of things she wanted to see and had based their negotiations on this list. Albert kept telling us he was the Man and would do whatever we wanted. So we set off towards the Pitons, tall, pointed mountain peaks, via fishing villages and magnificent views over the sea. We stopped on the roadside to taste the wonderful sweet small bananas, which is one of the main crops of the island. These villages seemed very poor, simple wooden dwellings in straight lines. Very few had glass in the windows, and Albert said only a very few had running water. Washing clothes was more often done in a river, if there was one near by.

These homes were in stark contrast to the luxury stilted villas dotted all over the hilly countryside. Albert explained about the 'rasta men' who lived in the rainforest, most of whom contented themselves and their families with a simple life, living off the forest on a vegetarian diet and smoking recreational dope. He said for the most part they were peace-loving people, but that of course some couldn't resist the temptation to make money and get into the murky world of drug dealing. The penalties for drug dealing were high on the island, but many young people fall into a trap and there is a high level of drug dependency, and an accompanying crime rate. I noticed a large sign for an HIV clinic on the roadside.

Hurricane Tomas had battered the island three months previously and there was evidence everywhere of broken roads and bridges, and mudslides. One particularly shocking outcome was a huge slide which took a house and its occupants (an island artist and his family), and there is no evidence that it ever existed. They were never found. It was eerie, as there was a tethered horse grazing on a narrow strip of roadside grass.

We stopped for drinks at a roadside café with a notice telling us that with Jesus's help they would make our stop a happy one. An elderly gentleman took out his violin from a battered case and started to play. The most excruciating sound erupted into the silence of this beautiful deserted hillside overlooking the Pitons as he attacked his instrument with gusto and a big toothless smile.

Albert, true to his word, took us to a bank in a small fishing village. While we waited for what I guess is West Indian Time, the local TV station was showing its obituary programme. Pictures of the deceased, with funeral details, are screened along with countless messages from friends and families. Our tour had grown from the promised three-four hours when Albert took us down to the beach at Marigot Bay, where we had a much-needed swim before a torrential storm cleared the beach. Albert the Man seemed determined that we would enjoy our stay on St Lucia and seven hours after we left Castries he deposited us back at the ship. We didn't make any headway with our fellow passengers, but it was a good day. Super performance of 'Bohemian Rhapsody' by Richard and Co.

by Dinah Read (Cabin 422)
I had a little more leisure this morning as my excursion was not called until 9.45. I got up and showered etc, and then lay down with Jack, as promised. We do need to confirm our love and affection at times, and I was leaving him again. When I did dress and go to breakfast and prepare to go, Jack was still at his ease. I went back to the cabin for my insect spray, but he had gone. I met him coming back again. He said he had been watching a massive P&O liner come in and turn and moor nearby – beautifully done, he said, and he could not help but admire these great cruise ships. I really, really dislike them. They look like an oversized block of municipal flats stuck on top of a giant shoebox.

I always think that everyone is born with their own fixed quantity of misery in them, and some people who have nothing to complain about will nevertheless find something just to complete their quotient. You can pick them out by their faces. Myself, I have been amused by the universal garnish of rosemary served with the meat here. You don't *have* to eat it. Today I heard a woman complaining that everything had rosemary in it and she didn't like it.

Then again, on the way back from the Pitons on the catamaran today, there was a woman sitting all alone on the foredeck. I was standing by the port rail and, as the boat changed course, my shadow fell across her. She asked me if I would mind moving away as she was trying to get the sun on her back! I politely moved two steps aft. There was of course nothing to stop her from moving over.

Actually, I was watching a plume of smoke on the sea which increased and darkened until flames appeared at the source. A boat on fire! A helicopter came to investigate and a small, fast launch with a blue flashing light and other boats were in attendance. After a while there were two successive explosions aboard her and that was that.

There is a big cruise ship in, and a Swedish topsail schooner. I tried to get a photo of them both in shot, as the size comparison is so striking.

by Jill Crocker (Cabin 514)
Steve [Ragnall] and I were here in St Lucia just before Christmas, so we organised a local minibus (the driver's name was Presidente) to take a few of us up to Pigeon Island, the site of the eighteenth century fort, and from where we could see Diamond Rock. We couldn't, the weather wasn't clear enough, but we had a good time anyway.

by Clive Leatherdale (Cabin 725)
We shouldn't be in St Lucia at all. It was not on the original itinerary that passengers signed up for. When the Orinoco part of the cruise hit the buffers, we were told we would be stopping in St George's, Grenada, instead. That was then cancelled because of the sea swell, and now we find ourselves in Castries.

As we were docking, one of those mega-cruise-ships, the 3,000 passenger P&O *Ventura,* edged in immediately behind us. All lines and rectangles, few curves, not easy on the eye.

Bernadine, Angela and I had agreed to share a taxi to the Pitons. Once off the ship we were besieged by taxi touts, each insisting we take them because everyone else was unlicensed. Eventually we settled on Anthony, who was cheaper but no less loud of voice, and we had to endure his ear-splitting tourist commentary from start to finish. I did not consider St Lucia the equal of Tobago for physical beauty, and its charms were not helped by finding each viewpoint lined with touts selling crap.

I spent the afternoon exploring Castries on foot. The public library occupied two floors and was wonderfully chaotic. It had no computerised catalogue of books, and the card index had not been updated for at least ten years, which meant no one had any idea of what books they did and did not have. The staff beamed happily from behind old wooden desks amid books stacked up from the floor like parchment stalagmites.

A regional capital like Castries has advantages for curious visitors. It would, for example, have its own law courts, and its British connection ensures its justice would be public. What better way to pass an hour than sitting in on a St Lucian trial? The two-storey court house was not far from the library. But now I made a mistake. Outside the court building a man and a woman sat behind a desk, selling or giving out papers of some kind. I asked to take a photo. The man said only if I paid! I was so taken aback that I jokingly replied that he should pay me. The woman barked: 'Why should he pay you? We don't know what you're going to do with it.'

I backed away. The court itself was on the upper floor. I was about to climb the stairs when the woman stood up to follow me. This was probably innocuous, but the last time I had taken pictures of official places without permission, in Ghana, I had been bundled into the back of a car by police. The thought of that scary occasion deterred me from further bravado. I spent the next hour peering round street corners expecting to be arrested at every moment.

The day had an unexpectedly dramatic climax. At the mouth of the harbour, a motor launch exploded in flames. [see page 154]

The wonderfully chaotic public library in Castries, St Lucia (Clive Leatherdale)

DAY 31. BRIDGETOWN, BARBADOS

'Barbados has much to see: Harrison's Cave, Flower Forest, and Gun Hill Signal Station to name a few. You could just head to the beaches, lay back and chill. Known for its beaches and cricket, Barbados is one of the most popular islands in the West Indies.'

'On the Buses' by Caroline Clifford (Cabin 468)

I hate Barbados – I always have. It's full of lobster-coloured, fat, ugly tourists wearing vests and shorts that they really should not. And then there are the rich, famous and, I think, talentless, such as Michael Winner, and the possible love-children of other rich, feckless, flatulent nobodies. And my Barbadian tenant who ripped me off for a considerable amount of money and allegedly died in two unrelated incidents. And the female 'official' at the airport who once confiscated my cigarette lighter and James's cellotape. And I hated the 4WD tour I took on my last visit, when the driver kept all the rum punch for himself.

So it wasn't a great surprise when the 'gentleman' in the tourist office at the cruise terminal was indifferent to my presence until such time as it suited him. He did, however, give me a free map and directed me to the right bus station, the one with the long walk from the port, across Bridgetown.

We queued for the 9am bus to Bathsheba with an army of school-children. The driver was a huge Bajan woman with thighs that could have supported half an offshore oil platform. James said she would have been more at home on a JCB.

There is no such thing as a 'full' bus in Barbados. They are charming, fun people, but it was a shock when not one of the smartly uniformed children on the bus stood up, or even looked remotely guilty, that we were standing, James in the stair-well. So we stood, hanging onto the handrail for dear life, like sardines waiting to be shot from a cannon. The kids were mostly punching each other or making mobile phone calls. It was a great relief when they finally got off at Grantley Adams High School, taking with them about as much knowledge of social graces as the average passenger in Marco's Bistro! The bus, incidentally, was meant to seat 42 with just 26 'standees'.

Travelling through acres of sugar cane and pretty villages with brightly painted houses, we crossed the rolling hills of the interior on Highway 3. The beach at Bathsheba would have been paradise to many, but we were aware that it was shortly to be invaded by 4WDs on tour. What luck – a bus leaving immediately for Speightstown, another government-operated public facility, with an excellent driver who ensured a speedy journey by clearing the road with persistent blasts on his horn.

Our final bus was a privately operated minibus taking us from Speightstown to Bridgetown. If you were to look at a map of Barbados, which would show the island to be almost pear-shaped, we had travelled in a triangle, and this, the last leg, was the hypotenuse. The bus wasn't much more than ten years old but was clearly knackered, with purple plastic seats ripped to shreds and reggae music blaring through the sound system, a little incongruous with the posh hotel area we passed through. The decrepit state of the bus was, however, reflected in the ticket price – a pittance for another hour's travelling time. So, after a triangular but almost complete circumnavigation of Barbados, we had travelled around 100km but spent just US$2.75 each.

And my quote of the day. I overheard two officials at the cruise terminal: 'There are two cruise ships in port today – and the *Marco Polo*!'

by Lizzie Mayes (Cabin 494)
Barbados. Holiday island of the rich and famous. We arrived early in the morning at Bridgetown. Shortly afterwards a huge cruise liner appeared, looking like a ghostly white block of flats. So that is what these monsters look like. The *Marco Polo* was positively dwarfed.

We decided to head up the coast to the beach on a local reggae bus. A strange lady in front of us from a Saga cruise ship took endless photographs of shanty houses, which were like wooden beach huts with peeling paint, until we got to luxury hotel-land. Gradually these turned into colonial-type mansions with grand-sounding names like Fairmount Royal Pavilion behind high metal security gates.

We were going to lunch at Mullins beach, but the menu was ordinary and incredibly expensive, so we caught the bus back to Bridgetown. The steel band on the *Marco Polo* was still playing as we waved the huge white block of flats off into the evening sunset. They must have been jealous to see us having such a great party.

We have six days at sea now. Richard Sykes has assured us that the gossip will get worse and people will get really mean with the claustrophobia of being on board. I actually love the sea days, especially when it's so warm.

by Neville Singh (Cabin 708)
Six weeks seemed like a long time, but it mainly passed quickly with mostly good memories and new friendships. Some of the crew I met in the gym for table-tennis at the end of their evening shifts. I was pleased to be asked to join them. Sport made up for language. We were delighted to be joined by the captain for a table-tennis challenge, when he won all but two of his games against the passengers. I, too, lost to him but enjoyed the session and the camaraderie of the occasion.

The waiters were also cool in the face of some passenger rudeness and impatience. To be at the receiving end of this for six weeks, every day, and still turn up next time ready, smiling and able, was wonderful to see.

The high point of this dedication came on the evening we left Barbados, when the captain delayed our departure for a lady who came running along the dock asking to wave her brother goodbye. She had just flown in and had rushed from the airport. It was touching to see Richard Sykes scrambling to find her brother and get him to the promenade deck to wave her goodbye, as the captain and others looked on in bemusement. It was truly a moving moment and a lasting memory. [see next]

by Jeremy Tait (Cabin 715)
By sheer coincidence, my sister Gillian flew into Bridgetown on the same day to join her cruise ship, *Saga Pearl II*, which was berthed a short distance from the *Marco Polo*. She managed to walk along the pier to our ship just as it was leaving, so we were able to talk to each other for a short while before we left.

by Mave Eaton (Cabin 616)
Bright, breezy and rough. The passengers stagger around. Many are bored, so sit in groups complaining. Choir practice is cancelled because of a leak in the roof of Scott's Bar where it is held.

More sad stories emerge of injured passengers. There is the poor man who slipped on the path on Île Royale – another victim of the pathway. He cracked his ribs and did other damage. He and his wife have been left behind in Barbados. I feel sad that their holiday ended this way.

by Dinah Read (Cabin 422)
It seems odd that Jack should have come this far to a place famous for its beaches, and cricket, and rum, and not want to go ashore and see them. However, none of these things appeal to me particularly – and anyway I missed the deadline for booking. So we are having a nice peaceful day on the ship. After lunch we went to our cabin for what Jack called 'make and

mend'. Apparently, when you have darned your socks etc, you can do whatever you fancy.

Dear Jack. He is such a gentleman in the old-fashioned way. He always gives me precedence and I feel like a queen walking in front of him. At other times he [85] leads me by the hand and I [a mere 80] feel like a little girl, but more often when there is room for us to walk abreast we go hand in hand, and in a lift, alone for a few brief seconds, he always puts his arms around me and looks into my eyes the way he does.

'You walk behind me, give me precedence
Like a queen.
You walk in front, leading me
Like a child.
You walk beside me, taking my hand
Gently, as a lover should.
Protective, considerate, holding me.
For I am yours
And you are mine.'

We went to the pool deck for a cup of tea. It is weird but I don't like it so much there, and eating at that end of the ship is a 'bit of a bun fight', as someone said. There is a man, nice enough but incredibly obese, whom I have seen about the ship. I think of him as the 'man mountain'. Today in the buffet bar at teatime I saw him eat a plateful of food – a doughnut and several biscuits and a thick sandwich, and then take three slices of Madeira cake and wrap them in a serviette and take them away with him. We, however, never have anything at teatime, or 'late night snacks', and I never fancy protein foods at breakfast. I never have more than four of the five courses available at lunch and at dinner either. It really is not necessary to put on a lot of weight on a cruise is it?

I can see a rainbow, a whole one. They always bring me luck – like kingfishers and humming birds.

'Birthday in Barbados' by Kay Rainsley (Cabin 543)
There's only so much pleasure that can be derived from staring at a box of chocolates. Even sniffing them doesn't really cut the mustard. For the real experience you simply have to dive in and sample the delights. And so it is with diving.

After weeks of staring longingly at the ocean, it was time to slip under the surface and explore. Michael, our skipper, had endeared himself to me by offering to carry my tank to the boat. I'm such a baby with my feet that as soon as the soft, silky sand changes to rocks I'm severely challenged. Les, my husband, is affronted by what he calls 'The American approach', whereby the crew often carry the gear, whereas I welcome it. St Michael was already a firm favourite. He told me that he used to dive but had stopped because he was afraid of the fish. I asked him to repeat it, just to make sure I'd heard correctly. 'In Barbados they come so close,' he explained. Great, I had my camera at the ready.

I had barely fallen in backwards off the boat on 'Pieces of Eight Reef' when I saw my first turtle. It swam past lazily, scarcely giving me a second glance. A puffer fish, about eighteen inches in length, hovered over a section of orange soft coral. Its black eyes peered out from its large head and ungainly brown body. Sadly they are sometimes forced to defend themselves by swallowing water until they puff up into a ball. Once puffed, looking like the tasteless ornaments offered for sale, they can barely swim. This one swam away unconcerned.

One of my favourites is the parrot fish, which are responsible for our white coral sand beaches. They bite off chunks of coral in their beak-like jaws, which they then excrete as sand. The one in front of me is an exquisite blue with flashes of pink and yellow, and I can hear it scraping algae from the rock. They are the grazers of the ocean. We finned past glorious peach gorgonia (sea fans) and pink Christmas tree worms. These flower-like creatures retract into their tubes when disturbed.

Hard and soft multi-coloured corals mingled with sponges and weeds as we explored the underwater wonderland with Jan, one of the Dutch passengers. We'd met earlier when we'd dived together in Tobago. Underwater sign-language is international although his English is excellent. We gazed at the fabulous angel fish with their long dorsal fins and elegant, shining, bodies, and their cousins, the butterfly fish.

Minutes before surfacing I spotted a large turtle, resting against a sea fan. Its beautiful carapace was angled upwards and it was silhouetted against the shafts of sunlight which were penetrating the clear, warm, water. A shoal of yellow-striped grunts flanked by a needle fish swam past. The turtle edged leisurely away.

On land, we chinked glasses with Jan and his wife, Poppy, to celebrate my perfect birthday.

by Clive Leatherdale (Cabin 725)
As we pulled in we espied another cruise monstrosity tied up alongside – *Carnival Victory* – and then something more like the *Marco Polo* steamed in – *Saga Pearl II*. She did not have the *Marco Polo*'s sagging deck line, though.

Taxi touts tell arrivals off the ships that it's five miles into town, even though it's only half a mile and an easy walk. It's a toss up today between taking a reggae bus or a taxi off into the interior. I join Bernadine and

Angela for the latter. Richard, our taxi driver wears a hairnet, which he takes off to show me.

As a virgin Caribbean visitor, I am struck by the contrasts between Tobago, St Lucia, and now Barbados. They seem to have nothing in common at all, other than being small islands. Most visitors to these parts stay in one destination, having neither the time nor the money to island-hop. To that extent, the *Marco Polo* has provided me with a welcome education. Three islands, one after the other. I feel something of an amateur expert on the West Indies already.

The Harrison Caves were our destination, slap bang in the middle of Barbados. When we got there it was a two-hour wait for the next tour. To fill the time Richard drives us up to St Nicholas Abbey in the north of the island, much less hectic than busy Bridgetown, and offering immense views of the wild Atlantic coast. Richard stops by a fruit field and calls to a man to fetch us some carambola, a five-sided yellow fruit that can be eaten unwashed.

The cave tour had progressed for only a couple of minutes when a young Frenchwoman was overcome by claustrophobia. The route was a series of *culs de sac*, so our 'train' waited at a junction for another heading for the exit, so that the unfortunate woman could transfer. Maxine, our unsmiling guide, told us the way to distinguish between stalactites and stalagmites was that 'g' stood for ground and 'c' for ceiling. I had an easier mnemonic: 'tights come down.'

Our return journey took us west to Holetown, then a little north to St James Parish Church, the oldest in Barbados. Children were coming out of school, traffic was clogged, and Angela remarked how smart the school uniforms are, even down to matching socks.

Back on board, passengers are exchanging anecdotes. One old man had marched into the sea with his walking stick. He wanted a pee, and the sea was the easiest way. He then fell over.

DAY 32. AT SEA

'13.45. Royal Navy & Nautical Get-Together in the Marco Polo Lounge. Join Susan and fellow passengers for this informal get-together.
14.00. Ab Blast. This 30-minute session of concentrated effort will trim, tighten and firm.'

by Margit Latter (Cabin 335) [continued from Day 30]

Amusement for many passengers about the rumour-mill, or the jungle drums. 'There are dead bodies in the fridge,' someone insisted. Indeed, we saw during one dark night two men with torches opening a hatch in the bow of the ship, climbing into the square hole. We wondered if the 'fridge' was down there.

The jungle drums had already, it seems, informed the whole ship that 'someone was bitten by a fish'. But it took two days for the drums to reach the safety officers.

At 5.20pm I received an official letter from 'Safety' to go immediately to Reception. The woman there, without a hint of a smile or any kind of charm, called the officers on the phone. Minutes later, two very serious-looking guys appeared. 'You must fill in this form, giving all details about the incident.' I felt I had to hurry, and I write very quickly, but the pressure was on. I tried to make a friendly gesture and attempted to joke: 'Aren't you glad, because I am German, that I can read and write?' I asked with my flirty smile.

'Fill it in,' was the curt answer. Quite intimidating. Maybe they had worked for the KGB in the past (they were East European). It was a good job I had not committed a crime, if they can make you feel guilty without out a bad deed.

They read what I had written but could not read the word 'thigh', so I showed them where mine was. They were still not amused. Then our gorgeous, charming Richard Sykes, the cruise director, appeared. 'What's going on?' I told Richard about the fish bite and he roared with laughter. But when he realised why I was sitting on the settee with two safety officers his face grew serious. I got a big cuddle and a kiss. What a super man.

'Have you seen a doctor?' the KGB asked.

'No,' I said, 'it's not necessary because I am okay.'

He then told me to sign a disclaimer, which I refused to do.

'It did not happen on the boat,' he said, in such a voice and a terrible tone that it gave me a jolt. My flirty smile disappeared and assertiveness crept in.

'You must see a doctor,' the KGB ordered.

'No,' I said. 'I am not prepared to pay vast sums of money for a doc to tell me that I am okay.'

'Come with us,' he demanded. They marched me down three decks to the ship's hospital.

'But I am not paying,' I repeated, my voice now as aggressive as theirs. They spoke to the doctor [Dr Papadakis] privately. Nice man, the doc. He wanted to see where the bite was. I dropped my trousers and the KGB disappeared rapidly.

I told the doctor I would not be paying, as I had heard about the extortionate sums being charged. He smiled, looked at the mole on my leg and said I was okay, gave me some antibiotic cream, and I went away a happy bunny. Nobody bullies me any more!

by Caroline Clifford (Cabin 468)

The shower water flowed out of its tray over the bathroom floor, stubbornly refusing to flow down the drain. Sick-bags decorated the handrails everywhere, water poured from the ceiling in Scott's Bar, and the public address system warned us not to wear heels. Yes, it was a little rough.

That did not stop passengers from walking sideways like crabs, staggering like drunks and slopping coffee on the deck; but all with a determined, if not apprehensive, look.

At the 'Twilight Zone' lecture, Tony Rice warned us that we were sailing straight into the wind and therefore 'lifting off' on the outside decks. I gatecrashed the 'nautical get-together', hosted by Susan the librarian. In her inimitable style, she told contributors that it wasn't necessary to stand up to talk, risking life and limb in the process. Come on, they are meant to be sailors! Of course, the first one to speak was, no, I shall not name him. In his 'normal' dictatorial and controversial manner, he said that the meeting was in the wrong venue. It should have been in a room with a bar.

I say 'normal', because his dining table is near ours, and at dinner we have overheard several loud outbursts concerning the food and the service. Actually, his table was earmarked for 'me', promised by the operations manageress at Cruise & Maritime. This was a 'thank you' for a 'kind letter' (her words, not mine) following a previous cruise with my mother. On boarding and finding our allocated table already taken by others, we were placated by a clever crew member who switched the table numbers for three days at the start of the cruise. But we weren't fooled.

Back to the nautical get-together. They were an aged audience, many were deaf, and consequently there was an irritating echo resulting from caring spouses repeating everything that was said. I listened briefly to some anticipated gossip concerning an infamous former deputy prime minister. But nothing to bother Mr Prescott, so I left.

This is the long bit across the Atlantic with more than 2,000 nautical miles to our next port of call. I did pop along to the final port excursion talk on the Azores. The poor chap seemed nervous and over-enthusiastic about the islands. He omitted to mention, whilst plugging the available tours, that the lakes and craters on San Miguel are usually shrouded in heavy mist – and that is all you see.

Richard Sykes was on top form, as per usual, with his 'Johnny Mercer' cabaret. Two people arrived late, very late, and groaned when Richard said the next song was to be his last: 'You've just joined us; get another watch.' The latecomers joined my table and started rabbiting about 'that horrible woman, she's over there'. I couldn't possibly look round or they would know I had been listening – but I did. The choice was enormous, but I think I've already got that t-shirt.

Two more days of 'moderate to rough' seas, according to the daily programme. James says it's fortunate we're 'pitching not tossing'. But if the weather wasn't extreme, what would we have to talk about at this stage in the cruise?

by Lizzie Mayes (Cabin 494)

Back into the old routine. Did the quiz – badly as usual. Choir club got us singing again after a long break – we are supposed to give a rehearsal concert at the end of the cruise, so we will have to do some work. Dick got inveigled to take part in – 'Just a Minute'. Richard Sykes cajoled him into taking part. As he didn't really know the radio programme, he was at a bit of a disadvantage but redeemed himself as the first subject was: 'The most interesting person I have met' – so the creep talked about Richard Sykes! The ship's esteemed ex-MP and Royal Naval Officer, Michael Brotherton, was on the panel too, so Dick happily got buzzed out and let him hold the stage.

I was sorry to have missed it. The 'basters' are now proudly strutting round the ship showing off their Caribbean sun tans – I still can't get over the lack of body awareness amongst the fatties – but at least they look better brown. There seems to be a new breed on the boat – the moaners moaning about the moaners. I don't know which are best – and

I am sure some of them are also the original moaners jumping on the bandwagon.

by Clive Leatherdale (Cabin 725)
Time is whizzing by. Although dozens of folk are making notes for the book, most prefer to send them in after they get home and have had a chance to tart them up. I try to resist this. There's a risk interest will fade and they'll lose the edge. I want their stuff as soon as possible, preferably now. The trouble is, not being forewarned, few have brought along any writing paper. Reception is dishing out reams of coloured card or anything that comes to hand, but the stuff shoved under my cabin door each night shows improvisation on a grand scale. Passengers have noticed that the puzzle pages prepared each day are blank on the reverse, so I am getting plenty of these – sudoku squares attempted on the front, scrawled diary entries on the back.

Whenever the sea is a bit iffy, the cabin staff line the handrails with paper sick bags. These are blue on the outside, white inside. Lazy passengers can open their cabin doors, pluck a sick bag from the rail, turn it inside out, and hey presto a sheet of writing paper materialises. Origami at sea.

The really indolent don't even need to leave their cabin. Loo paper is not really fit for the purpose, but with a steady hand, a racy thought or a limerick can be scrawled before it escapes the mind, using one's knees as a desk.

To capture every fleeting observation I have resorted to patrolling the ship, notebook in hand, and hijacking innocent passengers. I should have thought of this earlier. I bend down, put my mouth to their ear, and ask if they've anything they want to confess in the strict anonymity of this publication!

After a while I found that, rather than laboriously jotting down what I hear, it is easier simply to hand over my pad and pen. I tried this at breakfast, and this is what my first victim wrote:

'The banality of all this is driving me insane. I've got to the point where I'm actually avoiding people and withdrawing – craving isolation – but not quarantine in my cabin! When I meet 'strange' people (there are still some of the 750 we haven't met) I feel a surge of panic. More inane small talk with people I don't know, don't want to know, and don't care a f*** about.'

At another table I asked Sue Edwards what I'd discover if I spent five minutes inside her mind. 'If you were inside my head,' she wrote, 'all you would get are repeat showings of sensual pleasures. All I can think about is being surrounded by that gorgeous warm sea and wonderful turtles. It's like going back to the womb, being in the water.'

I button-holed Richard Sykes for twenty minutes, notebook poised. He does not shy away from his avowed atheism, but confesses to difficulties when carrying out his duties. One of these is to oversee the inter-denominational Sunday service. He does not conduct services – these are left to volunteer clergymen on board – but he does have to organise them. In so doing, Richard does his best to avoid all mention of 'god', and from time to time mischievously introduces Jacob Bronowski's atheistic masterpiece *The Ascent of Man* into the 'Best of British' programmes on the ship's Channel 3.

Richard quashed passenger rumours about facing ship hospital bills should they come down with norovirus or some other nasty onboard bug. Nonsense, he says. Passengers are never charged in such circumstances, but he acknowledged that fear of being charged can deter sick passengers from notifying the medical centre, which in turn helps spread any contagion.

He staunchly defends his staff. 'When passengers complain about a colleague for one reason or another, they often fail to realise that the crew member is not on a short cruise. The *Marco Polo* is their home. They live on her all year round, often for years. We all live together in this small vessel. It's like hearing complaints about a relative or a close friend.'

Our discussion sparked a flurry of further thoughts in my mind, but I'll postpone them for the next book meeting tomorrow. I leave Richard with one final question: does he try to avoid troublesome passengers? Quite the opposite, he said. If you avoid one passenger you might as well avoid them all.

At lunchtime today, on an unsteady ship, a man propped his walking stick so he could serve himself at the salad bar. A woman came along, inadvertently kicked away his stick, and did not even stop to apologise, let alone retrieve it.

Curiosity took me to the Royal Navy and Nautical chin-wag. I stayed to the end but learned only one thing. If fate had forced me to sea with such fellows, I would have found myself spectacularly miserable.

DAY 33. AT SEA

'The cruise has now entered the psychological stage. Could all Book Club contributors please attend Scott's Bar at 11.45am. Please note that the forthcoming book is not an official fairy-tale book, but an in-depth account of the highs and lows of this cruise.'

by Mave Eaton (Cabin 616)

I am becoming more docile the longer I remain on the ship. Is this because I am institutionalised? We have our rituals and routines. We usually have lunch down in the Waldorf restaurant where we are served by the waiters. The routine is unvariable. We arrive and ask for a table for two or four. We are usually informed that none are available, and they attempt to steer us to a table where eight sit elbow to elbow, making the same boring conversation they have already made a dozen times. But we stand firm and refuse to be steered. Immediately, a table is found, because we would otherwise stand there and block the entrance.

The lunchtime meals in the Waldorf are the preserve of the middle classes: not for them the indignity of queuing in Marco's Bistro. The food is pleasant and beautifully presented, although the lower classes enjoy moaning and say they are used to better things and compare it with Fred Olson's bounty.

'My encounters with other nations' by Margit Latter (Cabin 335)

A romantic trip on the Amazon in an old-fashioned ocean liner could have been spoiled if I had allowed it to. All chairs and loungers were occupied on the top deck, so I took a chair from a stack and placed it way behind the last row that was not shaded from the sun. I was about to sit myself down when a Dutch lady got up and told me I could not put my chair there because her husband, who was sitting next to her, wanted that space later! Bemused and thinking she was joking, I smiled and sat down. She repeated her demand and I just laughed, as I don't like arguments. Then she let rip at her poor husband in a very loud and harsh voice, something like – 'you stupid fool, you are always so slow, we could have had that space as well if you had put a chair there'. As a German, I can sort-of understand the Dutch language, and I could not stop laughing.

The poor husband, red in the face, got up and went away. I grinned about it all day.

Later in the day my chair was taken literally from under my bum while I was eating lunch at a table on the pool deck. I had stood up to reach for something three feet away. A man took my chair and was still holding it. When I said I was still eating, he said: 'It is not your chair!' Very aggressive as well. People around us looked at him aghast. I felt like punching him.

I had the opposite encounter with a delightful Dutch couple. They called me Frau Muller and did not use their native tongue, but mine. The lady was creating footware. No, not clogs. She was crocheting the most beautiful baby booties in white, navy, red, blue and green.

'It makes you want to have a baby,' I said. 'Please can I buy a pair as a a present for a friend with a baby daughter?'

The answer was, 'No, you can't buy them, I'll give them to you.'

In the end, we settled on payment of a can of Coca-Cola. She would not take more. This wonderful encounter restored my faith in the human race.

by Dinah Read (Cabin 422)

After our sea shanty rehearsal I picked Jack up and we went to lunch and came back down to read and have time to ourselves, he singing a version of 'Oh no John no!' that had me quite helpless with laughter. I tore myself away and went to listen to a parliamentary talk by Michael Brotherton, an ex-Tory MP and part of the Naval fraternity.

by Lizzie Mayes (Cabin 494)

Today we had choir club and a book meeting. Richard was in good form and assured us, along with Clive, that the book would be a warts and all publication. Dick has gone off doing his sea shanties with Steve Ragnall, who seems to be such an enthusiast for life and has overcome immense physical difficulties. His partner, Jill Crocker, has the prettiest face.

by Clive Leatherdale (Cabin 725)

The more one settles into life at sea, the more one realises the ship functions as a floating village, with all amenities and public services. It offers a library, doctor's surgery, a place of worship, and much else behind the scenes. What about its police force, I ask Richard at this morning's book club meeting. Suppose someone gets drunk and disorderly in the early hours, or takes a swing at a passenger who has got up his nose. What happens then?

Police duties are undertaken by the ship's security officers, he explains. They deal with anything necessary, such as keeping quarantined passengers inside their cabins.

Does that mean there's a prison on board? Obviously not, as cabins can serve that function.

What if someone goes do-lally? Off their head? A danger to themselves and others? The answer shocks us all. Would you believe there is a padded room in the bowels of the ship! A moment's thought shows this is not so extraordinary after all. The ship has to cater for all eventualities, however unlikely.

After lunch I was introduced to a world-travelled brother and sister. She belongs to the World Wildlife Trust and Durrell Conservation Trust. They, too, had refused to get off the ship at Boca da Valeria, describing the place as an outrage, insisting that the animals prettily displayed by the children would soon be dead. I was also enlightened in the secret ways of the ship's 'Benidorm Bunch', a group of passengers owning houses in Spain, while claiming benefits and attendance allowance from Britain.

Another couple, virgin cruisers, were having less fun than their permanently smiling faces suggested. It was a case of smile or cry, she said. She described life on board as like a Rowan Atkinson sketch: he finds his path downstairs blocked by a geriatric with zimmer frame; he dashes over to the other staircase and finds the same thing. The staircases on *Marco Polo* were a bit like that.

A man carefully transported a plate of pizza and salad up the steps in dreadfully strong winds. When he reached the top a gust of wind emptied his plate of everything except a slice of pizza, but rather than look for where everything went, he just stared at his plate, shrugged, and carried on.

Richard savvily enticed Michael Brotherton to entertain passengers with tales of being a Member of Parliament. Episode One was this afternoon. Brotherton was elected Conservative MP for Leith in Lincolnshire in October 1974. He offered juicy tidbits on political friends and foes: Labour's John Silkin (nice) and Tony Crosland (a friend, but political foe who dispensed with grammar schools); Jeffrey Archer (did not know fact from fiction); Ted Heath (misogynist).

Prior to his parliamentary years, Brotherton worked on *The Times*, and took credit for introducing Page 3 girls to that august newspaper before the idea was snapped up by *The Sun*.

The temperature is dropping day by day as we head north-east on a course of 46 degrees. I am writing this outside Scott's Bar on Deck 9, and the pool deck below is almost deserted.

'I Have a Recurring Nightmare' by Richard Sykes (Cruise Director)

I have a recurring nightmare. Having spoken to other cruise directors, it seems to be a common consequence of our career. I can be having a fantastic dream about, say, winning the Ashes. I'll have just collected the trophy, fireworks and fanfares sounding in my ears, experiencing absolute elation, when suddenly I'll glance at my watch and remember that the ship is now departing. The perfect dream is then sabotaged as I have to run, cricket bat, stumps and ashes trophy in hand, to the dock where the ship is nowhere to be seen. I'll then wake up in a pool of sweat, my heart-rate pumping ten to the dozen.

I think this particular situation haunts me because I'm usually on the flip side – waiting on the dock, staring at my watch, hoping the captain will hold his horses while one – and it is always just one – passenger ambles back to the ship, arriving shortly before they reach the embarkation deck.

Since my first days on *Marco Polo*, we've always waited. There have, in fact, only been two occasions that the ship has been delayed because a passenger hasn't made it back before the announced sailing time. Both in Bergen.

The first was a tense affair. You might imagine: 'Well, what does it matter? Surely they can make up the speed.' In most cases you'd be absolutely right, but the fuel required to increase the speed is prohibitively expensive. So as the time ticks away, it's akin to having a conveyor belt of money, piling the loot into an open furnace. Hence the tenseness. The Bergen dock is unusual in that there's only one route that passengers tend to take into, and back from, the city. The road winds along the water-side, so it's possible to see for about half a mile whether anyone is approaching.

On this occasion, one of our guests was over half-an-hour after the sailing time – a full hour beyond the 'all aboard' time. It was apparent that we couldn't wait any longer, especially as there was no sign of him as we all desperately scanned the road.

The procedure is that the guest's passport is left with the port agent, who is authorised to spend whatever money is necessary for the man – and it is always a man – to comfortably get to the next port of call, or get home. This had been done. The funds are then debited from his account.

The captain approached me and said that time really was up, and I agreed that we really couldn't wait any longer. So, the gangway stairs were removed and the engines were readied. I glanced back at the road, only to see a figure hurtling along the pavement. I asked the captain to hold everything, which to his credit, he did.

We had a photo of the gentleman and looked through the binoculars to see if we could identify him. The face was a lot calmer on the photograph, and not quite as close to heart failure, but the clinching moment was when we realised he was wearing the same red plastic mac as the one in his picture. So we held the ship. By this time, of course, the side of the ship had nearly the entire ship's complement looking on. We had made several announcements that became more and more urgent, and no one was in any doubt that we were about to leave someone behind to see the delights of Bergen at night.

He arrived, exhausted, to a round of applause which subsided a little as he was faced with a wooden plank – like asking Paula Radcliffe to walk the highwire after a particularly gruelling marathon – which he negotiated brilliantly. The port agent threw his passport up after him and *Marco Polo* moved off. The cheers rang out and the ship blew its horn triumphantly as it headed out into the fjord.

After he'd got his breath back, been thoroughly chastised by his wife – and there's always a wife – he was asked to the captain's office. Inability to find a taxi was the excuse, and profuse apologies were accepted.

The second Bergen incident was a far more surreal affair. Much the same situation, but this time only a few minutes had passed after the stated all-aboard time. The captain and I eyed each other nervously, but then we spied a lone figure walking – not running, not jogging – but walking. I proffer the word 'unbriskly' as a generous alternative to 'dawdling'. With the aid of binoculars we were sure it was him. The captain sounded the ship's horn to try to instil some urgency, but to no avail.

The gathered crowd got bored and wandered inside. The captain, staff captain and pilot looked casually at their watches and I stared in disbelief (in these situations they are not 'our passengers', but 'your passengers'). Eventually he ambled up to the ship and boarded without a thank you. He arrived at the captain's office and blamed 'the cruise director' for him not having altered his watch.

On previous ships, however, I have left passengers behind. After starting a two-week trip with a journey from Palma to Malta, a couple failed to reappear after going ashore. They contacted the company's head office when they returned home two weeks later, having deliberately missed the ship. They had been having such a good time, and thanked the ship for forwarding their suitcases.

Whenever you hear an announcement for a missing passenger, it's likely that the swipe card didn't work, or that due to a computer error they haven't appeared on the manifest. If you hear it a second time, they've often returned a little late or didn't hear the first announcement. If the call goes out for a third time, spare a thought for your cruise director, nails bitten, panic stricken, clock watching, silently praying on the bridge, trying to hold back a conveyor-belt of cash. If that doesn't give you nightmares, nothing will.

'Frangipani' by Sue MacPherson (Cabin 714)
Elderly ladies in colourful sarongs
　Float by like jaded butterflies
Leatherine skin exposed in small bikinis
　They don't give a damn
Tough tits to dermatologists
　These totties, once babes,
Now beyond the pale
　Of skin care, an anathema to others
Having got this far
　They'll go the last mile for a tan.

Dangers lurk everywhere on cruise ships. There are four warnings for those venturing down these steps: (1) Zig-zags, (2) 'Watch Your Step' (right), (3) 'Caution Use Handrail' (above left), (4) 'Caution Mind the Step' (triangle, above right) (Clive Leatherdale)

DAY 34. AT SEA

'Celebrate your love for one another, or even express your feelings for someone special. Jerri, your Cruise Services Hostess, is here to help you make Valentine's Day memorable. Why not treat your loved ones to 8 Wooden Red Roses. All for the loveable price of £15.'

by Mave Eaton (Cabin 616)
This day started early. Our elderly female neighbours returned to their cabin at 1am and talked and talked. Eventually I banged on the wall, and silence fell in the girls' dormitory. What had they been doing? The only possible activity was the late-night disco in the bar. They are the only noisy neighbours I have ever encountered in years of cruising. Their voices start at 7am and are unceasing: would that there was an Olympic gold medal for marathon chatter.

'At the Doctors' by Caroline Clifford (Hospital No 468)
Richard Sykes warned us that we would all go a little stir crazy at this stage of the cruise. Tempers fraying, sunbed fever at its height, no clean knickers (let alone any clothes that fit), food overload and boredom.

Having exhausted 'conversation' with my small and ever-decreasing circle of friends, I decided to visit the doctor. This is a little-known and scary area of the ship and one that no one wants to visit.

Dr Antonis Papadakis, from the wonderful island of Crete – what a kind man and so 'free' with his time. I wasn't expecting an immediate audience, certainly not without signing the charge form, so I found myself sadly ill-equipped for the interview. Of course, I realised I couldn't steam ahead with the questions I wanted answered. 'Does it really cost £1,500 for antibiotics?' and 'How many people have died on this cruise?' But skirting around the issue was more difficult than I had anticipated, and I ended up confirming my own theories.

'Insect bites, skin allergies and sunburn are the most common ailments.' No snake bites so far. 'Prevention is the best policy – spray with DEET and don't lie in the sun between mid-day and 4pm.' And, of course, sailing so long at sea, the medical unit must be ready for anything. 'This is a modern facility with an operating theatre, two beds, pharmacy and testing procedures quicker than those in the UK.' They can, and do, treat anything from the common cold to a heart attack. Of course, the doctor couldn't mention any names, or problems, but we had a few friends in common so piecing the jigsaw together wasn't rocket science.

As for the juicy gossip, I was sadly disappointed. No deaths on this cruise, or the last; although I had heard rumours to the contrary. Only three passengers and one crew member removed from the ship for health issues. But I believe that one particular woman has been warned that she will be 'put off' *Marco Polo* if she continues to behave 'irresponsibly' and dislocates her shoulder a third time.

I remain ignorant as to the number of malaria cases, drunken brawls, and as to the location of the morgue. James wanted to know what happens if a Jewish passenger dies and whether there is a coffin maker on board. He also said he hoped I hadn't given the doctor my cabin number. I've kept him guessing on all counts.

by Mark Edwards (Cabin 423)
How on earth do the cabin stewards cope with their jobs? Contracted for eleven months, they never seem to get a break. Unlike the bar staff, and outdoor deck staff, who can be rota'd to get a break of a day or even half a day, this doesn't happen to the cabin stewards. They work 7am to 2pm, or later if there is a difficult cabin, and then 6pm to 8pm. This goes on without a decent break, seven days a week, certainly for the six weeks we have been aboard. The longest our cabin steward, Oksana, can get off is for four hours when we are in port for a whole day. And even then it is on a rota basis, as the ship must keep a minimum number of crew on board.

I have no idea how she keeps so cheerful. She is known as 'excellent', because if you ask her how she is, she always replies 'excellent', with a smile and a twinkle in her eye. The only time she felt down in our six weeks was immediately after an afternoon on the beach at Barbados, when she got something in her eye and it got infected and wept continuously. One of her cabins had a lady medic/nurse with eye department experience who had some antibiotic cream with her and sorted it.

Oksana's unfailing good cheer carried us through our quarantine period in our cabin. How can you be down when someone is so cheerful. She wasn't allowed into the cabin, but we kept the door open, and when she passed she stopped and talked. Perhaps more importantly, she kept putting our predicament in perspective. 'It's only another day; I've got another nine months.' Talking with her, she finds the level of management oppressive. As she says, she is not a teenager, she is a mum, she's been around and she doesn't constantly need checking up on to see if she's done the job properly. Why is she here, working this way? She is Ukrainian, a single mum, with two children, a boy and a girl of 21 and 23, both at university. 'I need the money to put them through university, and they need money. So what can I do?' So here she is, cheerful as can be, watching us spend money, when she is saving every penny, and separated from her children into the bargain. How does she do it? It certainly does put it into perspective as to how fortunate we are.

We have a continuing set of running conversations. We are expected to find her a rich sugar daddy. In the meantime she looks after our teddy bear and keeps him safe and happy. Teddy is always tucked up, with whatever is appropriate, Sue's sunglasses, my cap etc. We have photo'd all of them. Because of my constant use of the camera, I am 'Mr Paparazzi'.

Nothing rattles Oksana. She soon realised that Sue's neck was giving her grief, and that at times she needed to be in the cabin lying down, which coincided with the time that Oksana needed to be in and cleaning. She would always enquire after Sue, and we would let Oksana know that it was okay to knock even if the 'do not disturb' sign was up. On the occasion when Sue really needed to sleep, Oksana just accepted that, and the two of us came to an agreement as to when I would help Sue get out of the way so Oksana could sort the cabin. I have to say that this was in contrast to another cabin of Oksana's, when she was left fuming in frustration because she couldn't get in because of the 'do not disturb' sign.

Oksana has been the star of the cruise for us. She has always gone above and beyond what she had to do. They will miss her when she goes at the end of this contract in November. Off to find a cargo ship, where she can be cook and housekeeper, with no one to look over her. I just hope that her children appreciate what she is doing for them.

by Sue Edwards (Cabin 423)
I had my neck massaged. He found lots of painful bits in my back but not in my neck. My neck was much worse afterwards. I went back to my cabin to lie down and had a very bad head episode that started with severe nausea. Consequently I was sick a few times – just liquid came up as I had nothing for lunch. [Five weeks after returning home, Sue Edwards was diagnosed with a malignant brain tumour the size of a large egg. It was surgically removed on 5 April. Editor]

by Dinah Read (Cabin 422)
We took advantage of an invitation to visit the bridge, Richard Sykes conducting us. There was a staggering amount to take in, the ship's history,

built in East Germany for the Soviets, as an ice-breaker and for military use during the Cold War, converted to a cruise ship, gutted and refitted. There have been a great many developments and updates where navigational and communication systems were concerned. An old ship, like an old lady, sees many changes during her lifetime.

by Clive Leatherdale (Cabin 725)
I lunched at the Waldorf, being pampered for a change. There were eight round our table. The other seven moaned incessantly about everything. I said I thought everything and everybody was fantastic, and the table went quiet. Eyes lowered to avoid mine. They must think I'm a head-case.

It was my group's turn for Richard Sykes' guided tour of the bridge. Built in East Germany in 1965, our *Marco Polo* was originally the *Aleksandr Pushkin*, the second ship of the 'Ivan Franko' class, and the only one still afloat. (Incidentally, the excellent website www.simplonpc.co.uk displays internal and external images of the old *Aleksandr Pushkin*, and informs us that her sister ships were *Ivan Franko* (built 1964, scrapped 1997), *Shota Rustaveli* (built 1966, scrapped 2003), *Taras Shevchenko* (built 1967, scrapped 2005) and *Mikhail Lermontov* (built 1972, sunk 1986).) One passenger reckoned he'd dived to inspect the wreck of *Mikhail Lermontov* off New Zealand.

In 1990, Orient Lines bought the *Marco Polo* for its only vessel. It was a 5-star ship in her time, but is now classified as 3-star, though I have been unable to trace any public 'star' ratings for cruise ships. It certainly doesn't appear on Cruise & Maritime's website.

Richard says our mid-Atlantic position is classified as a cruise lane, not a shipping lane, which explains why no ships are seen or satellite signal received.

'The *Marco Polo* is like Cher; lots of new bits,' he says. She has bow thrusters but no stern-thrusters, which is why she always has to do three-point turns when manoeuvring in and out of port. The dark windscreens on the bridge protect the crew's eyes from reflection off the water. Moving to the fire-warning system, Richard casually informs us that eight fires have been recorded today already, mostly from the rear passenger lift, and were triggered by smokers who lit up before they got outside.

Richard fields the inevitable question about whether our vessel is unsinkable. With reference to the *Titanic*'s 'watertight bulkheads', he says *Marco Polo* has ten watertight zones, eight of which need to be filled for the ship to sink. She could sail home if five were filled.

The ship stages regular anti-pirate drills, although it is inconceivable there could ever be a 'Pirate in the Caribbean' (his phrase), as any such attack would ruin the entire local economy. Richard is not permitted to say if arms are carried aboard to deter pirates, but did say they are allowed to use any methods to deter boarding.

This was not a cruise director running through a cribsheet; it was a man talking about his home. Richard Sykes spends 48 weeks a year living on the *Marco Polo* and evidently loves her.

Marco Polo (right) is dwarfed by the P&O *Ventura* in Castries harbour (see page 231). In Belem (below), demonstrators wait until the traffic lights turn red before unfurling their banner: (see page 95) 'Recovering lives from alcohol and drugs. We ask for your collaboration. Help us recover lives, because only Jesus saves. We are from the Army of Christ' (both Clive Leatherdale)

DAY 35. AT SEA

The Falkland Islands in Peace and War.
16.30. Guest lecture
Rev Dr Daniel Haines gives a first-hand account of life on the Falklands before, during, and after the Argentine Invasion.'

by Mave Eaton (Cabin 616)

This is the fourth day without land but it is beautiful, blue, sunny and calm. Husband explains that we are in the Doldrums. The passengers are happy and no longer huddle in groups to moan. People tell one another amazingly intimate personal stories on this ship.

I lie on the deck next to a single passenger. He has decided to visit unusual places. Unfortunately, in the Bay of Biscay coming out he felt unwell and worried that his heart was beating erratically. He paid one visit to the ship's doctor who gave him an ECG and placed electrodes on his chest and then tied him up to a saline drip. The visit cost £1,500. An expensive treatment for sea-sickness. I have heard mutterings about the excessive cost of medical treatment.

The passenger, a policeman, then tells me of the house he had built in Spain. When he went to move in, he found the builder had failed to put in the promised swimming pool. The builder laughed, because he already had the policeman's money.

The passenger went to Andorra and bought a gun with a silencer. He returned to the builder and placed the weapon on the desk, whereupon the builder wrote him a cheque for the amount paid.

The stress of building this house affected the passenger's wife's fragile state. He returned from a walk to find she had hung herself. He is a resilient man and now lives with his only son and adored infant granddaughter. I asked if I could write about him and he seemed pleased with the idea.

by Steve and Marion Wright (Cabin 617)

Welcome aboard Deck 9, Cabin 617. We were pleased initially with our cabin, and unpacked and settled in. Having survived the turbulent waters of the Bay of Biscay – just like being on a fairground ride, confined to bed, every time I stood up I threw up – 36 hours later things have settled down and we are looking forward to breakfast in the morning.

6.30am. I jumped out of bed, thinking someone was banging on our door, but no one was there. Just back into bed when I heard pounding across our ceiling. What the bloody hell is that? We lay there bemused. One minute, 30 seconds later, there it is again, 'bump, bump, bump' across our ceiling. What the devil is it?

I chuck some gear on, then go up to Deck 10. No cabins above ours, so I could see no cause for this noise. Suddenly, the mystery is solved – 'the fanatical exercisers' pounding the deck. I say, 'Do you realise that here at the front of the ship you are over our cabins and it sounds like an army parade ground?' And the sign says, 'No jogging before 8am.' I am told in a very curt and abrupt manner that 'we're only walking, not jogging'. Then they carry on, unconcerned, without any sympathy regarding our disturbance.

Same thing next day, 6.30am. I don't bloody believe it. Fuming, I quickly throw on some clothes and go up to Deck 10. I plead with them to stop this madness and let me sleep. Not interested, they carry on regardless. As they pass I call out, 'Why don't you go to the gym?' No response.

I go to complain at Reception. Days later, still the same 'bump, bump, bump'. I go again to Reception: 'When are you going to put a stop to this?' I'm told they will print a reminder not to jog before 8am. Well, we don't need our alarm clock on this holiday. Only another 36 days to go.

6.30am. 'Bump, bump, bump.' This is unbelievable. Some thoughtless assholes at it again. Up to Deck 10, armed with the daily programme as this woman [name withheld] comes round. I request she reads the kind reminder. 'I'm only soft footed,' she says, adding, 'It's not me that woke you.' I say, 'Well, I didn't set my alarm clock and there's no other walker.'

At this point her husband [name withheld] catches up. 'Don't listen to him. Carry on,' he says. And to my dismay, they do.

It was their inconsideration and selfishness that made me determined to get the '8am and not before' enforced. So, once again, down to Reception and demanded to know what they were going to do. They said they would leave a report of my complaint. 'Not good enough,' I say. 'Call Security or get the staff captain. This has gone on far too long.'

Day 35. Still the same. Oh, the misery of Deck 9, Cabin 617.

by Lizzie Mayes (Cabin 494)
Halfway to the Azores. We seem to be very lucky with the weather and able to be outside all day. I asked Richard if we could have a curry night,

as we have an Indian head chef who produces, not often enough, the most delicious curry. Richard said that there had been such a vitriolic response to the last 'spicy' evening (nasi goreng!) that they wouldn't dare. What a miserable lot of old farts there are.

Dick went to listen to the Rev Daniel Haines talking about his Falkland Islands experiences. He is apparently a police forensic surgeon, specialising in child abuse, a dental surgeon and a reverend. Dick found his talk very moving, while others thought it rather sentimental.

Chair-bagging has now become something of an art form – people thinking up all sorts of cunning ploys to hold on to their loungers, chairs, and tables, too. We have taken to having our lunch on our loungers, rather than get into an affray in the 'parrot house', with all the bumping and barging entailed.

by Dinah Read (Cabin 422)
Some of the grousers were at our lunch table – though I have to admit that they may have had some justification this time, as they were on the excursion where the 'bus got stuck in the mud on the way to an arboretum', and they felt that they were entitled to a refund! I am more and more convinced that the only people who deserve, and really enjoy this voyage are real seafarers – RN or MN or competent yacht masters.

'Where does Mr Margate go?' by Mark Edwards (Cabin 423)
I first spotted this gentleman and his wife after breakfast on the pool deck on the third warm day, sitting close to the rail, watching the sea and his eyes closing. He seems to have shrunk with age into his 1960s apparel. Enormous NHS specs that should have elastoplast on them, big hearings aids, a cap that slips sideways when he closes his eyes, and socks and sandals that are out of proportion to his skinny legs. After that, he and his wife were regulars after breakfast at the rail, always sitting eyes closed. He always appeared content, secure in the knowledge that if he had to do anything, his wife would gently point out what he had to do.

I never saw them at any other time anywhere else on the ship until, much later in the cruise, I followed the pair of them into Marco's Bistro at lunchtime, when she was getting his squirt of sanitiser organised. After that, I saw them occasionally at lunchtime in the Bistro, but never after breakfast anymore.

What do they do during the day, where do they sit or lounge, and what do they do in the evenings? Why did they stop sitting out at the rail, before we left the Amazon? What are they doing now we have left the Caribbean?

I've just spotted him coming out of the Marco Polo Lounge after the early evening show. No wonder I have been missing him. Washed and dressed, he no longer looks to be the seaside caricature, but is securely smart in his shirt and jeans. And, as ever, he looks quite content with life. Good on him and his wife, I'm sure that they are getting what they wanted out of the cruise.

by Jean McGinley (Cabin 229)
Then came the *Marco Polo* Masters Quiz. In spite of being keen quiz participants, we put our names forward, together with Bob and Barbara, our dining companions, with little thought of success. On the night of our heat, we four were strangely nervous. We very nearly didn't get to compete as Richard Sykes had forgotten that 'Team 3', us, had entered. I think Barbara was ready to lynch him. Feeling rather deflated, I ordered a glass of wine from the bar, but we weren't let off the hook as Richard found another scratch team for us to compete against. The wine must have oiled our brains because we won our heat (I can't remember answering any of the questions) after a tie-break on Eastern Bloc countries – remember Kazakhstan and any other Stan! Tomorrow, Valentine's Night, is the big final.

by Clive Leatherdale (Cabin 725)
At lunch in the Waldorf I put my foot in it. I was sitting with seven strangers, among them the Rev Dr Daniel Haines. He was sitting opposite, and I only deduced his name from overhearing a remark he made about the 'South Atlantic'. That could only mean the Falklands, and that could only mean the gentleman who took Sunday service on board *Marco Polo*, and who was giving a talk this very afternoon on his experiences during the Argentine invasion.

Across the table I foolishly asked him if it had been scary. My daft justification was that I had been in China and caught up in the Tiananmen crisis of 1989. I had not found that scary at all; rather, it was exhilarating and I would never have missed it. I regretted my presumption at once. I had not been arrested; he had. I had not had a gun put to my head; he had. I was blissfully alone; he had his wife and three young children with him. He probably thought me an ass. Of course it was bloody scary.

His afternoon talk was packed. This was partly because of the subject, but partly, too, a reflection of tedium among passengers, who had little else to enliven these long days at sea. Canny Richard Sykes, anxious to fill the void, had recruited 'guests' with unusual interests or life histories and offered them the microphone. An ex-Member of Parliament yesterday, a

Falklands veteran today, though he stopped short of suggesting I might enlighten passengers tomorrow with my insights into the wonders of Bram Stoker's *Dracula*.

Logging onto the online Medico-Legal Journal when I got home, I found this summary of Daniel Haines' life:

'Dr Haines has by any standards enjoyed an unusually varied and interesting professional career, both in Britain and around the world. He made a conventional start reading Dentistry at Guy's Hospital, but while still a student he became involved in the dental identification of air disaster victims. Having qualified in Dentistry he was invited by Professor Camps to read Medicine at the London Hospital. There he embarked on a career in forensic pathology but after two years of corpses and body fluids, he and his wife, Hilary, took off for 10 years of general practice with the FCO [Foreign & Commonwealth Office] in the Cayman Islands, Swaziland and the Falkland Islands. Caught in the Argentine invasion of the Falklands, where he was the Senior Medical Officer, he had some amazing medical and surgical experiences, followed by seven weeks in an Argentine prison (see his book, *A Dangerous Practice – Falkland Islands GP*, Memoir Club, 2005). Since returning to London where he now lives, Daniel divides his time between general practice and police surgeon work, with a little forensic dentistry to add diversity. He is also a bee-keeper and together with his wife Hilary he records, photographs and reports on the butterflies of North Cyprus and maintains the national collections. Daniel was made a Deacon in the Anglican Church in Swaziland and ordained Priest at Southwark Cathedral and is honorary Assistant Chaplain at HM Tower of London. He has served 45 years in the Territorial Army, served in the First Gulf War and was awarded the TD soon after his return from the Falkland Islands.'

His talk was enlightening, if a touch blimpish for some tastes. He had much to say about the Geneva Convention and general misbehaviour of the Argentines, but all was forgiven when considering the anguish he and his family must have endured. In fact, his emotions were still raw. When describing the sight of the White Ensign flying once again above Port Stanley, his voice broke and he had to pause. The silence was broken by sympathetic applause.

This has been a day of soothing contemplation. The sun shone and the sea was so flat as to suggest god was in a generous mood. As I pottered about taking notes, Brian Rawlings (Cabin 324) pointed to the beauty of the smooth sea on this day of worship and spoke the hymn: 'Eternal father strong to save, whose arm hath bound the restless wave, O hear us when we cry to thee, for those in peril on the sea.'

Earlier in the day, the ship had passed through large swathes of green algae. A woman near me asked why the ship did not carry a wide net to sweep it all up and leave the sea nice and clean.

On the pool deck amid the acres of brown, wrinkly flesh, I saw a wondrous sight. An elderly Dutchwoman sat facing me, eyes closed, with her head nuzzling against the ample belly of her standing husband. Damn! My camera was in my cabin. I dashed to fetch it, only to find the couple chatting normally on my return. But help was at hand. A woman near me said she knew the couple and they would be delighted to pose. Before I could stop her she went and asked them. I didn't get a clip round the ear; instead I got the picture I wanted. After I had taken it, the beaming Dutchwoman boomed, 'Photo one dollar,' in imitation of the urchins of Boca da Valeria. She, unlike they, was joking (see below).

Love on the *Marco Polo* (Clive Leatherdale)

DAY 36. AT SEA

The Marco Polo Masters Quiz: The Final
The final is here, come along and see who will be the ultimate winners of this general knowledge game.'

by Mave Eaton (Cabin 616)
Our fifth consecutive day without land. The ship hypes up Valentine's Day. On offer are eight wooden roses and a special dinner. I think husband will not be entranced by these specials.

I talk to Jenny, a gentle, fragile woman. She picked up a chest infection four days ago. It turned into bronchitis and high temperatures. She reluctantly visited the ship's doctor who informed her she was verging into pneumonia and might need to have an x-ray in the Azores. He has given her four treatments of intravenous antibiotics. Today she looks better and came on deck to see the ice carving [a *Marco Polo* ritual performed by one of the cooks]. A huge block of ice was sculpted into a heart and turtle doves. Does the sculptor regret that his work is so ephemeral?

The suggested dress code for tonight is 'formal'. Formal nights on the *Marco Polo* are a complete charade. Men put on dinner jackets reluctantly. Dinner is exactly the same as usual; there are no free glasses of wine or the opportunity to circulate and seize passing canapes. It is a pointless exercise to dress up on this ship – going through the motions of what is done on cruise ships. Husband would have been happy just to wear a tie and jacket.

Something odd. I switch on my mobile phone out of boredom and get a signal and then a text. 'Welcome to Iceland' and details of how to make a call. Iceland?

by Caroline Clifford (Cabin 468)
Valentine's Day – a really sweet poem from James about our meeting in Burma, ten years ago. It even made a mention of my mother's dislike for him. Needless to say, I won't be showing it to mother, who is affectionately and appropriately known as 'the dragon'. I gave James a nose and ear trimmer, used for removing unwanted and unattractive hair.

Our cabin was extremely cold this morning. The only advantage to this is that the water bottles remain cool. But it seems stupid when I would now be paying a fortune for heating at home. However, James still insisted the air conditioning was not working efficiently. I said it was cold enough. He disagreed. I reminded him that he wore t-shirts in the Antarctic. He said he was sweating. I pointed out that there was cool air coming out of the ceiling vent, and he said, 'What do you expect me to do – hang upside down like a bloody bat?' And so the maintenance man had to be called.

Five weeks into the cruise and I'm wondering whether so much time together is taking its toll. Although we have travelled together many times, we've never been away for such a long period at one time. Little things like leaving the toilet seat up, snoring, monopolising the washing line, and his fetish for crunching plastic bags, all seem to impact as time goes on. He's even started packing – a week before we get back to Tilbury!

Things you put up with for two weeks take on another dimension when you spend six weeks encapsulated together. We've never normally been short on conversation, but now we spend most of our time eaves-dropping for juicy gossip. We've even tried spreading a vicious rumour that the cruise is being terminated in Falmouth for essential ship repairs.

James is working on a design for his on-deck 'international chair strap' with the slogan, 'You'll never be without a chair again,' and the instruc-tions, 'Strap it on your back and you'll have both hands free for your cof-fee.'

I know I always rubbish James, but he is an innovator and spends a lot of time doing 'useful' DIY around the cabin. Any little problem and he'll sort it out – however much I protest. There was the bathroom door which is now fixed wide open to stop that claustrophobic problem. Now the problem is that the 'sick' people next door, who keep flushing the toi-let, cause a disturbance at night. James has also stopped the door squeak-ing by applying shampoo, eradicated the smell from the bathroom drains by filling up the water traps, removed the faulty strip lighting so that the maintenance man could not fail to miss it, and stopped the cabinet draw-ers flying open in rough weather. Where would I be without him? Every home should have one, and despite his protests, a home is where he will probably end up – quicker than he thinks.

by Jean McGinley (Cabin 229)
Valentine's Night loomed ahead for the final of the *Marco Polo* Masters Quiz. Sadly, Barbara was not well enough to take part, but Clive luckily

stepped in. I actually managed to answer a question right, and we narrowly won. However, the whole thing passed by in a blur. Richard congratulated us and bought all four of us a drink on the house, or ship. I don't think we ever received any *Marco Polo* 'prize points' for winning. I never did find out what they were – we never managed to win prizes.

by Lizzie Mayes (Cabin 494)
An air of excitement about the ship today. Dick obviously didn't attend the 'craft and creation' session for men to make Valentine Cards, and I didn't awake to a delivery of eight wooden red roses.

The clocks went forward again, and I woke late to a beautiful blue sky and warm sunshine. I will miss having breakfast outside when we get home – it is so lovely to be able to sit out every day. I went for our morning daily quiz, finding out how much we don't know, but then do I really care that *fucus* is a genus of seaweed (incidentally, it is pronounced 'foocus'). Romance is definitely in the air – menus festooned with hearts and flowers, ice carved into cupids wings and hearts, and a formal Gala Valentine's Dinner. Ladies queued at the beauty salon – time to get rid of the widening chasm of grey roots and get nails painted.

Another extraordinary assortment of evening wear at dinner – some very beautiful and elegant women, and some looking like drag queens. Then on to the 'Love Show' – the 'bolters' ensconced in the front row in eager anticipation. Will the men never tire of the scantily clad dancers prancing around the stage – no, I'm not jealous of their size 8 bodies and tiny firm bums. Afterwards, Richard invites us to 'go though those doors', or 'through those doors' for the rest of the evening's entertainment. If he ever writes his autobiography it would have to be called 'Go through Those Doors'.

Then on to the *Marco Polo* Masters Quiz – The Final. We were surprised to find our esteemed editor Clive taking part, sartorial as ever in shorts and check shirt. (Later he assured me he had been dressed up for the formal dinner but had changed back straight after – why?) He answered the final question correctly and his team were pronounced winners. What a relief, as I don't think he could have taken another defeat. He keeps promising to tell me about *The Krypton Factor*, which he took part in many years ago and which clearly had a huge impact on him.

But the highlight of today, apart from Richard's 'Gershwin' cabaret, was the visit to the bridge. The ship is evidently loved by the crew and in particular by Richard. The story of how a statue of Nureyev came to reside in the 'parrot house' overlooking the swimming pool was not as we had all supposed – that the great dancer had once sailed in her. It is, in fact, an analogy of the ship's transformation from former Russian ice-breaker into cruise ship, the *Marco Polo*'s defection to the west and that of the dancer. That is why the owners bought the statue. We were told that the ship would not be able to have stern thrusters added, which means she will have to cease sailing should these become mandatory.

We were shocked to learn that the ship needed nine miles to turn round if someone went overboard. Little chance of survival with that turn. Richard explained that if you see anyone go overboard, you should throw anything over the side for them to grab, and of course life-rings.

I am sure even if I never sail in the *Marco Polo* again I will think of her with affection, and remember the comforting creaks and groans in my cabin as she rocked me gently to sleep. Those towering white high-rise monster new ships will never steal the hearts of its passengers and crew like this old ship. But rumours abound that the company has gone bust.

by Clive Leatherdale (Cabin 725)

Tonight was special for me, if for no one else. In 1983, in an act of impetuous madness, I replied to an advertisement for *The Krypton Factor*. Weeks later, after several elimination rounds, 10,000 entrants had been whittled down to the requisite 48, and I was among them. Anxiety turned to panic. Nowadays, every television channel seems awash with quiz programmes. Back then, only two mattered – BBC's *Mastermind* and ITV's *The Krypton Factor*, which marketed itself as 'TV's Toughest Quiz'.

I shall not bore readers with the terrors of the army assault course, with its fleet of offscreen ambulances. Or the so-called 'intelligence test' in which the pieces of my apparatus refused to fit, as confirmed by the floor producer, who simply shrugged it off: 'It worked in rehearsal, mate.' All that mattered was the four-way blanket finish, but blanket or not, I was fourth. In other words, last.

Somewhere inside I once hoped for the chance to rewrite history, to recoup that handful of stolen points that might have transformed me from fourth to first. The real thing eluded me, however, and over time my sense of grievance faded, until Richard Sykes and the *Marco Polo* offered surprise redemption.

I never knew about the *Marco Polo* Masters Quiz and therefore had not entered. It was therefore as casual spectator that I turned up for the final in Scott's Bar. Then Richard comes over, bends down, and tells me that one team is a member short because of sickness. Would I mind filling in? Would I mind? I'm out of my chair in a flash.

In my mind I am no longer in Scott's Bar, with its packed audience of penguined men and sequinned ladies – this is, after all, a 'formal' dinner night. No, I'm mentally transported back to Granada's television studios in Manchester, with Albert Tatlock and Peter Ustinov wandering around the corridors. Instead of the studio's four swivel chairs, evenly spaced, with a private monitor behind each, Scott's Bar improvises. The dance floor is the studio. Our team of four sits lined up on red chairs; the enemy sit right behind us, perched on bar stools. Richard Sykes faces us, a fluffed up version of dour Gordon Burns, computer questions at the ready.

Each of us has a buzzer which, rather than emit a sound, lights up red when pressed first. I feel a surge of adrenaline. I score a quick point by knowing Billie-Jean King's maiden name – 'Moffitt' – and now the nerves have gone. I don't want this to end. Round after round goes by, and then Richard announces the scores level with one question left. This is it.

'What was the name of the ship in which Charles Darwin . . . ?'

It's easy. Surely eight thumbs have squeezed eight buttons simultaneously. But the only red light showing is mine.

'Clive?' asks Richard.

'*Beagle!*' says Clive.

'Correct,' says Richard.

Our team leap from our chairs, hugging like footballers after a goal. Redemption had taken 28 years, but tastes sweet. Our prize? Nothing.

The *Marco Polo* Masters Quiz Champions
from left: Clive Leatherdale, Robert Scott Johnston, John McGinley, Jean McGinley

A SELECTION OF VALENTINE POEM ENTRIES

'I've stalked you now for many years' by James Coleman (Cabin 468)
I've stalked you now for many years
   And followed you to many places
I saw you once in Harrod's
   Putting on your airs and graces.
I've trailed after you in Tesco's
   In Aldi's and Lidl too
You were rough and ready then
   But still I fancied you.
I'm the one who phoned you nightly
   With lots of heavy breathing
And I sent those filthy photos
   That must have left you seething.
I've been in your back garden
   I took your undies from the line
I peered in at your windows
   And wished that you were mine.
Time has come to confess all
   And I tell you Caroline
You're obviously just meant for me
   Please be my Valentine.

'The Valentine's Dance,' by James Coleman (Cabin 468)
I was feeling very romantic
   And went to the Valentine Dance
I saw her alone on a bar stool
   And thought, I'm in with a chance.
I approached and said, 'You're quite lovely'
   And I stood there, just like a toff
She said, 'You're old and you're ugly
   'Why don't you go and sod off.'

'Valentine Romance,' by James Coleman (Cabin 468)
He went to the Valentine Dance
   And met a young girl just by chance
There was a conclusion, to this instant infusion
   But she did ask for cash in advance.

'Reflections of Love' by David Mackenzie-Crooks (Cabin 641)
Oh Valentine, my Valentine
   You are so sweet to me

How glad I am that you're mine
  So strong and handsome too.
I see you in the early morn
  And in the evening light
I bless the day that you were born
  Oh vision of delight.
You know it's you whom I adore
  It comes as no surprise
For yes, I can the world assure
  My mirror never lies.

by Jeremy Tait (Cabin 715)
We danced together through the night
  and all the time I held her tight
It really had been quite a feat
  to find a girl so cute and sweet.

I kissed her at her cabin door
  We went inside, she asked for more
I put my hand upon her thigh
  And she turned out to be a guy!

by Norma Pascua Artajos (Cabin 715)
Barbados is behind us, and Tilbury ahead
  I've nothing much to do, because my library book is read
I'm single on this voyage, and lonely, truth to tell
  I lean upon the railings, to watch the deep sea swell
And then I see a figure, Pierce Brosnan could it be
  My little heart is pounding, but will he notice me?
He joins me on the railings, and puts his hand in mine
  The words he barely whispers, please be my Valentine.

'A Valentine's Lament' by David Mackenzie-Crooks (Cabin 641)
My colleagues really are absurd
  They tease me half to death
They say I'll never pull a bird
  Like a Mary, Jane or Beth.

They chant at me with cold refrain
  'You're bad for all time
And when that time comes round again
  You'll get no Valentine'.

But life is fickle, life is strange
    And if you kneel and pray
The hope is then that things will change
    And I'll find love one day.

So in the office I've a bet
    That this year will be mine
And for the first time I will get
    A lovely Valentine.

The day has come when life will start
    That day I fear the most
I'm at my desk with beating heart
    There, waiting for the post.

The post has come, the post has gone
    But nothing there for me
My colleagues have their cards, but none
    To ease my misery.

A bitter pill – it's really hard
    I'm back there on the shelf
Not even do I get a card
    When I send one to myself.

'Why It's the 14th of February' by David Mackenzie-Crooks (Cabin 641)
St Valentine was a bit of a cad
    Not quite all good, though not all bad
With his strong physique and long black curls
    He cast a spell over all the girls.

He set out in life with one great aim
    A girl a day – 'twould bring him fame
His final target, so we hear
    A girl for every day of the year.

The fifteenth of Feb, the day he started
    Big Liz was his, big tits, big-hearted
Then onwards into April, May
    A damned good life, this girl a day.

The summer passed and autumn too
    Even in winter's cold he knew
Through Nell the nymph to Pearl the peach
    His target was in easy reach.

On Feb thirteenth, just two girls more
    He sought out number 364
She was tall and beauteous, quite a catch
    But it seems our Val had met his match.

As if now cursed by heaven above
    Poor Valentine, he fell in love
His mission failed, though oh so near
    St Val could never complete his year.

His heart in chains, he solemnly swore
    Feb fourteenth would be for ever more
A day of love that he'd leave free
    For other souls, like you and me.

'Hand in Hand' by Kay Rainsley (Cabin 543)
This entry won the ship's prize for best Valentine poem. Kay met Les, her
first boyfriend, one week after her fourteenth birthday and married him
two weeks after her sixteenth birthday. He was seventeen. In the years
that followed they both studied for degrees at the University of Warwick
as mature students whilst working full-time. They also took up scuba diving which has been a shared passion for over 30 years. They have now
been married for 41 years and have one son and one daughter and three
perfect granddaughters.

This world can be a lonely place
    without a kind and friendly face
Someone to love, someone to care
    Someone with whom our lives to share.

I wear your ring and you wear mine
    We live like grapes upon a vine
yet free to flourish as we grow
    in love's continuous ebb and flow.

As life goes on and time goes by
    I ponder on the reasons why
My life would surely never be
    the same without you close to me.

We've both matured and understand
    we're stronger when we're hand in hand
Life's not plain sailing but it's true
    I'd do it all again for you.

DAY 37. AT SEA

'15.00 Radio Theatre. Our radio theatre is simply a chance to sit back, relax and listen to some of the best in radio comedy. Today, there's an episode of Yes Minister with Paul Eddington as Jim Hacker. Then it's The Goon Show with Spike Milligan.'

by Mave Eaton (Cabin 616)
Sixth day at sea. The sun shines out, but passengers are becoming more irritable. One lady complains of another who took two oranges. Another rages about the woman who kept a sunbed for 40 minutes for her husband, when 30 minutes is the maximum. I snarl at a woman who asks me to return a book to the library I did not borrow. Our dinner takes an hour and a half, so I start to leave before dessert is served, to the horror of our harmless waiter. We'll all be better behaved after reaching Ponta Delgada.

by Lizzie Mayes (Cabin 494)
Morning quiz, choir club – trying to get everything right for the dreaded public choir performance. I can't believe we're still sitting out on deck in warm sunshine. We missed the 'Rule Britannia' bash in the 'parrot house' – Clive told me it nearly caused World War III, with the Dutch getting stroppy about the noise spoiling their sunbathing on the 'puffin deck' and the 'broiler deck'. They are now taking every opportunity to turn themselves into pieces of old leather before returning to the winter climes of northern Europe.

Rumours abound that the shipping company is about to go bust and that the owners are coming on board today to tell us that we have to find our own way home from the Azores, as the ship can't return to the UK. Couldn't get too excited, as Richard seemed to be as positive and exuberant as ever, the staff seemed unruffled, and the pace of life on board unchanged. I still keep seeing people I have never seen before – really strange when there are only 800 passengers on board.

by Caroline Clifford (Capsule 468)
Emerging from my capsule there was a wonderful feeling of camaraderie – 'good morning', 'morgan', 'morning, sleep well?' – quite uplifting. And

feeling uplifted I broke the 'table for two' routine and shared my table at luncheon with a famous publisher, er, Clive. This totally fazed the waiters who were, now, all aware of my solitary preference.

It's not that I'm totally anti-social, but all that small talk! It's tedious and serves little purpose. 'Have you cruised with *Marco Polo* before?' I once replied: 'If I had, do you think I'd be here now?' Not true, but it was quite a conversation stopper.

'Did you go ashore today?' 'Did you see the cabaret last night?' Of course I saw the cabaret, I'm Richard Sykes' biggest fan. Then the meal drags on for an age with some people demolishing an extraordinary number of courses. Another problem on a big table – I can't secrete my leftovers to James' plate, which is my food disposal system.

Finally, I'm never sure what 'little gems' James will come out with. This usually involves commenting loudly on the lookalikes at the next table, the bits of shrub on his plate, or people dancing 'like his dad' in Scott's Bar. Yesterday, he said, 'last time I saw so many old people it was in a graveyard.'

I reminded him that at 75 *he* is old. 'At least I'm alive,' he replied. 'Only just,' I said, reminding him that if the pillows weren't so skinny I would have suffocated him by now. So, as a rule, only on deck do I share a table (if I can get one) and swap gossip over a cigarette, which makes it easy to escape.

It is probably for this reason that I haven't reached the 'psychological state' mentioned in the daily programme, and haven't felt a need to avoid anyone – yet. I enjoy a smile from a fellow passenger and I loved a comment heard earlier: 'She's alright, she's a smoker,' whilst they guarded the endangered ashtrays. It does seem that there are either ashtrays and no chairs, or chairs and no ashtrays.

I was possibly in some danger, walking round deck with the most valuable book in the library – the only copy of Bradt's guide to the Azores. I had camped in the library well before the lovely Susan was scheduled to open up the locked cabinets, and was bent on procuring the book the minute it was returned. As a rule I'm not a selfish person, but Darwin (according to my mother – a distant relative) promotes the theory of the 'survival of the fittest', and sometimes that is what I feel this cruise has taught me. I was made painfully aware of this at the deck party. Spotting two free chairs together, I sat on one and the other was abruptly snatched away by a passenger whom I would have considered to be above such appalling behaviour. I know it was 'just a chair', but his action was rude. I'm only glad my protestations were witnessed by astonished and sympathetic onlookers.

by Jill Crocker (Cabin 514)
Saelesh (our cabin steward) is treating us to the towel sculpture treatment. It was a monkey hanging from the air-conditioning fitting last night. It was so good that we left it up there, which gave us a bit of a shock when we saw it this morning.

'Gyms on Ships' by Mark Edwards (Cabin 423)
Now we are on the last leg, it's only the addicted exercise idiots who are left. Strangely, the numbers exercising in the gym have steadily dropped from the heady days at the start, when we all had to wait in line to do our stuff. The early-morning session has dwindled to the absolute regulars: at 6.15am, the 'nice lady' who rows for 30 minutes, the 'colonel' with his strange exercises probably taught to him by a PTI 50 years ago, and 'shopping bag man' who walks for 30 minutes on the treadmill leaving his shopping bag on the window ledge.

I arrive at 6.30, and at 6.45 Australian 'Mr Pilates' and his wife move into the table tennis area, followed shortly by his three lady followers. They latched onto him when they discovered he has a very good 40-minute stretch routine that is a hybrid of Pilates, T'ai Chi, Yoga and other disciplines. It could be his promise to get rid of facial wrinkles, if they keep it going for five years, but he is a retired PE teacher. Then the three Dutch couples arrive, who bumble though a few simple non-taxing routines. I wonder what happened to the 'lean brown running machine'? He used to come most mornings, and I can't believe that a 50-year-old in such good shape isn't running.

The mid-morning session early in the cruise started with passengers walking in, looking around in a bemused way, and trying the exercise machines for a couple of minutes. I think it is their one and only opportunity to have a free go in a gym. Some of them vaguely got the hang of it, but what's the point of walking slowly on a treadmill, when you could be outside walking on the deck? They don't even put the telly on. So far I have only numbered six of us that actually raise a sweat.

But then the plonkers pop in and out. So we have several 'Mr Walk in Confidently'. They pop in, pick up a pair of heavy dumbbells, do ten repetitions of an exercise and then leave. What was that all about? 'Mr Bullfrog,' a Dutchman who looks like a Boer/bore. He is so proud of himself in his perfectly ironed white trousers and shirt, who exercises all his boxing muscles for 25 minutes, but never raises a sweat or creases his clothes. 'Mr Explode,' who does ten repetitions of a heavy weight slowly without breathing, going redder and redder in the face – please breathe because I don't want you to explode all over me. 'Mr Abs' doing his 30 minutes on the 'ab curl' machine: Christ knows, exercise is boring enough without expertly wrecking your back.

Then there are the dutiful wives, who come to watch and/or wait, who are likely to have a weight dropped on their toes, when they stand six inches away from my heavy weights. They obviously don't have any lateral vision or they would see the 80-kg pile of weights on the bar that I'm swinging around. Actually, the best time for the ladies to come and watch bottoms is about 3.30ish, when one or more of the ship's male dancers are doing their weights.

And then there are the power walkers, who dutifully start after 8am. Hi folks, as I lap you every third turn round the ship, I'm only walking: it's good for you to get the heart rate up just a touch.

A couple of us trainers have postulated that you should have a physical before you get a gym pass. We have mentally reviewed our 'resusc' training, and probably ought to ask where the external cardiac defibulator is kept. Hopefully not in the hospital, as that is the furthest part of the ship to the gym. Is it the nurse in red who comes along and shouts 'stand back'?

by Dinah Read (Cabin 422)
We have just come from another of Tony Rice's deeply engrossing lectures. This one was on territorial limits, 3 mile, 12 mile and further, based on coastline, or continental shelf, or other criteria, with national and financial and therefore political implications and effect. I was fascinated and look forward to asking my son, who is an oil geologist, for his take on these matters.

Another snippet. Every day when I walk along the Pacific Deck corridor I have noticed that one of the young Indonesians, who cleans and tidies the cabins so efficiently when waiting for the next one to be vacated, is always reading a small book. I have been wondering what he is reading with such concentration, so I asked him today and he showed me, *The New Testament and Psalms.* I had thought it might be the Quran. In fact, I feel a slight sense of relief.

by Clive Leatherdale (Cabin 725)
I reached breakfast in the Waldorf just before it closed. Serving herself slices of melon, the woman in front of me dropped the tongs on the floor. Rather than ignore them or hand them to a waiter for washing, she retrieved them and placed them next to the melon tray for me to use.

Richard had just announced the rare sighting of a container ship on our port bow – the *Orient Cavalier.*

This afternoon I observed an inflammatory incident. At 2.30 Richard hosted a raucous English deck-party, complete with *Rule Britannia*, Vera Lynn, and other staples of Englishness. Scots, Irish and Welsh were implicitly, nay, explicitly uninvited. The Dutch weren't mentioned.

I positioned myself on Deck 9, looking down on the action, as from a balcony. Richard Sykes knows exactly what he is doing, of course. Most passengers relish this kind of thing. The question is, what about those who don't? I did my 'pass-around-my-notebook' trick to four couples nearby. Here is what they wrote in it:

'What a load of rubbish!'

'The louder the noise is not a measure of quality.'

'Good for football fans and other miscreants.'

'Incidentally, Britain is a slave to the USA!'

I even witnessed a bit of argy-bargy. A beer-bellied English idiot started prancing around in front of The Hook of Holland (the Dutch smoking ghetto) nearby. Strong words were exchanged, but when I sidled along to eavesdrop, everything had quietened down. The first 'murder on the *Marco Polo*' will have to wait.

Ever since my unexpected introduction to the ship's hospital, I've known I have three vital interviews to conduct – with Dr Papadakis and the two nurses. I can hardly collar them when they are treating passengers, so I bide my time until I see them on deck, relaxing before their next shift. I spied my chance and nabbed the nurses, separately, this afternoon.

Nurse Daisy was born Desislava Doncheva in Varna, Bulgaria in 1983. 'Desi', as her friends call her, found her name slipped into 'Dizzy' in English, so she anointed herself 'Daisy', from the Disney cartoon character Daisy Duck, and because she likes the flower. She studied for three years at medical college in Varna, and still sees herself as a 'theatre nurse', even though she fainted on her first day as a student. She spent 2005-06 working in theatre. She learned her English at high school, but only as a second foreign language. Her first was French, as her grades were not good enough to give her preference in English.

Daisy's dream to work abroad was initially frustrated by her diploma not being internationally recognised. She was offered work only as a 'sanitary nurse' or 'orderly', which she declined. Her two older sisters are still in Varna, as is her mother, who encouraged her in her quest to leave.

Applications for medical appointments on cruise ships are submitted via the internet. Daisy faced the usual problems. Cruise lines prefer nurses with cruise experience, so how can a newcomer get that experience? A vicious circle. The bigger lines even demand at least three years' 'emergency room' experience.

By cruising standards, Daisy is now a veteran of the high seas. The *Marco Polo* is her fourth ship, following work on the *Albatross* and the *Van Gogh*, until the owners became insolvent. Her experience on a sailing clipper, the *Star Flyer*, brought particular hardships. With just 150 'guests', there was no doctor and just one nurse. She had almost no facilities and also had to double up as a waitress. Despite exotic destinations such as French Polynesia, sea-sickness afflicted her terribly.

Her worst moment in her years at sea was when an elderly patient died because the doctor arrived too late to be able to apply CPR. Daisy was at the time working as crew purser, not a nurse. On the *Marco Polo* she is on 24-hour call, which means her cabin is right next to the medical centre. As her phone is liable to ring at any time, she rarely goes to onboard shows, almost never goes ashore, and tries to sleep whenever she can.

Daisy loves her job, but admits she prefers patients with a sense of humour. In three years' time, when she turns 30, she thinks she might be married with children, and in the meantime she saves all the money she can.

That concluded our interview, but there is more to Daisy than the bare facts related. With her tumbling blonde hair, pressed tunic of pink or green, deliciously strong Slavic accent, and charm acquired from years of dealing with cruise patients, Daisy wins affection from everyone she meets. As our interview ended and I stood up to leave, I remarked to someone nearby that I had just interviewed Daisy.

He corrected me: 'You mean delightful Daisy,' he said.

Nurse Lily is a different character. Liliana Paceagiu is Romanian, born in 1985 in Constanta on the Black Sea. Half the crew of *Marco Polo* seem to hail from Constanta, which has seemingly been drained of its young people in the service of Cruise & Maritime Voyages.

Lily's Constanta and Daisy's Varna are separated by just 75 miles on a direct Black Sea coast road, but their native languages are mutually unintelligible – Romanian being a Romance tongue, Bulgarian is Slavic – which means they can only converse in English.

I ask her why she prefers to be called Lily, when she has a beautiful name, Liliana. She winces. 'I hate my name,' she says, 'it takes forever to get out,' a reference to all those tiny syllables. She had gone straight from high school to nursing college, then to university to be a kindergarten teacher. She then worked for three years in cardiology and gynaecology. Unlike Daisy with her Bulgarian diploma, Lily's qualifications are more widely accepted, giving her greater opportunities.

Lily is comparatively new to cruise ships. As she is free to work anywhere, across Europe as well as at sea, she is unsure where the future will take her. At times she seemed a little preoccupied, but I knew why. When tending to my intravenous drips at the end of January, she would come by every few minutes to check progress or change one sachet for another. She looked low and I asked what the matter was. Her father had died that week. She had signed up for this cruise to earn money to help pay for his treatment and had last seen him two months previously. I reached out my hand to express sympathy. She seemed on the point of tears but fought them back. She shrugged: 'It's life.' That, I sensed, was very much Lily's outlook. You get on with it.

Now, speaking to her on deck, I enquire about her proudest moment as a nurse on a cruise ship. She does not hesitate. Some months ago a lady presented herself to the medical centre with symptoms of bronchitis. Lily, however, noticed an erratic pulse in the woman's neck, which her cardiac training taught her might be dangerous. She called the doctor urgently. Atrial flutter was suspected, and the ship 'turned around'. Patient confidentiality meant Lily was unable to tell me more.

The best part of Lily's day is when passengers say, 'Thank you.' The worst part is when some are rude to her, particularly those quarantined in their cabins when she goes to check up on them.

She has had a seven-year relationship with her boyfriend, an officer on a container ship, and has learned to be wary of trusting people, as most think only of themselves. Her dream is to be happy. A thoughtful yet spontaneous person, she believes life is for the living. She ends our interview with her philosophy: 'It is better in life to regret what you did than to regret what you did not do.'

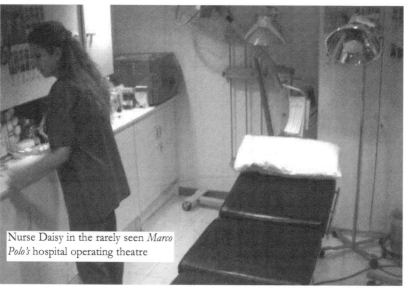

Nurse Daisy in the rarely seen *Marco Polo's* hospital operating theatre

Day 38. Ponta Delgada, Azores

'The archipelago of the Azores consists of nine volcanic islands situated in the middle of the North Atlantic, 932 miles from Europe and 2,423 miles from North America. The largest of the islands is São Miguel, or the Green Island.'

by Mave Eaton (Cabin 616)
Ponta Delgada – good weather, a charming small town in the Azores. We take the *Marco Polo* excursion and go by bus to a beautiful viewpoint. Our local guide is one who never stops talking; all facts, figures and statistics. He ignores historic buildings as we drive along. We are taken to a pineapple plantation. I had seen many in my years living in Borneo. This one is certainly different. It consists of about twenty greenhouses with the glass painted white. Inside are pineapple plants, but there are fewer than twelve that actually have full size but unripened fruit. We are given a free drink in the shop, which is part of the 'plantation'. It sells souvenirs. Perhaps this is the reason for the plantation visit – to get captives into the shop? Husband gives driver and guide a small tip, but no one else does.

by Caroline Clifford (Cabin 468)
Armed with my timetable from the tourist office, we caught the 11am 'Caetano Raposo' from Ponta Delgada to Nordeste, a pretty town ironically situated at the north-east corner of São Miguel. I can only imagine that 'Raposa' refers to the breakneck speed that the comfortable bus/coach tore along the roads and round the hairpin bends. There were just two other passengers from *Marco Polo* – Dutch – who smiled but didn't talk much. The views from the elevated road of the seascapes were stunning (when I dared to open my eyes). It was too early in the season for many of the flowers, but there were still splashes of colour between the shrubs and ferns. I had tendered €10 and the driver patiently counted out 98 cents in change, the fare mysteriously set at €4.51 each.

There was much squealing of brakes and a judder from the gearbox, which James explained was caused by well-worn mountings. 'Not a difficult job,' he said. We passed via the popular town of Ribeira Grande, Porto Formoso, Maia, Santana, São Pedro, Lomba da Fazenda and many small hamlets. We dived down narrow streets to pick up and deposit locals piled up with all manner of produce. The lanes all had blue and white tiled nameplates, and the house doors all opened onto the street, making our progress akin to the running of the bulls in Pamplona, pedestrians running for cover in shop fronts and driveways.

I would like to say the local women were exceptionally pretty, at least the ones we saw, except the opposite is nearer the truth – weather-worn, distorted faces, greasy hair, and one proudly supplanted by a badly trimmed beard. James put most of it down to too-much inbreeding. He supposed that these particular features could be attributed to ancient mariners returning to Europe having played 'whose turn in the barrel' for more than eighteen months. Whatever that means!

Everyone drove without fear, at high speed and apparently blind, around hazardous sharp corners. It was a relief to arrive safely in Nordeste at 1.30pm. We had hoped to complete a circuit of the island, but unfortunately the bus timetable given us at the tourist office bore no resemblance to reality. The bus to Povoação (back on the south coast) did not run on Wednesdays. We were stranded in unremarkable Nordeste until the 4pm bus, which was the last one back to Ponta Delgada. We arrived early at the 'terminus'; it was remarkable because, although in essence it was just a car park, the shelter had clean toilets and a memorable view down to the sea.

I felt sure we were in pole position for the front seat, although James suggested that a few cretins had camped in the carpark overnight. He was right; I was beaten by a determined pensioner, no more than four feet tall – and wide – who shot onto the bus like a cannon ball.

This time we had the right change for the cheery driver, and once again we set off at a speed more suited to Brands Hatch and to ear-splitting sounds of 'popular music'. This was just as well – James was very critical of the driver's skills and had not realised that Pedro spoke excellent English.

With a sudden jolt and an expensive scraping sound, we mounted the pavement and hit a wall. Evidently, both Pedro and the approaching juggernaut had failed to correctly judge their braking distances. I would describe our driver's reaction as, 'Not too bothered.' Pedro had damaged the front trim over the wheel arch. James confided: 'It's a Volvo. It's tough.'

Back on the road, it would be remiss not to mention the spectacular cascading waterfalls, the obstacle course up and over the construction works of the new highway, and the sheer drops, five or six hundred feet above the sea. 'It makes Cornwall look featureless and flat,' said James.

Then an extremely loud bang – the indisputable sound of a blow-out. Now the driver looked worried. He cut his speed considerably but there was nowhere to stop, so we limped into the next village, Pedro muttering 'pneu' to himself. A phone call was made, and several cigarettes later we continued slowly with the radio volume reduced, but still two hours away from Ponta Delgada. We had no idea what would happen and – if repairs were necessary – when and where they would happen. 'We've missed dinner,' observed James.

The wheel was 'looked at' again at Ribeira Grande bus station. Pedro smiled and said we would be leaving in twenty minutes; just enough time for ten more Marlboro. James gave me a lesson on how to change the wheel with the aid of a greased plate. 'You'll never get that off without one.' Not that I had any intention of getting my hands dirty.

And when we finally got off the bus on Avenida Infante d'Henrique, Pedro winked at me and said, 'Only one minute late.'

by Lizzie Mayes (Cabin 494)
The ship arrived early, so we decided to make an early start by public bus to Seta Cidades, only to discover the one and only bus had left at 7.30am – even too early for us. We decided instead to go to Ribeira Grande – by bus at 11.30am. While passing the time, we wandered around the strange shops – lots of them selling masks and dressing-up clothes. I thought some of the local girls very plain, so maybe that's the only way they can catch a man. Not that the men were any beauties either. The island seemed rather sterile – everywhere very clean, no graffiti and little litter. Perhaps it livens up in the tourist season. It seemed also to be very well policed by menacing men, with guns and handcuffs on display.

The sea was huge at Ribeira Grande, enormous white-edged breakers crashing against the shore – the noise deafening. It was a strange little place – kind of empty and ghostly, with the few shops hidden by huge brown wooden doors and very dark inside. The people are dark-eyed and generally unsmiling. Such a contrast to the happy and vibrant West Indians. Churches looked down on us from every corner – perhaps the demeanour of the people reflects that god is watching their every move and looking for sinners. The churches were often built in the traditional black and white, with lovely bell towers, as are so many of the official buildings in the town, reflecting former grandeur and wealth. The prison occupied prime position on the sea-front in Ponta Delgada.

Back in Ponta Delgada we went to the market and met a strange English lady who communed with the spirits to keep the island 'safe and beautiful'. She hadn't succeeded in bestowing any of this physical beauty on to her son and daughter-and-law who ran their market stall. They were selling their own produce but had to import a lot.

It's been a strange day really, which didn't evoke a single emotional response. Back on ship, I chatted with the Polish women with a west African husband who is very sick. He was the community physician for Leicestershire when he was struck down with a massive stroke eleven years ago. She finds cruising an ideal way of getting a break, as he sleeps a lot and is safe in the cabin, so she can take some of the shorter shore trips. She is so glamorous and has such a kind face. She tells me she has brought a different dress for every night of the cruise.

The rumours don't seem to have come to fruition – it looks as if we will have to brazen out the last four days in raging storms. Everyone is preparing us for a terrible time, and we are to leave the Azores two hours early tomorrow morning to try and avoid the worst. Olga and Liliya were singing Richard's praises – is there anyone on this ship who doesn't love this affable, larger-than-life genius who keeps the whole show on the road?

by Jill Crocker (Cabin 514)
Steve Ragnall and I took a walk along the portside in the morning. Steve is escorting a tour to Fire Lake this afternoon. He fancies the Portuguese tour guide (he fancies anyone if he can see over the top of their head without a box). I teased him by asking if the man in the red t-shirt would be with us today.

by Dinah Read (Cabin 422)
This morning we moored at the cruise terminal at Ponta Delgada in the Azores. Jack elected to go ashore and look for *The Times* newspaper – the first time he has set foot on shore for 37 days. So, of course, I went with him. We emerged from the terminal onto a purpose-built range of eating places and tourist outlets. We walked up a ramp onto a harbour-side road with municipal and office buildings, and a church, but no newspapers in sight – let alone British ones! So we went back again. The fact is that Jack really cannot walk freely, though he tries to conceal it.

I later went off to join the excursion to Fire Lake. When I had awoken at dawn, my first impression of the island we had arrived at overnight was purely white. I thought, 'This can't be snow?' Then I realised that everything here was *painted* white. At full daylight I saw that almost all the buildings were also picked out in black. The only other colour was a green as bright and clear as any in England, and the regular fields of the lowland areas were bounded by neat dry stone walls of black basalt. Not only that, but they were stocked with the biggest and best herds of black and white Friesian cattle that I have seen for years. This perhaps came as the greatest surprise to me in the whole of this voyage. Amazing that the remote and volcanic Azores should go in for dairy farming on such a scale. How and where did they market the milk?

by Clive Leatherdale (Cabin 725)
Breakfast in the Waldorf, where I was joined by Sue MacPherson, the Scottish artist and poet. She said she couldn't believe the colonels-of-the-raj conversations she was overhearing onboard. She took my notebook to relate an incident whereby a Dutch passenger became irate with an Englishman hammering out noises on his cellphone.

'Said the Dutchman to the Englishman, "You're beeping, sir, it drives me mad. Please desist or go elsewhere."

'The Englishman to the Dutchman replied – with his back.

'My neighbour chuckled. I snorted, "Will this in fisticuffs resolve?"

'Silence.

'Ten minutes later, William of Orange explodes. The Essex swain splutters in the face of continental wrath.

'"You stop zis now or pay zee price," Mr Holland screams. "Don't you understand English?"

'English subsides in a whimper. Detente is restored, of sorts. My neighbour's muffled giggle the only sound.'

Murder on the *Marco Polo*? We're getting nearer, I thought to myself.

I did not leave the ship until 10am. The quayside is plush and modern. I found the tourist office and there was no queue. I had three lady attendants to choose from. The first bus going anywhere would be the one I took. It would leave in ten minutes for Mosteiros on the north-west coast, an hour's drive.

Empty roads, prosperous countryside, recognisably Portuguese. Signs of comfort everywhere. All the walls were black basalt. The further west, the wilder grew the sea. Rock stacks were pounded by waves higher than I have ever seen.

Two couples from *Marco Polo* alighted at the terminus, a patch of gravel, and we pooled together for a taxi to take us to Sete Cidades and the volcanic lakes. On our return I was then left with 90 minutes in Mosteiros before the bus back to Ponta Delgada. The village was dead, the only life outdoors being unsmiling old ladies. As in Cape Verde, Portuguese influence dictated a bandstand in the centre. I found a café-bar, inside which men played dominos underneath an immense, wall-mounted digital television. A pool table and bar-football table stood unattended nearby. But my lingering memory of Mosteiros is the waves. Park benches were positioned at the best points to sit and watch.

I met the other couples for the 2.45 bus back. One couple were having a great time overall; so – on balance – was the other, with the caveat that they had nearly been left behind on an Amazon excursion. The wife had to be transferred from one boat to another in mid-river. She nearly fell in, and the experience had left her traumatised.

Ponta Delgada is laid out like so many other port-towns we have seen on this cruise. Streets parallel to the water, rising higher as one moves inland. Narrow streets, no life, no action. I wandered into a school playground to photograph a football match, but the man at the security gate shooed me away. I thought I'd have better luck in the law courts. I was allowed in, but the courtrooms were empty. This can't be through lack of crime. Police cars were everywhere. The young take drugs, I was told.

There is a little-known mine of information on *Marco Polo*, which is pinned to the notice board opposite the excursion desk every evening. These are the latest charts from the website www.PassageWeather.com and they show what lies in store for unwary or nervous passengers. They take the form of two small coloured maps, one showing wave height, the other surface windspeed. They're full of arrows and pointy ticks, and might be dismissed by ladies as 'a man thing'. In fact, at times I thought of them as simply 'a Clive thing', for seldom did I find anyone else examining them, at least not nearly as intently as I did.

A helpful scale shows how to interpret the splodge of colour on the charts. The nice colours are white and pale blue – for these show flat seas and windless skies. The scale then passes through the spectrum until, at the far end, we meet a nasty deep red – signifying waves up to twelve metres and winds up to 50 knots. But next to it is a colour that represents hell, a ghastly purple, shown on the scale as tapering to infinity. It reminded me of the sailors' maxim for the South Seas: 'In the 40s [latitudes] there is no law; in the 50s there is no god.' Deep purple marks the end of the scale, the end of the road, the end of life.

I go and have my regular evening peep at the notice board. Just north of the Azores, where the *Marco Polo* will shortly steam, sits a tumour of purple. Not red, not even dark red, definitely purple!

In my cabin I find tomorrow's day sheet. It contains an insert: 'We have received advanced weather forecast which highlights the possibility of adverse conditions that could delay our passage to Tilbury. Taking all factors into consideration, we are taking the precaution of bringing forward our sailing time from Ponta Delgada by ninety minutes, and therefore *Marco Polo* will sail at 1030h on Thursday 17th February.'

DAY 39. PONTA DELGADA/AT SEA

'As we say our farewell to the Azores, take a look at what activities we have in store for you today. Cruise Director's Corner: Richard Sykes is on stage to answer any questions about onboard life, and talks about his experiences over a decade of cruise ships.'

by Judy Chapman (Cabin 419)

That's it. We've just sailed away from our final port of call. Talk about saving the best till last. The Azores were well worth waiting for. We headed for the nearby car rental booth. Mike had mapped out a route which took in the stunning lush green scenery, hot springs, unspoilt villages and fantastic ocean views of the island of São Miguel.

But now we've left the islands behind. Our cruise is almost over and shipboard talk is of home and supermarket shopping, laundry and child care (next week is half-term). What treats have I got to look forward to? A committee meeting; work; leading a 'walk for health'; a hospital appointment for mother [aged 94], provided she's strong enough to make the journey; and next week a trip to the dentist for a root canal filling. Can't wait.

We have virtually forgotten the Canaries and Cape Verde Islands. They seem so long ago. It will be some time before I forget the image of a barber in Scarborough [Tobago] trimming Mike's hair with one hand whilst holding his mobile phone in the other, talking on it all the time to his girlfriend.

In the course of the past 39 days, we've managed to avoid stomach bugs, insect bites, seasickness (so far), muggings, broken limbs, chest infections, over-spending, and piling on the weight.

We've also done our best to avoid listening to moaning passengers. And there's plenty of them. I can't quite believe what some of them find to moan about. Lumpy pillows, waiters who won't jump to attention when commanded, lack of fresh bananas in the middle of the ocean, the excessive number of transfers ashore by tender, the number of days at sea, the size of the cabins, the lack of an automatic laundrette, the absence of tea and coffee facilities in the cabins. Some even complain about the quality of the lectures and entertainment. This I cannot believe.

The shows have been superb. Who can ever forget Christian's sexy rock and roll performances? And the lectures have been varied and fascinating.

I sometimes wonder if these moaning passengers bother to read the cruise brochure before booking. And have they ever worked out how much – or rather how little – they are paying per day? To us, the cruise represents excellent value for money.

We have laughed at the gossip going round the ship. Five people have died! Their bodies are stored in the meat fridge. Just two more cases of norovirus, or whatever this dreadful bug is called, and we'll be quarantined. Several passengers have been flown home, some with Legionnaire's disease, others with pneumonia. The ship's owners have gone bankrupt and the ship will be impounded. Several female crew members have formed lesbian relationships, and the male crew members are all sleeping with female colleagues. I sincerely hope there are enough females to go round. Maybe some of this gossip is based on truth, but much of it must be down to fertile imaginations. Who are these people?

by Lizzie Mayes (Cabin 494)
Left Ponta Delgada in driving wind and rain, so there was a definite feeling around that the holiday was over and we had four days of misery to look forward to. We were told the weather was deteriorating, that we were getting caught in storm systems, and to be prepared for rough seas on leaving the shelter of the island.

We had breakfast inside for the first time in weeks. Undaunted, we went up on deck in waterproofs, hoping to see an elusive whale. We had to hang onto everything for dear life in gale-force winds and rain. No bloody whales. Took part in the 10am quiz and we won with fourteen points. I enjoyed chatting to Jose and Wilhelm out on deck this afternoon when the weather eased. They are really funny and have that dry Dutch sense of humour, which is so compatible with the British. They don't sit in the 'Hook of Holland', as Jose doesn't smoke and Wilhelm has his cigar in the 'parrot house'. We seemed to miss the storm, and then I found I'd missed Richard's talk on life onboard ship. How maddening – I'll have to get it all second hand.

We went to see the new comedian, who flew out to the Azores to join the ship – laughed all the way through – had heard some of them before but he had great delivery and kept going for 45 minutes. Not good for the laughter lines.

I have mixed feelings about the end of this journey. Surprisingly, from my feelings at the beginning, I have really enjoyed so much of it and many of the kindred spirits we have met (though others are odious and abhorrent) and will miss it all when I get home. DinoRod, the always cheerful and mild-mannered Australians, John and Sue, the rocks who have underpinned the whole cruise, Clive and his nagging about the book, while swapping observations about all sorts of things, Mr Clarke (and his constant rumour-mongering) and his lovely wife Elise, laid back and smiley, retiring to her cabin when Mr Clarke becomes too much, Bob and Pauline from Minorca – wish I had the courage to ask if they are newlyweds – they seem so sweet together.

Drs David and Michelle, in their Kenya khaki, holding no prisoners, and coming unprepared for any formal, or even semi-formal occasions, but David amusing us with his humour and poems; Robert and Sheila, Sheila calmly sitting reading a book with a cigarette in her hand, and Robert in his state of restless anxiety; Wilhelm and Jose (who loves The Dubliners and has a little bit of England in her heart) looking forward to their world cruise later in the year; David and Chrissie Cobbold, and Pattie; Lynsey de Paul; and ever-smiling Helen and placid husband Lawrence, propping up the bar with a book.

After six weeks it has become easier to sort out the more kindred spirits. I'm still bothered when I am cornered by the 'been there, done it all and haven't seen a bloody thing' brigade – there are plenty of them. I have realised a change in my emotions. The first five days were mixed – panic, horror, dread, and would Dick ever forgive me for landing him in this mess. Then the realisation that I love being on the sea, the vastness and emptiness of it all, the silence on deck at night with nothing but stars reaching right down to the sea.

Then there was the anticipation of reaching the magical Amazon. The overwhelming and mighty river, with forest as far as one could see for mile upon mile, the stilt houses and floating homes, the smiling children of Almeirim, the colourful river life, boats festooned with hammocks, the opera house and performance in Manaus, the butterflies, moths and birds, the dolphins, the markets full of exotic produce. Then the horror of the cities, the baseball hats and football shirts, the total westernisation of the people with nothing in their houses, no water, furniture or glass in their windows, but the 42in TV powered by a generator if there was no electricity, forest trails worn down by endless tourists tramping through them, and the endless talk from the guides, animals and wildlife long gone to safer places, the herding on excursions.

As we left the river I felt a huge surge of relief – I had seen the Amazon (albeit only the tiniest fragment) and had no more expectations, and I was on the way home and I suddenly realised I was having fun. A holiday. No more expectation, no more disappointment if I didn't see clouds of parrots, pink dolphins, sloths, or monkeys, no pressure to hand over a dollar to a grasping child and the guilt of not doing so. No more listening to other passengers' Amazon experiences.

The West Indies, which was refreshingly relaxed and seemed to be full of happy vibrant people. Who wouldn't be happy, living with crystal clear waters, beaches, forests and sunshine and an abundance of fresh fish? I love to be on the ship, finding a quiet shady spot, a good book, and the sea changing every day, a good dinner followed by first class entertainment.

At the same time, I'm really looking forward to getting home and seeing everyone and the garden. Have we missed the snowdrops; is there any sign of the daffodils and primroses? Are the chickens laying and have we still got fifteen ducks?

by Dinah Read (Cabin 422)
Lunch we had with a woman I shall call Gargantua and her similarly built husband. I found nothing to like in either of them, as she had not a good word to say about anything or anybody. I cast my eyes to heaven.

by Clive Leatherdale (Cabin 725)
This morning I was told that one passenger was so terrified of the projected storm that she disembarked yesterday in the Azores and intends to fly home. This is the sort of rumour that I have learned to dismiss, so I went to ask Richard to confirm or deny, and he confirmed. She was a solo passenger. He had come to my cabin to discuss what will be the last book club meeting. He said two passengers intended to get off at Barbados 'because they were bored', although they were dissuaded from doing so. With regards to British 'guests' (Richard never speaks of passengers, only guests), he noted that those who pay the least complain the most, the opposite of American 'guests'.

It's not been a good day for the morale of one particular crew member. It was her turn to take the 10am daily quiz. There were mutterings when she asked a question about King 'Meedas' (Midas), but when she asked the name of the first Poet 'Laur-ee-ta' (Laureate) the poor girl was howled down with grumbles about modern educational standards.

Passing ex-MP Michael Butterworth in the corridor, I asked if I could take his photo. He said yes, but kept mumbling his 7-times table as I took it. He said he had been taught to do this!

This afternoon Richard Sykes gave his much-anticipated cruise director's talk. The theatre was packed. He admitted to being atheist and gay, which earned him a round of applause. He quipped that twenty years ago a confession to being gay would have seen him stoned. He had studied music at Derby University, and as a graphic designer had worked on football programmes at Rochdale and Barnsley. Following the stress of a norovirus outbreak on *Marco Polo* in 2009, he suffered a minor stroke, which left him with one pupil larger than the other, but otherwise none the worse.

He gave a good offering of daft passenger comments:

'Can I get off to film the ship leaving harbour?'

'Do the crew sleep on board?'

'We're sailing up a fjord, how high are we now?'

'The swimming pool uses sea water, not fresh water. That's obvious because it looks a bit choppy.'

Richard was scornful of guests' wristbands and white stickers behind the ears to prevent seasickness. 'The only thing that works is Stugeron 15', he insists.

I took one at 11am, another at 5.45pm, and don't feel at all seasick.

Not murder, but 'Terror on the *Marco Polo*', as Donna (secretary), Susan (librarian) and Louise (fitness) catch an unexpected sight of cruise director Richard Sykes in the nude

DAY 40. AT SEA

'Important Book Meeting:
The final meeting of the book club
with Clive Leatherdale will take place at 13.00h.
Many passengers are still unclear what this book is
about. To find out more please attend.'

by Lizzie Mayes (Cabin 494)
I got dressed in warm clothes to face the promised storm (that's the wonderful thing about having a 9ft square cabin with no window or porthole – you have no idea what mother nature has in store for you when you step outside). So what a surprise to see a soft blue sky and not a cloud in sight. I had breakfast outside with about ten others – Marco's Bistro inside was packed, as many passengers believed it wasn't safe to go outside!

I heard the best news today, about the toilet police. Apparently the cabin stewards have to say if there is evidence of diarrhoea in the pan. If so, they have to report it to the senior steward, who then reports to the doctor, who will decide if you are to be confined to cabin or not. Is this rumour or is it true? Can anyone tell me? No one seemed to know.

Our daily hymn sheet predicted a temperature of 12 degrees and a rough sea. In fact, the temperature was perfect, about 20 degrees. Went to choir practice. To appease Welsh passengers, we are singing *Men of Harlech* – where does Richard get his ideas for songs?

Gradually people realised they would not die of frostbite if they came outside, and the 'broilers' and 'basters' started to strip off, giving us one final glimpse of their bronzed bodies – bloody annoying, because they came down a deck to where we were. It was a bit chilly right up on top, so it was hard for the regulars to get a place. I notice a coolness between the Dutch and Brits, as it is mainly the Dutch who are obsessed with the suntan and they are a bit aggressive about the sunbeds.

After lunch I went to our last book meeting. Clive seems happier, with people now queuing up to take part, and there are some pithy and amusing anecdotes which he now receives on a daily basis. That's good – the pressure's off me and I am sure there are some proper writers amongst us, rather than witterers like me. Clive and Richard said how difficult it is to separate fact from fiction as so many rumours abound – the latest is that there are five dead passengers on board.

Later, I was chatting with Clive over the railing when he announced he was going to take my photo – I had no time to get the glasses off or run my hand through unruly hair. Snap, about a foot away. I had pointed out the most elegant woman on the ship sitting just behind us. Whatever the occasion – torrential rain, hot sun, she always looks immaculate, with beautiful coordination. I thought she must have been a model and I had nicknamed her Super Model.

Clive suggested I stay put and then walked over to her. Next thing she was posing for photos, so I went over and said I was going for a sulk and a cup of tea. Clive had switched from the scruffiest person on board to the most elegant by a mile! Bastard!

Later, when Clive had disappeared, I went over and chatted to her. She was really pleasant and said I should see her at home mucking out horses and gardening (I still think she would look immaculate). [See page 303]

I went to Richard's 'Tom Lehrer' afternoon cabaret – great fun. At the end he came over and put his arm round my waist and said to be prepared for three hours of rough-as-hell the following morning.

by Caroline Clifford (Cabin 468)
Dear Diary, I'm trying to write yesterday's entry today; luckily today's was partly written yesterday, and I started tomorrow's yesterday because it's the last day tomorrow.

If James mentions, once more, how old the gangplank is, or that the ship's exhaust system needs cleaning, he will lose more than his endearing smile. But all in all I was in high spirits and looking forward to the last book meeting with Clive at the helm. Was it due at 1pm or at 1.15? The daily programme said both in different places. Either way, it would curtail lunch and interrupt Stephen Smith's penultimate 'blast from the comedy music past'. I was glad I went, if just to hear Richard say definitively that no one had died on *this* cruise. He failed to confirm the number(s) for the preceding Caribbean cruise. James said it was a statistical improbability that – given the average age on board, 65 – no one has died.

The highlight of the day was to have been Richard's renditions of the songs of Tom Lehrer. Tom is James's idol, for his sardonic humour, so I was hopeful for a little respite from his persistent complaining. As I sat down I overheard a 'nice' lady next to me comment 'only 63¾ hours to go' before we get home. She knows who she is!

Nothing else to do, so James and I played *Coach Trip*. If you haven't watched the Channel 4 series – seven 'strange' couples travel together by coach and at the end of each day one couple is voted off by the others. James said he would be changing the rules today and was voting off two couples – not including those that had left voluntarily in the Azores – 'Mr and Mrs Pastry, and Private Godfrey and his son.' For my choice, I'm still bitter about the 'gentleman' who took my chair at the deck party, and the other vote was for the fraternity that sit around the ashtrays and complain about the smell.

The evening marked the final formal dinner and a faultless piece of 'cow'. The low spot was this: earlier on in the cruise I had seen paperwork suggesting that we should be invited to dine with the captain, but the invitation had not materialised. It wasn't that I desperately wanted to dine in his company, after all English is not his first language, but I would not have said no to the free wine. I put it down to the confusion/deception concerning our dinner table number and the clever switching from 78 to 80.

After dinner I found Daniel, the Romanian audio-technician and brilliant guitarist in the ship's orchestra, smoking in 'Dutch Corner'. It is my favourite spot for mature conversation. He mentioned that most of his friends among the crew were British. He impacted on me how hard the entertainers worked, and he had nothing but praise for Richard. Surprisingly, he told me how nervous he had been at the 'Eurovision Song Contest' show, as he had rehearsed very few of the songs.

I told Daniel I had voted for Italy because Christian had the tightest 'bottom'. Just to watch Daniel in his control box in Scott's Bar, jumping around behind the scenes like a lunatic, you wouldn't guess he's quite insecure and feels isolated by the passengers. I'll have one of what he's on.

And so to bed. To my great embarrassment I had left a bottle of cheap vodka, purchased way back in Parintins on the Amazon, jammed upside down between my bed and the chest of drawers, to drain the very last drop. It's an economy measure my mother taught me. Dear Patrik had found it and put it, right way up, on the bedside table.

by Dinah Read (Cabin 422)
We went up together to listen to Steve Ragnall talking about the *Bounty* mutiny and the mutineers who were rounded up and returned to England for trial, those who were guilty and those who were not, family influence, and the characters of the people involved. I had read a fair amount about this before and agreed with Steve's analysis. I have always thought that Captain Edwards, who was sent to Tahiti to capture them, was far more ruthless and cruel than was Bligh himself.

'The Politics of Cruise Quizzing' by Jill Crocker (Cabin 514)
It is a given that you can expect most guests aboard a traditional cruise ship to have pursued a professional calling, and that an even greater number will be retired. Couple this with the ever-present need of ageing man, whether home or away, to daily achieve an acceptable level of cerebral activity and display of knowledge, and we have a competitive, nay volatile atmosphere for the onboard quiz.

In the formation of the quiz team, strategy is king. There are those who wish to shine alone, who lack the confidence which allows them to answer alongside others, or who simply set themselves a personal challenge, but the teams, oh the teams.

Rule number 1: don't choose your team members too soon. The pleasant couple with whom you share your dinner table may well sit with you for the early-evening quiz. Don't commit too soon. There's a risk they may not engage at your level and will drag down your score. Give it a day or two to find out the best membership combination.

Rule number 2: keep an eye on the numbers in the team. There may be no hard and fast rule, and while there is an advantage when several team members each boast a specialist subject, there will also be a number of contradictory answers, leading to the final answer being changed several times (and finally being wrong).

Rule number 3: if your competitive spirit is overwhelming your judgment, hide it! If dissatisfied with the performance of your everyday team, suppress the urge to poach the best members from elsewhere. The reward of the winners' prize of a *Marco Polo* pencil is not worth the slur on your character brought about by this social *faux pas*.

As the quizmasters become younger and, in doing so, highlight the variations in the education systems of different periods in our history, it is increasingly obvious that it won't be long before there is no one left alive who knows that Cliff Michelmore was the first presenter of the *Holiday* programme!

by Clive Leatherdale (Cabin 725)
The boat was not too rocky after all. It has, in fact, been a glorious day – passengers basking on the pool deck for perhaps the last time. Richard says this is because we are sailing in the gap between two storm systems, and it could yet change for the worse.

Richard and I hosted the last book club meeting. Contributions are now flooding in. Strangers come up to me and ask, 'Are you Clive?' They hand me envelopes, quiz sheets, bits of scrap paper, and now I'm thinking that, rather than having too little material, I might end up with too much. The book club even had our photo taken, so faces can be put to names and no one can hide.

Later, I had my long-awaited interview with Dr Papadakis down in the hospital. We are almost home, and his waiting room is no longer over-flowing, so I don't feel I'm intruding. I still feel like a patient, however, for he sits behind his desk, sideways to the chair I know so well. The first time I had sat here, it was to hear the dreaded words: 'Mr Clive, I do not have good news.' The second time, a week later, it was to hear the uplift-ing: 'Mr Clive, I have good news.'

This is how he speaks, fluent, but mannered, with favourite phrases, a bit like a Greek José Mourinho. If his expression changed one jot between being a prophet of doom and a merchant of joy, I did not notice it. This is partly because of cultural differences. Bedside manner may be important in all medical situations, but across different cultures it is sometimes difficult to interpret.

He hands me his silver business card: 'Dr Antonis Papadakis MD GP. Member of the Swedish Medical Association. Cruise Ships Medical Consultant.

The unexpected Swedish connection seems a suitable place to start, considering that Dr Papadakis was born in Crete in 1968. He trained in Athens in general medicine and worked in the public hospital in Crete for six years. He followed that by being a military doctor for two years before transferring to the Uppsala University Hospital.

Reasons for wanting to work overseas are easy to explain for a Greek doctor. Greek medicine has always been highly regarded and its practi-tioners eagerly sought after. Add the fact that, back home, a Greek GP can expect to earn perhaps €2,500 a month – perhaps £25,000 a year – and you can appreciate the exodus.

Dr Papadakis also has considerable experience of A&E at St Thomas' Hospital in London, and still works there as a locum for several months every year. In fact, it was while living in London that he saw the American sitcom and movie *The Love Boat* and realised that cruise ships have doc-tors. He applied via the internet to several cruise lines and found that, with his CV, it was not difficult to get a posting.

When he had diagnosed my kidney infection, I made one of my inane remarks: 'What a fantastic job you have,' I quipped. I did not know the half of it, otherwise I would have kept my mouth shut. He, too, had been initially blinded by the salary, the holidays, the quality of life, seeing new places. It seemed like occupational utopia for a doctor.

Five years later he no longer sees it that way. The responsibility on his shoulders is huge, the stress almost unbearable. Cruising in the North Sea or the Mediterranean is comparatively straightforward. Should an emergency arise, it is not too difficult to transfer the patient ashore to a modern hospital. But on cruises like this, no such easy solutions are at hand. The moment we left Tenerife, heading south to Cape Verde and then across the Atlantic, he tells me, he dreads what might lie ahead. Should a patient present difficult symptoms, he has no second opinion to call upon. He is alone, with his two nurses, and god – and he glances up to the ceiling to make his point.

'And what if I get ill?' he continues. 'If I have a heart-attack, who will treat me? And what will happen to the ship's patients?'

For this reason he has regular medical check-ups throughout the year. He also has an unexpected back-up, a small list of names and cabin numbers pinned on his noticeboard. The first thing he does with every cruise is check the passenger list for active or retired doctors or nurses whom he might summon in an emergency.

Richard Sykes had already explained that, despite the huge 'H' on the top deck, helicopters are never allowed to land on the moving *Marco Polo* at sea. It's too dangerous. Therefore a critically ill patient either has to stay on board or the ship has to divert.

These decisions, Dr Papadakis, confides, can wreck an entire cruise. Should he diagnose a patient with a life-threatening condition – he lists heart attack, stroke, major bleeding – he has to inform the captain, whereupon a rapid decision has to be taken on what to do. To carry on or to turn back to find the nearest hospital?

I ask what happens in the event of a conflict of priorities. If the captain wants to carry on and the doctor wants to turn back, who wins?

'I do,' he says quietly, but he immediately qualifies himself. 'What if I make the wrong diagnosis? What if the patient recovers quickly? Then I have ruined the cruise for all these people.'

All of a sudden, I see that being a cruise-ship doctor does not seem such a rosy career choice.

Dr Papadakis rises from his desk to take me on a tour of the hospital wing. It is vast, stretching the entire width of the *Marco Polo*. Sick passengers arrive through the carpeted front door, so to speak, whereas injured crew enter via the spartan crew's quarters on the other side. Beyond the waiting area and private surgery, a couple of siderooms are used for blood tests, delivering antibiotics, setting fractures etc. Further on, I am shown into what serves as an operating theatre. The entire hospital is windowless. Doctor and nurses see natural light only up on deck. For them, it is a bit like living on a submarine. This only adds to the contradictions, for the venerable *Marco Polo* is clearly blessed with a spanking medical centre in which patients are seen within minutes and laboratory results are returned within seconds.

On our return to Dr Papadakis's office, I turn our conversation to the mundane aspects of his routine consultations. He sees an average of 25 patients a day, which over a six-week cruise amounts to over 1,000 consultations – though obviously many of these will be repeat visits. Most patients come with predictable ailments, seasickness, sunburn, insect bites, although the advanced age of many passengers and the peculiar hazards of ships at sea ensures he sees more fractures than most land-based doctors.

In Britain, I tell him, the fact that the NHS is free means many GPs find much of their time consumed by frivolous complaints. Is it the same on a ship?

No, he replies. The fact that passengers have to pay means they seldom see him unless the problem is important.

There is one aspect of life on *Marco Polo* that vexes Dr Papadakis more than any other. Being a closed world, cruise ships are acutely vulnerable to contamination by bugs and germs and anything else. No matter how diligently passengers wipe their hands with antiseptic gel, the risk of an outbreak of norovirus or something worse is ever-present. Right now, he says, one ship is holed up in the Canaries with 200 cases of norovirus on board. If *Marco Polo* reaches a certain number of contaminated cabins, he has to inform the port authorities, who have the power to impound the ship. Every day when in port the ship's captain and doctor must sign the Maritime Health Declaration, detailing the range of illnesses on board. Otherwise, no one gets clearance to go ashore.

There was a gastro-enteritis problem on *Marco Polo* last week, he tells me, and many passengers didn't realise how serious it might have been. When told they must be quarantined, they were sometimes verbally aggressive to him and his nurses. Even though there is no cost to see the ship's doctor when an epidemic threatens, some passengers with symptoms waited until the ship had left Barbados and was heading home before going to the medical centre. He describes such passengers as 'egotistical, thinking only of themselves'.

It is difficult to match such strong words with such a mild-mannered man. Dr Papadakis peppers his conversation with folksy homilies. He says that in Greece a perfect family has three sons who will grow to be a priest, a lawyer, and a doctor. In his family, however, there were two doctors and a priest – no lawyer, the most important job of all!

I had already ascertained one rule of cruise ship recruitment. Crew or staff dealing with guests must be competent, of course, but they also need social skills. A lecturer might be blessed with a brilliant mind but deliver dull performances, in which case there is no place for him on a cruise ship. A doctor might be gifted, but might also be a sourpuss. Think of Gregory House! Hugh Laurie's misanthropic character, *House*, could never get a job on a cruise ship.

I make this point because it would have been fun to dish the dirt on the ship's hospital. I could have said that passengers privately sneered at the care offered by East European doctor and nurses, that they snootily insisted 'British is best', that they complained the medical facilities provided onboard were sub-standard.

Except that none of this would be true. Everyone I encountered who had visited the doctor was full of extravagant praise. He is probably the most liked and highly regarded man on the ship. 'That wonderful doctor,' they would say; 'Dr Papadakis is such a lovely man,' etc. One lady showed me her mobile phone. She had got her husband to fix a photo of the good doctor on it.

Popular he might be, but the burden of professional loneliness sometimes wears him down. He's going on extended leave when we get back to Tilbury: he says he needs weeks to recharge and unwind after a long cruise. And I can understand why.

Nurse Lily (left), Nurse Daisy, and Dr Antonis Papadakis in the waiting room of the *Marco Polo* hospital. Thank-you cards decorate the walls

'My Rock, My Dad' by Marie Martyn (Cabin 627)
The following verse was written at the request of cruise director Richard
Sykes, who had been teaching music composition. Richard asked people
to write lyrics that were personal to them. I chose to write about my rock,
my dad. He died in May 2010, and this has been my first major time away
without being able to contact my family, especially my mum. These lyrics
were performed by Richard, and they had music put to them. I want to
thank him for what was a moving experience that I will never forget.

My dad was a man of substance
   Who did not take a thing to chance
He guided me through life's highway
   Through the happy times till he died in May

Knowing that he had his two clubbed feet
   But he was the nicest person you could ever meet
He liked his sport, especially football
   But his knowledge would make him look so tall

If you want to see him or just call round
   It was a pleasant, happy, cheering sound
Just wish that he could have travelled around and about
   He loved his nature for sure, there is no doubt

If I need a memory or time alone to think
   I'll just sit and ponder over a nice warm drink
A flower, an insect, a moment I want to recall
   Was when I got married, he made me feel ten feet tall

So now he's gone, I will have good times and bad
   All I have is memories of my unforgettable dad.

Day 41. At Sea

'10.00 Guest Lecturer Tony Rice will be discussing The Shipping Forecast: The Story of the Beaufort Scale. 16.15 Guest Lecturer Steve Ragnall Join Steve for his Marco Polo Shanty Crew Concert.'

by Mave Eaton (Cabin 616)

Calm seas, but passenger unrest at attempt at compulsory gratuities. They are £4 per person per day; for 42 days that is a total of £168 per person. The majority of passengers wish to tip individuals who have served them personally.

Talked to another passenger – a single, elderly woman who explained her reason for this voyage was to make her peace with Brazil. She had backpacked around the world four years ago and had been attacked and almost killed when in Brazil. She had been unable to speak the name of the country. She regained her serenity only after sailing up the Amazon.

Today is my birthday. I was horrified to see it was revealed in the daily programme, but the sea-shanty concert organised by maritime lecturer Steve Ragnall was a memorable highlight.

I met gentle Jenny's husband, Ian. He had just received her medical bill for £3,000. He went to Reception to explain that he did not have enough money in his current account and would need to ask his bank to pay. He said it was like the Gestapo. He *had* to pay tomorrow, Sunday. How was he expected to organise this? Common sense eventually prevailed and he will be allowed to pay on Monday [before we disembark at Tilbury] after contacting his bank. He will [he hopes] be able to reclaim the money from insurance but he was upset at being treated like a criminal. Very few people have thousands of pounds in their current accounts.

by Lizzie Mayes (Cabin 494)

Another glorious day – still warm enough to sit outside. Don't know what happened to the promised three hours of hell, but I said to Richard maybe he had had a word with the Almighty, or was *he* the Almighty?

I was amused to watch a man spend half an hour rubbing sun-cream into his wife, and at the end of each rub he gave her a cheeky smack with a lascivious look on his face. I have noticed her around the ship – she never smiles. Anyway, having got her well greased, the sun moved round and she was plunged into darkest shade. She was surrounded by the Dutch so at least the Brits are keeping their end up!

The Limpet resembles a piece of leather more by the day, but she's obviously delighted with the result of spending hours on the broiler deck – strange, really, as I think it's really smoky from the funnel up there. The best place for all reasons is the front of the ship – no engine noise, no 'parrot house' noise, and the only passing traffic the dedicated deck walkers. Dick did his last practice of the shanties for a performance later on in the day.

I couldn't believe my eyes when I went onto a deserted pool deck around teatime and saw two men buffing up [the statue of] Nureyev – or touching him up, as a member of the medical profession said, as she was passing. Told Sue and John about it at dinner, and Sue said she hoped he came up nicely!

by Mark Edwards (Cabin 423)
One slip-up by the management was the failure to change the weather forecast whilst we were at Ponta Delgarda. The last forecast posted before we arrived was horrendous, showing horrendous wave heights and wind strengths. This was acted on by the ship advising us that we would leave port early the following morning. Everybody was walking around saying, have you seen the forecast. I spotted on that forecast that the bad weather was one day's sailing away, and that we were going to be in port for over 24 hours, so that put the rough sea 48 hours into the future. As an experienced weather watcher, that is plenty of time for it all to change.

I kept an eye on the notice board, but the forecast wasn't changed, and nor was it removed, despite it steadily going out of date. We set sail as planned, and the noonday message from the bridge warned us that in an hour the sea would be getting worse. It didn't, and when the new forecast was posted up 48 hours after the previous one, it showed that the situation had changed considerably. The bad weather was tracking north-east in front of us, and the next day showed that it was going faster than us. Luckily the bad weather behind us wasn't catching us up.

To my way of thinking, the failure to show a changed forecast during our stay in Ponta Delgarda caused undue stress to many passengers.

by Sue Edwards (Cabin 423)
It must be morning, the drawer-bashing from next door has started. Our neighbours are like larks. Their dawn chorus would waken the world. It

starts with the coughing, perhaps they are smokers. They have good lung-fuls to clear every morning before they start talking. They must either be the tidiest or most forgetful pair on board, because their drawers crash in and out dozens of times before they are set for the day.

Noise is one thing, but as their drawers back onto our cabin, the crash shakes the wall, and therefore my bunk. It is with relief that I hear them in the corridor greeting our cabin steward, so I brace myself for what I hope is the last crash – the slamming, quite unnecessarily, of their cabin door – so loud the whole corridor shakes. Then they are gone, taking their chatter with them until tomorrow morning.

At all times the ship continues to have its distinctive sounds, so there is no place that is really quiet. Going back to the cabin is no guarantee of peace. My cabin sounds have changed since this morning. A carrot-chomping demon now inhabits my personal space, but at least it is more tolerable than the tortured cat that wailed for twelve hours last night.

'Clomp' replaces 'wail', as 'groan' replaces 'creak'. Is it a cycle of bits? or the life force of the *Marco Polo* – 'I creak therefore I am?' This language changes according to the wind direction and sea conditions. I am sure there was a southbound repertoire, now replaced by a northbound one.

Each noise is more irritating than the last. Especially so are the ones on the bedside table that are so close to one's ears at night time, irritably because I am sure they are caused by some ill-conceived arrangement of one's own – book against hairbrush or something rattling on a tray.

The drawers seem to rearrange themselves according to their con-tents. I am sure my knickers are disgruntled by being squeezed up against a bra – they are used to better conditions at home, a scented drawer. And the socks just have their noses put out of joint because they have to share the drawer with other unsavouries. I can hear them moaning about the change of status in the underwear world.

by Jean McGinley (Cabin 229)
One annoying habit I have discovered about myself on this cruise is that I have a tendency to leave books lying around. I had hardly got into my own copy of *The Girl with the Dragon Tattoo* when I discovered that I had misplaced it. Worse still, I had left my little metal bookmark clip inside it. It had been out of a Christmas cracker many years ago, but had accom-panied me on numerous holidays. Imagine my delight when Susan the librarian asked if anyone had lost it. I was reunited with it and was able to finish the said book.

Sadly, the same did not happen to the library copy of *The Rough Guide to Trinidad & Tobago*, which I had mislaid and was never returned. If the person who picked it up and kept it reads this, I hope you are ashamed of yourself.

Feeling guilty about the loss of this book, I volunteered my services to Susan at the end of the voyage. She had bemoaned the fact that she needed to get the library in some order as she was going on leave and the person taking over from her was not a trained librarian. It seemed a good idea at the time to offer my services. After all, wasn't I a nurse who was obsessed about filing medical records in the right order? My obsession even went as far as to sort out donated paperbacks, which were now coming in thick and fast.

An enjoyable Saturday morning was spent doing this, with only one problem – there were still 125 books outstanding to be returned. We had visions of all these being submitted at the same time – deadline 12 noon Sunday. Worse still, they may never be returned. I was fired with enthusiasm for going round knocking on people's cabin doors demanding their return! I never did find out whether Susan received all her books back – last time I checked she was down to 25 missing books.

by Dinah Read (Cabin 422)
I joined Jack in the cabin for the early part of the afternoon and we relaxed together and drifted off to sleep, warm and comfortable as ever. At 4pm we went up to the Marco Polo Lounge, where Jack found a seat, while the 'Shantymen' rearranged the stage for the 'choir' and soloists, and set up the film screen for the sailing footage that Steve Ragnall uses. There was a good audience and the whole thing went very well. Any performance always ratchets up when there is an audience, as a matter of course.

Finally, there was a brilliant condensed version of *Joseph and the Amazing Technicolour Dreamcoat* with all the show team (including Richard as Jacob). A crowning glory, this show. I have to say that I had half-expected to be glad that our cruise was coming to an end, so that I could get back to my own home again, but really I have been, and am, very happy on this ship with Jack, and also in the real friendships that I have made and the company of people that it has been a real privilege to meet.

by Caroline Clifford (Cabin 468)
The cruise is almost at an end, and we just have the 'disembarkation dance' and the 'shore-bound shuffle' to look forward to, if you catch my meaning. There is a mood of discontent around the Reception desk, and a number of passengers, including 'Troopship Bill', have raised their voices because the anticipated onboard accounts were not delivered under

their cabin doors overnight. Something to do with the fact that credit cards had been lodged, giving the ship carte blanche to charge what they wanted.

This didn't worry me, I have trust in the accounting system, but the consensus was that passengers wanted to adjust their 'compulsory' gratuity on the grounds that the vessel was understaffed and the staff overworked. Previously, I had heard a few people boasting how little they had bagged the cruise for. No pleasing some people. So be it. I could tell you what James said – how long have you got?

On deck, I complained to Alison at the excursion desk that we had been promised a rough voyage from Ponta Delgarda and that didn't happen. I don't care how skilfully the captain had navigated between the two hurricanes, I had been looking forward to a bumpy ride. I am thinking of demanding a refund on the grounds of misrepresentation. Alison assured me that on the approach to Tilbury conditions would deteriorate [they didn't].

James, meanwhile, was busy replacing the chairs missing from outside Scott's Bar, causing maximum inconvenience to their users. I spotted Clive hanging over the deck rails like a vulture waiting to swoop on the next would-be Samuel Pepys.

I watched with interest an engineer freeing a passenger stuck in the lift. He levered open the lift doors on Deck 7, revealing just an empty shaft. The lift was stuck several floors below. The old man, imprisoned, once released, far from being grateful was actually oblivious to the fact that he had been trapped at all.

I am proud to say that I have not yet used the lift – not because of any fear for my safety, but as an aid to minimising the inevitable weight gain on a cruise such as this. Other things I haven't done include learning the British monarchs, and reading at least one Shakespeare play on those long days at sea. I have, however, completed a collage of our ports of call, a few missives to my mother, and an unanticipated activity, keeping a diary!

James completed his passenger 'comment form' and suggested there should be a lecture on 'euthanasia made easy'. He advocated a 'sitting and staring' area, and suggested that chairs on deck should be tied to their respective tables. Other activities for the over-80s to include skinny dipping, pole-vaulting, archery, and 'old people's charm school'. I, on the other hand, think it's wonderful that people no longer fit enough for a Saga holiday can enjoy a cruise on *Marco Polo*.

And finally, 'Nureyev' (the statue) got a thorough scrub-down after someone, not James, had dressed him in shorts the night before.

Quote of the day: overheard from dinner table 74:
'Are you on this table for your follow-on cruise?'
James said: 'The mere thought of anyone staying on is certifiable!'

by Jill Crocker (Cabin 514)
Steve's sea-shanty concert was a great success. He had a full audience, all
went well, and bits of various shanties could be heard around the ship for
the rest of the evening.

The Pushers, The Peasants, and the Perseverers' by Jeremy Tait (Cabin 715)
After experiencing 40 days of standing in one or other of the two food
queues in the *Marco Polo* self-service restaurant, I have concluded that my
fellow passengers can be divided into three separate groups. These can be
loosely categorised as the Pushers, the Peasants and the Perseverers. I, of
course, fall into the last category. The queues are generally quite orderly
and move quickly, but occasionally one will meet a pusher who insists on
walking in the opposite direction, and my advice is to persevere and to
give way gracefully.

The food itself is adequate, with different choices of meat, fish and
vegetarian main dishes served each day, although the choice of salads
does not alter and the desserts are similar, with artificial cream predomi-
nating. However, some inconvenience was experienced, as is usual with
many buffets, so here are ten tips for future passengers who decide, like
me, to use the buffet onboard the *Marco Polo* for breakfast and lunch.

1. Avoid using the small glasses next to the fruit juice stands. When
the glasses run out (as they do each day) simply fill up an empty soup cup,
which not only holds three times as much juice as the glass, thus avoiding repeated visits, but also has two handles to facilitate drinking. A coffee mug is also a suitable alternative to a soup cup.

2. Bananas and the small sachets of honey are very popular, possibly
because they fit easily into the peasants' handbags, so be sure to arrive
early if you want either of these delicacies. However, if the supply is
exhausted when you arrive at the dessert counter, be persevering and ask
the waiter behind the counter for the missing item, and he will invariably
produce what you ask for.

3. Do not waste time queuing for tea or coffee at the self-service
counter. Instead, place an empty tea cup or coffee mug on your table and
it will be filled up, and replenished, by a bevy of waiters whose sole task
is to satisfy the demands of thirsty passengers.

4. You will sometimes forget to help yourself to a particular item
while loading your plate in the food queue, such as a knife and fork,

which are not provided on the tables. My advice is to join the end of the queue to obtain the missing item, and not to queue-barge under any circumstances. Overtaking people in the queue is frowned upon, and you will not be popular with your fellow passengers. Perseverance is a virtue to be encouraged. Do not be a pusher!

5. If the weather is warm, some food such as barbecued spare ribs, pizzas or hamburgers may be served outside the restaurant around the swimming pool, and this food will not be available inside. Be sure to check this out, as you can always bring your barbecued food back to your restaurant table.

6. To reserve a table, do not just put a drink on it as several people do, because when you return with your food you will probably find your table occupied by peasants and your drink removed. However, if you drape a sweater or a shawl over an empty chair, you will find your table unoccupied and awaiting your return.

7. If you feel that you absolutely must take some food out of the restaurant and back to your cabin, don't be a peasant and try to hide the food in your clothing or in your purse. Instead take a tray and load it with as much food as you want and nobody will stop you from taking it out of the restaurant!

8. If you enjoy a bottle of wine with your meal, it is a good idea to order it the day before if you want to start drinking it with your first course. If you wish to avoid the formality of tasting it before your glass is filled, bring your own corkscrew. Don't be afraid to order the house wine. It is very good value.

9. By all means chat up the waiters, provided you don't mind hearing their life histories. If you address them by the names they display on their uniforms, you will be surprised at the response, and an occasional small cash tip will guarantee you special attention, and will set you aside from the pushers and the peasants.

10. Remember that sharing a table with strangers when the restaurant becomes crowded can relieve boredom and can often lead to new friendships. However, be sure to choose your table with care in order to avoid the peasants.

I hope these tips will be of use to future passengers who use the buffet in the *Marco Polo* and will help them enjoy their meals as much as I did.

'The Elegant Lady and the Missing Son' by Clive Leatherdale (Cabin 725)
Yesterday, while clocking some gossip, I had noticed 'the elegant lady' sunning herself on a chair by the gym. I call her the elegant lady because there is no better way to describe her. Female passengers routinely call her

'immaculate'. Almost six weeks had passed and we had never spoken, so notebook in hand I went and introduced myself. I wondered how she would react to this strange man pulling up a chair beside her, flicking a pen in one hand and with the other positioning a notepad on his knee. Some people clam shut in such circumstances, others talk freely. This lady opened up in ways I could never have predicted and in directions I could never have expected.

Our conversation started innocuously. Pauline Velten is 70. Her looks and effortless poise, my words, not hers, had led to modelling work in her twenties, catwalk and fashion shows, not photographic stuff, partly because she did not think she was photogenic, partly because most of the photographers she met were only after one thing. She did pose for yachting magazines and suchlike, but nothing racier. Her modelling heroine was her exact contemporary, Jean Shrimpton. Pauline's parents were hoteliers, who expected their daughter to always appear neat and tidy at home when guests were around. And the habit stuck.

As the years passed, she did some ocean sailing (working as cook) but her love of horses took her into the world of dressage – ballet on horseback, she describes it – and eventing. She remains a dressage judge and keeps herself busy designing gardens.

I know nothing of horses or modelling, and am struggling for questions to ask. Pauline helps me out, telling me that one young model she worked with, Kim, was a bit of a wild child. So wild that she ran off with Keith Moon, the even wilder drummer of The Who, whom she eventually married. Kim later married Ian McLagan of The Faces.

Pauline is an admirer of Monty Roberts, inspiration behind the novel and film *The Horse Whisperer*, and has attended his displays in Britain. She also knows the jump jockey Bruce Gregory, who was offered the chance to ride Foinavon in the 1967 Grand National but turned it down, partly because he wasn't offered enough money, partly because the horse was hopeless. Foinavon won, of course, at extraordinary odds of 100-1.

This seemed like a cosy interview that had just about run its course. I had stopped taking notes, but Pauline had not stopped talking. She mentioned her daughter – something of hers had been published – then her son, and suddenly I felt a tightening in my stomach. Did she say that? Or had I misheard? I thought I heard a word joltingly out of place, given our easy conversation on the sunny deck of a cruise ship.

That word was 'missing'. I asked her to repeat herself. And then it came tumbling out. Pauline's son had vanished.

I suggested we move inside, out of the blinding sun. We found a quiet corner where there were no distractions. I took pages of notes.

Pauline's son Christian had the world at his feet, multi-talented, a free spirit. He was a gifted photographer and had written a book on the fauna of the West Indies before he chanced upon a personal odyssey. Two hundred years ago, the Scottish surgeon Mungo Park had made two pioneering journeys to the Niger river in west Africa. On the second of these he vanished. Christian Velten, likewise a graduate of Edinburgh University, decided to trace his footsteps, literally, planning to follow the river from Mali to Nigeria, on foot, by donkey and by canoe.

Armed with a video camera, Christian, then 27, had flown to Banjul, Gambia on 7 February 2003 to begin his quest. He estimated the journey would take no more than five months, for he had a ticket to London from Lagos, Nigeria, with Virgin in late July. Like all good sons, he promised to write and phone when he could, though this might be difficult. He telephoned from Kita, Mali, six weeks after he departed, on 23 March, sounding fine and upbeat.

Christian Velten was never heard of again. No more letters, no more phone calls. By May his family started to get anxious. Perhaps he couldn't find a phone, but would nevertheless turn up, safe and sound, on a Virgin flight as planned. But he didn't. Pauline and her husband, now frantic, had to find help, but where to turn? When Sussex Police were notified of a missing person they came and searched under his bed! This infuriated her. The Foreign Office put its West African desk in contact with her. 'Worse than useless,' says Pauline. It was her local Sussex MP, Gregory Barker, who finally kicked ass (my words, not hers).

In September 2003 the *Daily Telegraph* ran a feature, followed by other British papers. BBC television and World Service radio interviewed her. She hired an ex-Army Gurkha officer, who was recommended to her, to go to Mali and organise a search, but she was advised not to go herself as 'it would only make things worse'.

The publicity alerted Richard Branson. Learning that Christian had been due to fly home with Virgin, he phoned Pauline – and got cut off just as she entered Sevenoaks tunnel! Branson rang back with the offer of a satellite phone and £1,000 of free calls in west Africa to assist the search. Finally, in March 2004, British police also went to Mali, but drew a blank. Locals, she learned, always told investigators what they wanted to hear, so the trail went cold.

Christian Velten would have celebrated his 30th birthday on 7 July 2005, the day of the London bombings. Many friends had arranged a birthday celebration, but with the ensuing transport chaos only a few were able to attend. Eight years have now passed since Pauline last saw her son. With no body, he is not considered legally dead. There has been no inquest, and the agonising state of legal and emotional limbo drags on year after year.

Like any mother in her situation, something deep inside prevents her believing her son is dead. Pauline comes across as the most pleasant and rational of people, but she confesses to consulting mediums – who insist Christian is 'alive and getting better and will return'. She admits she clings to anything. She also admits to the pain of human insensitivity. Over the years she has become hardened to barbed comments, about her looks, her privilege, and how can anyone with her good fortune know anything about suffering.

I am numbed by what I hear but slightly puzzled as to why I am hearing it. Pauline knew before meeting me that I am preparing a book, but intruding into such intense personal anguish is not what I had in mind. I ask if she wants her story in print. She consults her husband and says yes. She would do anything to put Christian back into the public eye. She also knows, as I know, that the *Marco Polo* is full of well-travelled, retired people with time on their hands. Some may go to west Africa, and you never know . . .

Full details of this case can be found on the internet by searching 'Pauline Velten' and 'Christian Velten'.

Pauline Velten and her adventurous son, Christian. He vanished without trace in west Africa in 2003 (photo of Pauline by Clive Leatherdale)

DAY 42. AT SEA

'Our final day at sea can be as relaxing or as stimulating as you want it to be. For the journey home we've got some wonderful activities and entertainment to keep you enthralled. However you choose to spend your day, we hope it is a fitting finale to a wonderful holiday.'

by Mave Eaton (Cabin 616)

Our last day. We will arrive back in Tilbury early tomorrow morning. What have I felt about this cruise? What will I say when I am asked in my small home town?

I thought about the actual things which had irritated me. They are surprisingly few. The cabin had appalling sound insulation but that is a problem with an old ship. I wish the cabin windows had been cleaner. I missed TV news for a month [there was no signal once we were out in the Atlantic]. There were small niggles: the maitre d' could have given us a table for two, as one was available. The cabin's TV map of the Amazon was inadequate. The ship's three lecturers were stretched too far in producing material to cover six weeks. The 'Crossing the Equator' ceremony was pathetic – no King Neptune and his court. The delicious curries were too few.

But the good things outweigh these irritations. The cabin was pleasant with good air conditioning and bathroom. The food was well presented and the waiters were the best I have known. The library was small but well-stocked. The entertainment was the best I have ever encountered on any cruise ship – the east Europeans are so talented. Richard Sykes, cruise director, is becoming a legend for his many talents and abundant energy. The journey up the Amazon affected many people with varying motives.

Dear Clive, use what you want from this. I tried my best. Mave.

by Lizzie Mayes (Cabin 494)

Our last day. I am really looking forward to getting home, but at the same time feeling sad that this little chapter in our lives is coming to an end. It has been fun, relaxing and what an opportunity to see so many places and things, albeit for a short time. Nureyev is still being polished with great vigour – the verdigris disappearing by the minute. One of the buffers spent at least an hour on his inner thigh.

John went to the Prize Point Redemption for our team winning the quiz on two occasions. We were proud recipients of *Marco Polo* biros.

I then got pinned down by a ghastly woman who announced she had had an interview with the chef and put him right about certain things. That he shouldn't serve curry, as most of the people on board were over 65 and couldn't digest curry after that age. She then went on to tell him that his salads looked like dog-sick and why didn't he make a potato salad. She castigated him for garnishing beef with rosemary – English people just don't do that. He didn't know what vegetables to serve with any particular dish and, at his tender age of 32 and Indian, he should have no business being a chef on a British passenger ship. This diatribe was delivered without a breath, but I managed to extricate myself to say I wanted to hear Richard's 'Victoria Wood' cabaret.

I managed to cram everything into suitcases for collection outside our door – how wonderful not to see them again until we have left the ship.

'Ladies First' by Mark Edwards (Cabin 423)

Another good game to play was trying to get the crew, and especially the females, to come past you in narrow corridors when there wasn't room to pass two abreast. I never managed it, except when the waiters were carrying loaded trays. In a way it upsets me, because why not ladies first?

Today is the last full day, breakfast time in the Bistro first thing, shortly after 7.45. I had taken my camera to grab a few photos of the staff there, which went fine, but they were all in exuberant mood. All stood in their normal line together, but joking and joshing each other and then bursting into song, so quietly you had almost to be part of them to hear it. Sailors the world over love the voyage to be over, even if the next one starts tomorrow.

by Caroline Clifford (Cabin 468)

The last day of the cruise and my roots are appalling, but I'm not alone. 'Raucous red' has become true grey, 'burning brunette' also grey, and 'bubbling blonde' grey, too. It feels such a long time ago that we were obliged to attend the fire drill, with the interesting twist of shuffling along, with one hand on the shoulder of the stranger in front – a little like a sober conga.

Packing – what's that? I know I am the scruffiest person on the cruise, but I always take clothes on holiday that I can 'wear and throw', and so travel home with less luggage than when I arrived. This trip I shall have space for a duty-free bottle of Drambuie at the giveaway price of £9.90. Incidentally, a 10 per cent increase in six months.

So what have I gained from this cruise, apart from two stone in weight? Education? Yes, 46 intriguing and thought-provoking lectures from three top speakers. Yes, I enjoyed the Amazonian destinations, but I feel the real Amazon is deep inside the continent, away from the scruffy ports – in Ecuador, probably. And food – I have consumed three steaks, 45 pieces of pig, too many cubed vegetables to mention, sixteen bread rolls, three prawns and 86 cups of coffee. I've not done any washing up, but I've made my bed 42 times.

I've been to one 'tea time', and also enjoyed the front seat on the tour coach once. I've watched James's feat of falling asleep on a bar stool and I don't think I've upset any passengers yet, but I can't talk for James, who thought an invitation for bridge had come from the captain. I'm hoping as he grows older (he's 76) he will calm down a bit.

What shall I miss? Smuggling cheap vodka on board, purchased at the Amazonian ports. The anticipation of each menu and of mulligatawny soup, Woody Woodpecker's smile, her infectious laugh, and her husband's poem for Valentine's Day.

I shall miss many of the crew, all the head waiters, especially Stalin, Lwin (our waiter from Burma) and Andrii, whose sense of humour is amazing for a Ukrainian. Who else could have recognised James's 'bollocks' tie? Carmen with the 'rear of the year' and Susan from the library, always laughing, not always at the right place. And the staff at Reception who equipped me with stationery to write this rubbish on – they know who they are. Patrik, who cleans up after us, brings ice at 5.30pm, and kept quiet about my vodka bottle. Then there's Harold Bishop from *Neighbours* (alias Steve Smith), Mr Hope from *Holby City* (Tony Rice), and 'This Way Up' – not my words, but those written on Steve Ragnall's hat. Last, but certainly not least, our incomparable cruise director, Richard.

I shall not miss the creosoted passengers who give their sunbeds up only to 'book and bag', the anti-smoking lobby, men with trousers too tight under the armpits, the smell of TCP, mothballs, and Sterident, putting the lavatory seat down, small talk, people who use their walking sticks as primitive weapons, *Dad's Army* and *Allo Allo* on the ship's TV, and James in his shorts. As James has said, 'You couldn't make it up.'

But finally, what I should ask myself is this. What do the crew think of us, and what do they say about the 'pantomime' that is us, when we're fast asleep, with full bellies in relative luxury?

Now I'm thinking, this time tomorrow I shall be alone. Just my photographs for memories. How sad.

by Margaret Atkinson (Cabin 504)

Today, looking out at a dull foggy sea and sky, seems the perfect time to reflect on the past 42 days.

Forty-two days ago there were hopes, fears and doubts. The hope was that this cruise would be the trip of a lifetime. Fears that it would be more than we could manage because of husband Ron's heart attack. Doubts that maybe the cruise would not live up to expectations. Would we become disappointed and disillusioned, possibly bored, and bad-tempered? Maybe bored, because fourteen days had been our maximum cruise before. What would we do for 42 days?

With hindsight, I ask myself why did I put myself through that mental torture? From the very beginning, wonderful memories have been retained. Memories of each port of call and of people met. Memories of different ways of life. We have been inspired by what we have seen.

Paramount are the memories of the mighty Amazon. The size of the river's mouth. The water colour. Seeing the equator moon rising on the horizon, as if from the river itself. We were spellbound as we watched the lush rainforests slip by, where the sun's reflection glistens on the finest smooth water. We survived being hot, sticky, and soaked to the skin in the rainforest.

Bored? Never! Not with entertainers like Richard Sykes and the brilliant show team.

Bad-tempered? Never! Not even by the small cabin, the creaks and groans of this old ship.

Having sailed 12,000 miles, been rocked and rolled, we can truly say this was a voyage of a lifetime.

'Passenger Prizes' by Valerie Waite (Cabin 223)

MOANERS: Mrs Tiltnose and Husband. They only came on this cruise to visit the Orinoco and, when that wasn't possible, they wished they had left the ship in Amsterdam. The excursion office got fed up with their complaints and said they didn't want them on the tours anyway. They cancelled all their bookings.

MISERY: The couple from the Isle of Man who scowl all the time. She refused to move along one seat in the Marco Polo Lounge so that a couple could sit together. She was then upset when people refused to move for her on a catamaran.

ANGRY: There was an incident outside Scott's Bar when technicians were setting up the audio for Richard's deck party.

RUDE: The Admiral and His Wife win this prize. All in one breath she ordered two glasses of tomato juice, two glasses of water, one bowl of porridge, one pot of hot water, a plate of lemon slices, and a teabag with ne'er a please or thank you. No wonder the poor waiter was bewildered.

GREEDY: The man who leans across you and takes a handful of cakes and biscuits without using tongs. When confronted by a fellow passenger, he told him to mind his own business.

FUNNY: Two ladies who complained that the ship was rocking too much after leaving Barbados. They said it was because the captain was 'driving too fast'.

by Clive Leatherdale (Cabin 725)
My last entry written onboard *Marco Polo*. The crew have been touching up the statue of Rudolph Nureyev out by the pool. Ian Loughran (Cabin 632) told me a joke at breakfast.

A paper bag goes to the doctor and says it's not well.

The doctor says he will send the paper bag to the hospital for tests.

A week later the paper bag returns to the doctor, who tells him he has bad news.

'But I'm only a paper bag, there can't be anything wrong me.'

'I understand, but your parents were "carriers".' Boom, boom!

This afternoon I attended Michael Brotherton's second lecture on his time as an MP (1974-83). Of House of Commons Speakers in his time, Selwyn Lloyd was a 'forbidding character', George Thomas was 'in awe of the front bench of both parties', and Bernard Weatherill was 'the best of modern times'.

Brotherton's first ever question to Harold Wilson during Prime Minister's Questions ended, in football parlance, Wilson 6 Butterworth 0. This was fitting, as Wilson had an encyclopaedic knowledge of sport. In 1982 Brotherton demanded to know why *HMS Endurance* was being withdrawn from the South Atlantic, whereupon Douglas Hurd, then No 3 in the Foreign Office, said it was not the job of the Royal Navy to protect piddling little islands in the South Atlantic. Weeks later the Argentines invaded.

Amongst his gentle character assassinations, Brotherton described Nigel Lawson as 'not the world's most pleasant man'. Tony Crosland, Labour Secretary of State for the Environment, was Member for a neighbouring constituency in Lincolnshire. Brotherton liked him for his 'can do' approach to making things work. Ken Clarke said he could strangle bloody Brotherton for voting against the Care in the Community bill. Willie Hamilton, the arch-Labour republican and atheist was 'a tremendous chap'. Ted Heath was part-author of his own downfall because he treated back-benchers with contempt. When the Conservatives were in opposition, before Margaret Thatcher (whom he voted for) became prime minister, Brotherton always sat behind Enoch Powell in the House. Tony Benn was another great parliamentarian. Of James Callaghan, can you trust an Englishman with an Irish name who represents a Welsh seat? Yet Callaghan was 'a very friendly man'. So was Labour's Eric Heffer: 'I like you, Brotherton, you are a proper Tory.'

Brotherton described Cherie Blair's attitude as disgraceful for a PM's wife, unlike Sarah Brown, who conducted herself properly. His own wife had once heckled him: 'I'm not going to stand and make speeches, because one fool in the family is enough.'

Brotherton reminded his listeners of the brilliance of Brian Walden, who 'nobody now remembers'. I do remember Walden, who in 1998 had delivered a coruscating attack on Nelson Mandela in a series of broadcasts called *Heroes*. Whether or not by coincidence, Walden has rarely been seen on our screens since.

Brotherton poured scorn on some modern politicians – including the current prime minister – 'who had never done a day's work in their lives', and concluded with a rousing bit of patriotism: 'I thank my maker I was born under the UK Parliamentary system.'

Ex-Tory MP Michael Brotherton mumbled his '7 x table' as he posed for this photo. 'It's what I was taught to do!' (Clive Leatherdale)

Happy motorcyclists in Mindelo, Cape Verde, photographed through a taxi window (Clive Leatherdale)

DAY 43. TILBURY

'On behalf of Cruise & Maritime Voyages, Captain Zhukov, his officers, staff and crew, we would like to thank you for cruising with us onboard Marco Polo. We wish you a very fond farewell and we hope to see you again soon for another wonderful cruise.'

'Final Wash-Up' by Mark Edwards (Cabin 423)
I keep taking photographs right to the very end. As I work from visual cues, they will be a reminder of the good things. The bad things don't really matter, and my mind is good at only remembering the highs. A quick look at the photo will be the memory jog.

This was our first cruise, and halfway through was likely to be our last. But is that fair? My wife Sue had had several torrid days with motion sickness, and then there was our confinement, which crucially forced us to miss one of the highlights of the whole cruise – the flora and fauna of Îles du Salut.

What did I expect of the cruise, and did it meet those expectations? Sue and I are not people persons, and I have low socialisation skills. We have only ever done one package holiday in our life, and yet we still were prepared to commit ourselves to a long cruise. Having spotted the advert for the cruise, I did my research. So I knew that it fitted our needs, sun and warmth during the dead part of the British winter, small size ship, no children, the excursions sounded right, we had never been to any of the countries visited, and it was good value for money. The real clincher was the Amazon.

So, with all the questions I had posed and answered myself, I had judged pretty well. The cruise did meet up with expectations. There were questions I didn't know to ask, and they proved to be the areas that tripped us up because we hadn't planned mentally or physically for them. The ratio of sunloungers and chairs to passengers was disproportionately low. Not being package-holiday folk, we were not prepared for the energy, organisation and pre-planning required to get, and keep, a chair or a sunlounger. A further surprise was that two thirds of the passengers were mentally and physically dopey. So most of the time it was not possible to stride at even half my normal pace down the corridor.

More important was the problem with the cross-infection control on board and I developed severe professional worries about this. In future I would not board a cruise ship without surgical standard face masks, latex tactile examination gloves, surgical quality surface disinfectant, rehydration mixture and all known medications for gastro-enteritis. Interestingly, in everything that I read up beforehand there was no mention of the possibility of quarantine, and that was a severe shock to the system.

I set out with six aims:

1. To enjoy the cruise, whatever happened. Mainly achieved.

2. To get an inkling of new countries and their way of life. Achieved.

3. To have a decent photographic record of the cruise and the countries for my memory. Achieved.

4. To use the ship as a warm training camp to get significantly fitter to be able to start getting properly race-fit for rowing. Achieved.

5. To relax in sun and warmth and get away from the stresses and strains of my professional life as a rowing coach. Achieved.

6. To continue with writing my rowing coaching manual. Didn't even get started.

Five out of six is not at all a bad score, so despite the blues during and after confinement, it has to score as a success. Would I do it again? A qualified yes, as long as I picked the correct cruise.

by Caroline Clifford (Cabin 468, Empty)
The very last breakfast and I was not in the mood for a scrum. I settled for coffee – not prepared for another 'pineapple gate'. Why is it always the women fighting for the tongs and the fresh fruit, and the men opt for 'stewed'? Unashamedly, I put a piece of ham into one of those delicious rolls, stole a pat of butter and 'handbagged' them for later. How sad is that? Anyway, James had called me Porcine. What did he expect after six weeks at sea? Up until then I had stifled my urges to comment on his ample waistline and 'hands on' features.

This was sadly the end of my relationship with . . . my diary . . . but checking the daily programme, I couldn't put my pen down yet. There were very clear printed instructions on how and when we were to disembark.

But read on: allegedly on 'this cruise we have consumed 2,957 kgs of pork' but an incredible '3,580 kgs of beef'. Bullshit – no pun intended – where was the beef? We had pork every day on the main menu, not to mention the bacon and sausages regularly pigged at breakfast. I put my hands up. I had once ordered a mixed grill at dinner and, by asking the chef to forget the 'mix' and just give me a cow, I had a lovely steak.

A second occasion – I made a plea to Antonio – and two perfect pieces of beef came from the kitchen. Both served with a cordon bleu sauce, and so blue and bloody that the dear animal could only just have ceased kicking.

But what happened to the other 3,570 kgs? Perhaps the supplier is making a few bucks. If I was really bitchy I would also question 'ice cream 2,378 litres'. Ounces, maybe! Where else have you seen such tiny portions served up in cocotte dishes? Loved the food but, at least tomorrow, when I ask for 'two scoops' the waiter won't look at me and suggest, 'Don't you think you've had enough?'

Disembarkation is everyone's worst nightmare. For me, the only problem had been the midnight dash to get the suitcase out of the cabin door into the corridor for collection. I couldn't believe it when the zip failed. It was a new case – another job for James – but not tonight! So, fingers crossed, I watched this morning from an upper deck as the suitcases were offloaded. Not my best idea. It was reminiscent of Bangkok Airport, where the handlers just don't care a damn. Someone shouted from a deck above me. 'That's the one with the camera in,' as the trolley sped round the corner, depositing yet another case onto the quay.

The disembarkation procedure was akin to a perfect military procession – full marks to the *Marco Polo*. I was particularly sad to say goodbye to the 'top male talent aboard' – the wonderful security officers, always smiling at the gangplank. I said, sincerely, that I really hoped to see them again. Even I can wipe the odd tear away.

Still smiling, and crying a little, I had failed to realise that my 'pale blue' luggage tag was probably the same colour given to the majority of passengers, all travelling on the 'special' cruise coach service from Tilbury to Victoria, London. This was a recipe for bruised ankles and crushed tits. The cases were stacked far too close, and it presented the perfect opportunity for many of us to vent our anger on fellow passengers. I left James to do that and I whispered a sad goodbye to the crew, and without too much regret, my 2ft 6in bed.

I should end my diary now, safely aboard a comfy coach to London. Not the front seat, of course; James still insists that was taken before the ship even docked. I had the seat behind the toilet – the toilet door that read, 'Get key from driver.' Well, I'm not a typical Saga traveller, nor have I ever suffered from incontinence, but after staring at that door for an hour I had my legs crossed and I knew what my first job in Victoria would be.

I did the patient thing, letting most people off first, so I was a little perturbed to be met by a uniformed officer asking if I minded if his dog sniffed me. Yes I did, actually. I have mild dog phobia, I was busting to go to the loo and I was still in possession of a stolen ham sandwich. I looked at him pleadingly, mumbled that this coach was full of geriatrics smelling of this and that: 'We are not drug traffickers,' I said. He laughed at me and said, 'The last lady carrier I stopped was 70 years old. She used the excuse that it wasn't illegal because she had grown it herself. So please, stand still, don't touch the dog.'

Travelling overseas and meeting people from so many backgrounds and with so many interesting stories, I've often wondered what 'meets' them when they get home, after we've said our goodbyes.

For me it was Bus 148 to Notting Hill Gate. I kissed James goodbye and said I'd had a lovely cruise – he said he hadn't.

So home, alone; no change there then. I pushed the door open against a barrage of post. Then, not seasickness, but that real stomach-churning moment – I'd been burgled.

by Lizzie Mayes (Cabin 494)
Arrived alongside in Tilbury early in the greyest, dullest, mistiest morning – oh, to be in England now that spring is here. Spent some time looking for people to say goodbye to and couldn't find anyone. No sign of Clive but guess he jumped ship as soon as it landed, as he has no luggage! Last statistic: we have covered 11,866 nautical miles [that's 13,655 miles to you and me]. I started to talk to a lady in the cloakroom as we were sanitising our hands for the last time:

'I expect you're looking forward to getting home now' (mastering the art of inane small talk after six weeks' practice), to which she tearfully replied, 'No, I wish I'd got off in Amsterdam.'

'Oh, dear,' I said, 'Why?'

'I hated every minute of it – the noise, too many people, the entertainment, everything,' she replied.

'Oh, I am sorry, I said, 'Is it your first cruise?'

'Oh, no, I've been with Fred Olsen, and that was even worse!'

I thought the bugger would get the last word.

POSTSCRIPT
THE ORINOCO: WELL, NOT QUITE

The Vanishing Orinoco' by Clive Leatherdale (Cabin 725)
Except it isn't the last word. The last word belongs to the vanishing Orinoco, given joint star billing, but never seen. The cruise was marketed as the 'Amazon & Orinoco Discovery', and these words adorned the day sheet's masthead for six weeks, all the way out and all the way back. This book is sub-titled, 'A Cruise up the Amazon and the Orinoco,' followed by the teaser, 'Well, not quite.' So, what happened?

Some passengers were relaxed about missing South America's second greatest river; others were livid. A few had visited the Amazon before, but not the Orinoco, which was for them the main reason for signing up. Some had booked a year in advance, dreaming of Venezuela.

And what if the Amazon rather than the Orinoco had been cancelled? Could the cruise conceivably have gone ahead? Losing the Orinoco and substituting three well-trodden islands in the Caribbean was hardly offering like for like. It was akin to promoting a pop concert with The Beatles and The Rolling Stones, then having the Stones pull out, replaced by Piggy and the Piglets, Lily and the Lollypops, and Billy Bollocks and the Gooseberries. Cruise ships often vary their itinerary for all sorts of reasons, and passengers generally accept them but, in the view of many on *Marco Polo*, striking out a headline destination encroached beyond what is acceptable. Why weren't passengers given a last-minute opportunity to cancel and claim a full refund?

Knowing the passenger jungle telegraph would invent countless 'real' reasons for the late change of itinerary, perhaps Cruise & Maritime should have tried to still the rumours with a detailed and comprehensive explanation before there was time for them to build momentum. Among the lurid explanations reaching my ears for the vanishing Orinoco were these: fuel costs were rising, and a few miles could be shaved off by avoiding it; the crew were there last year and didn't enjoy it; there isn't a decent hospital in Puerto Ordaz; taking on fresh supplies could not be guaranteed; the last time *Marco Polo* went there, they filled her water tanks with contaminated water. Apologists for the company, by contrast, insisted the ship would never cancel all its pre-booked Orinoco shore excursions without good reason. In short, no one knew anything, and everyone guessed everything.

The first source for anyone venturing into dodgy parts of the world is the travel advice issued by the Foreign & Commonwealth Office. The

FCO's website is notoriously cautious, preferring to say 'stay out' rather than 'come along'. Not being a travel agency, it has nothing to gain from welcoming travellers in, but everything to gain by avoiding the hassle should anything go wrong. For that reason, hardened travellers generally take its advice with a pinch of salt.

What did the FCO say about Venezuela in January 2011? It noted that the only parts of the country best avoided for 'all but essential travel' are the drug-fuelled border states with Colombia to the west. That's the opposite side of the country to the Orinoco delta. The FCO offers these figures: '13,000 British nationals visit Venezuela every year. 25 British nationals required consular assistance in Venezuela in the period 1 April 2009 to 31 March 2010.' That's one in every 520 visits. And it's surely improbable that guided and escorted cruise ship passengers, who aren't spending the night ashore in dingy hotels, could join that number. It would make headline news if it did.

So, if the warning did not emanate from the FCO, where else could it have stemmed from? The first indication that *Marco Polo* might skip the Orinoco was a letter dispatched to passengers by Cruise & Maritime on 17 December 2010. It admitted the FCO had *not* added the Orinoco delta to the areas best avoided. It referred, instead, to local sources claiming an inability 'to guarantee the minimum security of disembarking passengers'. This, the letter added, was an interim statement only. As *Marco Polo* was not due into Puerto Ordaz until 8 February, nearly two months away, there was plenty of time to clarify the situation.

The second letter, dated 10 January, was not posted but awaited passengers in their cabins as they embarked at Tilbury. This confirmed that 'it is currently not possible for cruise ship tourists to visit Puerto Ordaz'. Tobago, Grenada and Barbados would be substituted. This was a bit of a party-pooper, to say the least. But the wording seemed cut and dried. *Marco Polo* was not being singled out, as the ban appeared to cover all cruise ships. But did it?

Venezuela, largely because it is not perceived as safe, attracts far fewer cruise ships than does the Amazon. Indeed, that was part of *Marco Polo's* appeal. If Amazon cruises are, comparatively, two a penny, cruises up the Orinoco are platinum plated.

So, back home in Britain I did a bit of internet digging. I found another cruise line advertising Orinoco voyages; one cruise had apparently just finished, and another was set to depart. I emailed the company with two questions: a) were their ships stopping at Puerto Ordaz; b) had they received any official Venezuelan warnings about the deteriorating situation in that country. I say 'deteriorating' because *Marco Polo* had sailed up the Orinoco without incident twelve months earlier, so something serious must have happened in the interim. I received a prompt reply, which I condense. Their cruises *were* stopping at Puerto Ordaz and they had *not* heard any reason for not doing so. They emailed attachments of their various shore excursions and invited me to book ahead for their next Orinoco cruise. Either that company had not received the warnings sent to Cruise & Maritime, or it had chosen to ignore them.

In the meantime, I had been busily emailing the British consulate in Venezuela at the address on its website – consular.venezuela@fco.gov.uk

As no reply was forthcoming, I also sent faxes to the British Embassy in Caracas, with no greater success. I prepared to report to readers that I could shed no further light on the mystery. Then, weeks later, an email arrived from the consulate. It is long and detailed, so I shall report only the essentials, paraphrasing where necessary:

'I am afraid I did not find your email messages in our inbox. Perhaps our spam filter prevented your messages from reaching us. Please accept our apologies. The information you were given by *Marco Polo* is correct. Cruise & Maritime Services approached us in mid December. The Venezuelan immigration authorities, SAIME, informed the local port agent contracted by them, Agencia Naviera Silva, that the tourist port of Palau in the Orinoco/Puerto Ordaz area would be closed during the days the *Marco Polo* was to arrive to Venezuela. This port did not comply with the structural safety facilities necessary for disembarking. We have no information that suggests that this decision had to do with any criminal activity in the area. Cruise & Maritime asked if there was anything the embassy could do to help them complete their visit to Venezuela successfully. We tried to contact SAIME officials in Puerto Ordaz, but as they were running understaffed for the Christmas season, they were only able to reply by January 5th. They confirmed the information. They added that the rest of the ports in the area are only for cargo ships and were not fitted with immigration facilities for controlling the entry of tourists. The only exception to this would be through special permission issued by the central offices in Caracas. We then approached our contact in SAIME Caracas, asking what was needed from us in order to get such permission for *Marco Polo*. He said unfortunately this was an extremely bureaucratic procedure and that any permission for February needed to be submitted in December. It was already January 7th and the information we had was that *Marco Polo* would sail from the UK on January 10th. In the light of this, we felt we had no choice but to inform CMV of the disappointing news. I hope you find this information useful. Please let us know if there is anything else we can help you with.'

This seemed pretty conclusive, except for the fact that another cruise ship had, apparently, docked at Puerto Ordaz in the same time-frame. I emailed back to the consulate seeking clarification. This time they replied swiftly. Again I paraphrase:

'According to the information we were given, both cruise ships, *Marco Polo* and ***********, were contracted to the same shipping agent in Puerto Ordaz. In the letter sent by SAIME to the port agency, dated 15th December 2010, they specifically informed the agency that the other cruise ship, ***********, would not be allowed to dock. We don't have any more information about what transpired after that.'

Naturally, I then emailed back to the other cruise line, enclosing these consular warnings. I received no quick response, so I emailed repeatedly, until I regrettably concluded that no response was ever likely.

So there we leave it. The reasons given for *Marco Polo* never venturing up the Orinoco were entirely valid, although Cruise & Maritime might have saved itself awkward questions by a fuller account of the problems it faced, and in so doing forestalled the inevitable passenger rumour mill.

As expected, the Amazon did indeed 'wow'. Murder on the *Marco Polo*? Well, not quite. But, from what I saw, if looks could kill, the ship might easily have returned to Tilbury with far fewer passengers than had set out.

The core of the 'book club' which brought you *Murder on the Marco Polo:* From left: Front: Steve Wright, Neville Singh, Jean McGinley, Richard Sykes (cruise director), Marie Martyn, Mark Edwards, Steve Ragnall (lecturer); Seated: anon, anon, anon, Valerie Waite, Clive Leatherdale (editor), Malcolm Whatcott, Jeremy Tait; Ladies standing: Margaret Atkinson, Marion Wright, Daphne Carden, Kay Rainsley, Judy Chapman, Caroline Clifford, Margit Latter, Sue Edwards, Lizzie Mayes, Vivian Walsh, Dinah Read; Men standing: anon, James Coleman, Piet Pieterse, Jack White, anon

Printed in Great Britain
by Amazon

52086798R00192